IMAGES OF RACE

THE VICTORIAN LIBRARY

IMAGES OF RACE

EDITED WITH AN INTRODUCTION BY
MICHAEL D. BIDDISS

Articles by Alfred Russel Wallace, Francis Galton,
John Elliot Cairnes, Charles Mackay, John William Jackson,
Frederic William Farrar, Thomas Huxley, Kelburne King,
Herbert Spencer, Edward Augustus Freeman, and Grant Allen

Holmes & Meier Publishers, Inc., New York

First published in the United States of America 1979 by
Holmes & Meier Publishers Inc.
30 Irving Place, New York, N.Y. 10003

Introduction copyright © Leicester University Press 1979
Printed in Great Britain by
Unwin Brothers Limited
The Gresham Press, Old Woking, Surrey
A member of the Staples Printing Group

Library of Congress Cataloging in Publication Data

Main entry under title:

Images of Race

  Includes bibliographical references and index.
  CONTENTS: Wallace, A. R. The origin of human races
and the antiquity of man deduced from the theory of
natural selection. — Galton, F. Hereditary talent and
character. — Cairnes, J. E. The Negro Suffrage. [etc.]

  1. Race – Addresses, essays, lectures. 2. Ethnic
attitudes — Addresses, essays, lectures. I. Biddiss,
Michael Denis.
GN269. 14   301'.0422   78-31825
  ISBN 0-8419-0482-0
  ISBN 0-8419-0483-9 pbk

CONTENTS

PREFACE

There are a number of ways in which a selection from Victorian writing on race might be made. The approach adopted here has been influenced by the desire of the Advisory Committee of 'The Victorian Library' to encourage reprints from periodicals of the period and to ensure that each resulting volume should be composed of substantial items rather than shorter snippets. On this basis I have selected 11 essays, most of which are presented whole. The limited excisions made elsewhere, principally to remove matter of particularly ephemeral interest, have been appropriately indicated in the text. I have endeavoured to keep a balance between items drawn from the more specifically anthropological and ethnological journals and ones taken from the rich hoard of general periodicals so avidly read by contemporaries. In both cases we are dealing largely with opinions expressed by and for an educated middle class, and any claim to wider representativeness would have to be carefully qualified. The chronological range of the selections has been restricted to the two middle decades of the Victorian age. In matters of race this period, running from the first repercussions of the Darwinian revolution to the eve of the 'scramble for Africa', has a marked unity. I have concentrated on these years with a view to enhancing the coherence of this collection. The chosen pieces reach very diverse conclusions; what draws them closer together is some measure of consensus about the issues which debaters of race needed to confront at that epoch.

While preparing this book I have been fortunate to enjoy valuable advice and encouragement from a number of friends and colleagues. It is a pleasure to mention particularly the kindness of Michael Banton, Peter Boulton, Lorna Duffin, Greta Jones, and Douglas Lorimer. To my wife, and to Paula Wheatley, go thanks for help in preparing material for the press. I am happy to acknowledge also assistance from the Research Board at the University of Leicester, and from librarians there and at the University of Cambridge. Some of the preliminary work was done during a visit to South Africa, and I am especially grateful to friends and temporary colleagues at the University of Cape Town for enabling me to study at first hand a society in which images of race – many reminiscent of those found among Victorians themselves – have come to affect so strongly every aspect of life.

M. D. B.
January 1978

INTRODUCTION

Victorians used the term 'race' no less readily and confusingly than their twentieth-century successors. As the President of the Anthropological Society of London lamented in 1863, hardly any two persons were fully agreed upon its meaning. The concept obviously had something to do with classification, but this was only a beginning. On one level, people still talked of 'the race of men' just as they did of 'the race of birds'. On another, concerned with divisions inside mankind, the word continued to be used for many groupings not based essentially on shared ancestry and it appeared thus in such phrases as 'the race of lawyers'. Even in its more regular context, associated with attempts to sort men according to patterns of common descent, the term was anything but precise. Before 1800 it was used generally as a rough synonym for 'lineage'. But over the first half of the nineteenth century 'race' (and its equivalents in a number of other European languages) assumed an additional sense that seemed, initially, tighter and more scientific.

This usage was evident, at its simplest, in the growing conviction that there were a finite number of basic human types, each embodying a package of fixed physical and mental traits whose permanence could be eroded only by mixture with other stocks. Much debate ensued about the circumstances under which such crossings might work out for better or worse, and about the long-term fertility or sterility of these alliances. Here was an interpretation of race which, often co-existing with the looser usages, haunted most popular discussion throughout and beyond the Victorian age. It managed, at this level of discourse, to survive both Darwin's revolution and Mendel's. One of the chief elements in the confusion which it engendered was a broad failure to agree even upon the number of types involved and upon the nature and significance of the distinc-

11

tions between them. In the following selection of articles no single
point is more amply illustrated.

There were good general reasons for a heightened interest in race
towards mid-century. Even the British had felt something of that
urge to identify the origins and uniqueness of the national community which had loomed so large in the Continental romantic
movement, and their country's political and economic stature in the
world at large encouraged them constantly to analyse the characteristics and capacities of distant peoples. But when the concept of
race began developing along the lines just hinted there were also
more particular reasons why the resulting debates had to assume
increased importance. Once the idea of type was firmly linked to the
notion of innate racial characteristics some were tempted not only
to equate mere classification with social explanation but also greatly
to exaggerate the scope of this new interpretative tool. Here race
would be treated not as merely one of the influences upon behaviour
but rather as the dominant conditioning factor. Thus there was
emerging around mid-century, in Britain and elsewhere, a racial
determinism so grandiose in its claims as to demand attention and
response.

Isaiah Berlin has rightly noted the high value which nineteenth-
century social theorists placed upon the quest for 'a unitary pattern
in which the whole of experience, past, present, and future, actual,
possible, and unfulfilled, is symmetrically ordered'.[1] Even while
Marx was building a total explanatory system around the concept
of class, there were others asserting no less passionately the significance of race as supreme determinant of civilization, prosperity, and
power. The mood was reflected in Benjamin Disraeli's *Tancred*
(1847), which includes the remark: 'All is race; there is no other
truth.'[2] Three years later the Scottish anatomist Robert Knox
attempted in his *Races of Men* a remarkable systematic elaboration
of the same sentiment. 'That race is in human affairs everything',
he proclaimed, 'is simply a fact, the most remarkable, the most
comprehensive, which philosophy has ever announced. Race is
everything: literature, science, art – in a word, civilization – depends
on it.'[3]

During the 1850s this kind of view was ever more commonly
voiced. Although few expressed themselves so sweepingly as Knox,

or as Dr Kelburne King 20 years later (Selection 8), there were already many who betrayed sympathy at the level of half-articulated assumptions. Such support was eased by the fact that racial determinism appeared to provide an authentically 'scientific' explanation of social development. This was important because of the broad contemporary consensus about the need for the human sciences to be modelled on procedures already established for investigation of the physical world. As Philip Curtin comments: 'The vast majority of the educated public appears to have accepted at least some aspects of the new racial doctrine, if only as a vague feeling that science supported the common xenophobic prejudice.'[4] In the current state of knowledge it was not at all unreasonable to be examining an hypothesis about the possible determination of culture by race; the real error lay in assuming that it had been successfully confirmed. That the whole matter was so hotly contested is not surprising in view of the huge issues necessarily raised. Among them was the place of man, and of different kinds of men, within the natural order – a topic with religious implications no less delicate than scientific ones. There was the question as to whether racial determinism could be kept compatible with belief in freedom of will and moral choice. Or, as another example, we might note how crucial it was to settle whether qualities of race did indeed explain the extent of European, and more especially British, global authority.

The sheer range of possible dispute on these and related issues can be appreciated from the proceedings of the two learned societies that were most deeply concerned during the 1860s.[5] The first was the Ethnological Society of London, founded in 1843. It originated among certain members of the Aborigines Protection Society who felt that the latter was promoting its missionary and charitable concerns rather at the expense of dispassionate scientific enquiry. Among the E.S.L.'s early leading figures were James Prichard and Robert Latham, two doctors with philological as well as racial interests. By 1860 the Society had recovered from a lean period and was prospering under the presidency of John Crawfurd. But soon there came secession, and the establishment of a rival body. This, the Anthropological Society of London, held its first meeting in January 1863. The groups wrangled for the rest of the decade, not least over the right claimed by each to dominate the relevant subsection of the British Association for the Advancement of Science. Until the death in 1869 of the A.S.L.'s Founder-President Dr James Hunt, the chances of general reconciliation remained slender. Only in 1871 did the two bodies reunite, as the Anthropological Institute of Great Britain and Ireland. None the less, the new organization had to deal in 1874–5 with another secession, involving a London Anthropological Society which during its brief existence offered comfort to the more intransigent members of the old A.S.L.

Membership lists indicate that such societies appealed particularly to medical men, and also drew in no small number of lawyers, colonial administrators, journalists, clergymen, and amateurs of geography, geology, zoology, and similar subjects. Some enthusiasts chose to belong simultaneously both to the E.S.L. and to the A.S.L. (which met in the same rooms on different nights), and even when official relations were strained there could be exchange of speakers. Thus the two societies' images of race must not be contrasted too starkly. Of the E.S.L. we can certainly say that during its last years the defenders of Darwin were gaining in influence upon proceedings. Also clear is the fact that it never failed to reflect something of its Quaker and Evangelical origins. Traditionally its tone was humanitarian, and most of its arguments favoured a common origin for all mankind. Resorting readily to linguistic and other cultural data, it was more willing than the A.S.L. to go beyond mere physical evidence. Within two years of seceding the latter organization had a membership of 500 and was promoting an ambitious programme of publication. Even so, the A.S.L. attracted fewer major figures than its rival and never won the same degree of acceptance from the scientific establishment of the day. It concentrated much more than the E.S.L. on racial classifications derived from comparative anatomy, in the tradition of Knox. Broadly speaking, the A.S.L. was the more harshly deterministic in tone, the more illiberal in politics, the more inclined to doubt any common origin for all branches of mankind, and the more resistant to accurate assessments of what the Darwinian version of evolution might imply for the study of mankind. Much of the Society's spirit is captured in the attack of 1866 by J. W. Jackson upon John Stuart Mill's whole approach to social understanding (Selection 5).

The mid-Victorians who discussed race in these and other settings were far from agreed on the relevant principles of classification. There was dispute even over the particular level of taxonomic activity involved, in so far as a substantial minority preferred to treat races as different species within one genus rather than as different varieties within one species. Confusion stemmed too from the invocation of very varied classificatory criteria. Herbert Spencer's article of 1876 constituted one notable plea for the consideration not only of physical but also of mental features (Selection 9). One of the commonest non-physical pointers was language. This proved vital especially to the diffusion of belief in Aryanism, which drew strength during the early nineteenth century from the supposition that the kinship of the Indo-Germanic tongues must be matched by some marked community of blood.[6] Linkages of this kind were very influentially promoted from Oxford by the great Sanskrit scholar Friedrich Max Müller, whose belated recantation on the same point was inadequate to repair the damage already done. The use of philology as an instrument for ethnological investigation survived quite strongly into the 1860s and 1870s when, of the authors represented here, Frederic Farrar and Edward Freeman – the latter very explicitly in his essay of 1877 (Selection 10) – were much concerned with this approach.

Yet linguistic criteria, when employed, did not stand in isolation from a variety of more physical tests of race. Gradations of skin pigmentation were obviously given much importance, not least through being so readily visible. There was also concern for the colour and texture of hair. More broadly still, a great deal of potentially relevant data was being generated from the developing science of comparative anatomy. During the early nineteenth century there had been increasing study of 'facial angles' – involving classification according to degrees of prognathism and orthognathism – within a tradition first pioneered by the Dutchman Pieter Camper. The years from 1820 to 1850 also marked the heyday of phrenology, with its assertion of correlation between mental faculties and the contours of the cranium. George Combe, the most influential British phrenologist, asserted unhesitatingly its relevance to racial study.[7] Among the writers featured in this volume, Spencer experienced an early infatuation with Combe's ideas; Jackson remained a faithful phrenologist to the end of his life; and as late as the last

years of the century Alfred Wallace could still declare that here was
an unduly neglected field. But even as the more specifically phren-
ological doctrines waned in influence the significance of other kinds
of skull measurement grew. Specially notable was the cult of the
'cephalic index', first presented in 1840 by the Swede Anders Retzius.
During the rest of the nineteenth century there was to be live debate
in many countries about the relative merits of long-headedness and
broad-headedness, and about the implications of such dolichocephaly
and brachycephaly for the assignment of racial categories.

It was only a short step from classifying races to describing them
as unequal. Disraeli betrayed the nature of this facile and perilous
progression by declaring in 1849 before the House of Commons:
'Race implies difference, difference implies superiority, and superiority leads to predominance.'[8] Few doubted that there was some
such racial hierarchy, and few refrained from constructing it in
terms of ethnocentric self-flattery. This vision of hierarchy could
encompass not only a gradation of worth within the ranks of white
men themselves but also distinctions of value made upon a still
wider basis. No racial idea was more universal than that of European
superiority over the mongoloid and, lower still, the negroid stocks.
Farrar's essay of 1866 gives it particularly clear expression (Selection
6).

Whenever the language of hierarchy was employed it became vital
to ask whether the disparities thus asserted were fixed for all time;
and, if they were not, to question how far and how quickly these
could and should be reduced or even removed. A minority of
'degenerationists', led in the mid-Victorian period by Archbishop
Whately of Dublin and the Duke of Argyll, approached this matter
with the conviction that the lower races had regressed from earlier
higher forms. More usually, however, the debate was conducted
according to the rhetoric of progress. Here the mid-Victorians were
clearly less inclined than eighteenth-century commentators to view
all stocks as being capable of upward development, and less generous
in estimating the sheer extent of any improvement which might
indeed be envisaged for racial inferiors. Attitudes like these followed
very readily from the concept of race as type and the accompanying
notion of innate differentiation.

In these debates on classification and hierarchy another crucial question concerned the origin of races. Confrontation centred on competing ideas of monogenesis and polygenesis. Was all mankind ultimately descended from a single union, or did the major races each have an independent point of origin? The polygenists stood in a minority, but they were far from insignificant, especially when during the 1850s their cause was so vigorously led by Knox and Hunt; and the article from Farrar on differential racial aptitudes is symptomatic of the survival of this general approach into the following decade. Clearly polygenists were more likely than their opponents to play up the discrepancies and inequalities between stocks, to doubt the long-term fertility of mixed breeds, to view mankind as composed of more than one species, and to embrace racial determinism. On the other hand, a commitment to monogenism did not necessarily compel belief in the equality of races. As John S. Haller remarks: 'Almost the whole of scientific thought in both America and Europe in the decades before Darwin accepted race inferiority, irrespective of whether the races sprang from a single original pair or were created separately.'[9] In short, many monogenists felt able to assert that the tribes of humanity had developed, over the period since their common creation, such inequalities as could not be ignored by those engaged in social and political explanation. The precise degree of harshness stemming from this stand depended on what attitude was taken to the desirability, the practicability, and the pacing of any policy aimed at reversing this trend towards ever greater differentiation in worth.

At no other point in mid-Victorian discussions of race were religious issues more unavoidable. Most particularly, the controversy between monogenists and polygenists brought into question the literal accuracy of biblical references both to common descent from Adam and to the time scale of Creation as a whole. In the first half of the nineteenth century the orthodox interpretation of the latter issue still supported the kind of calculations which, 200 years earlier, had led John Lightfoot and James Ussher into suggesting that man had existed for rather less than six millennia. This chronology proved embarrassing for monogenists whenever they were pressed to explain the sheer speed at which mankind must have been diverging over such a brief span. There was something unsatisfactory about their frequent and speculative justifications in terms of catastrophes and convulsions occurring soon after the Creation. Certainly it did not seem that environmental or other factors were any longer working at the required rate.

It is easy to see why, in this situation, many monogenists took comfort from the revolution in geological and palaeontological thinking which gathered strength during the middle third of the century.[10] The pre-eminent influence here was Charles Lyell's *Principles of Geology* (1830). This attributed to the Earth, and potentially to man, an antiquity far greater than that allowed by Ussher. However, the use of Lyell by Christian monogenists brought perils of its own. The new geology promoted a looser and more poetical interpretation of biblical information which, if then applied to the tale of Adam, threatened to play into the hands of polygenists by casting doubt on the literal truth of the unitary human creation presented in Genesis. Moreover, an enlarged chronology only made easier the argument (monogenetic more in form than substance) that any common origin was so remote as to be negligible when compared to the racial distinctions subsequently established. Similarly it was now easier to accept that any possible reduction of inequality must be, at best, a painfully slow process.

The value of this whole wrangle between monogenists and polygenists was questioned most strikingly through the work of Darwin. The very titling of his two leading books, *The Origin of Species* (1859) and *The Descent of Man* (1871), gave warning of their relevance. Darwin, strongly supported by Wallace and by Thomas Huxley, criticized the polygenists for over-rating the permanence of species and for so rashly treating taxonomic labels as essences. 'It will be seen', he declared, 'that I look at the term species as one arbitrarily given for the sake of convenience to a set of individuals closely resembling each other, and that it does not essentially differ from the term variety, which is given to less distinct and more fluctuating concerns.'[11] This view was obviously hard to square with the polygenists' belief in race as fixed type. More disputable was the measure of benefit that monogenists could derive from Darwin's observations on the vital issue of human origins. He was certainly proposing an ancestry common to all men – yet not to all men alone. If humans were indeed descended from some lowly form, which might itself also belong to the pedigree of an ape, then there would be great difficulty in continuing to treat man as the object of a separate act of creation. Darwin was not merely denying purposeful design in the development of species but also threatening to destroy the most traditional, Adamite, basis for belief in unitary human origins. Perhaps he was leading the monogenists towards only the most pyrrhic of victories.

This doubt was confirmed by racial polygenism's refusal to succumb. Plural origins, in any literal sense, were plainly enough dismissed by Darwin. But, in so far as these had often been invoked merely to justify convictions about extensive differentiation in the present, his work might be adapted to the spirit, if not the letter, of polygenism. From this broader point of view, writes George Stocking, 'polygenism and monogenism can be regarded as specific expressions of enduring alternative attitudes toward the variety of mankind. Confronted by antipodal man, one could marvel at his fundamental likeness to oneself, or one could gasp at his immediately striking differences. One could regard these differences as of degree or of kind, as products of changing environment or immutable heredity, as dynamic or static, as relative or absolute, as inconsequential or hierarchical. Considered in these terms, polygenist thinking did not die with Darwin's *Origin of Species*, nor is it entirely dead today.'[12] One of the most elegant examples of the strategy which aided such survival is Wallace's essay of 1864 (Selection 1). It demonstrates particularly how Darwinism, in conjunction with the newly enlarged chronology of human development, could be used to stress the importance of present racial distinctions rather than the significance of some remote community of origin.

Darwin's own thoughts on the races of mankind were rather inconclusive. Especially in *The Descent of Man* he argued that human differentiation was effected predominantly through sexual selection, which gave greater reproductive opportunities to those who possessed whatever physical traits were deemed most alluring. He denied that any such trait must confer advantage always and everywhere, and thus refrained from asserting the universal superiority of any single conformation and the preordained supremacy of any particular breed. He sought to write neutrally of adaptation not of progress, to deal in terms of contexts not absolutes. Yet this did not prevent him from suggesting that some form of racial

hierarchy had in fact evolved, albeit blindly, and was now showing
a large measure of stability. Such a notion rendered far less effective
Darwin's effort to argue that among humans, who had developed
moral qualities unique to themselves, natural (as distinct from
sexual) selection and the struggle for existence were no longer the
most significant factors in evolution. Other writers were soon
vaunting the persistent relevance of these very factors both within
and between societies. In such circumstances it was all the more
readily supposed that conflict amongst races – let alone nations or
classes – had the sanction of nature, and of the science revealing
nature.

It was soon evident that most political doctrines, old or new,
could gain in plausibility through being presented in the jargon of
so-called social Darwinism. So malleable was this creed that any
accurate reliance upon Darwin's own views became increasingly
peripheral. Jacques Barzun comments: 'It was good social Darwinism
for the white man to call the amoeba, the ape, and the Tasmanian
his brother; it was equally good social Darwinism to show that the
extinction of the Tasmanian by the white colonists of Australasia
was simply a part of the struggle for life leading to the survival of
the favoured races by natural selection.'[13] We should not be surprised
that, among those plundering Darwin, racial determinists should
have been so prominent, for none were more committed already to
a scientific, indeed biological, conception of politics. Social Darwinism fortified the tendency to judge morality chiefly in terms of its
contribution towards improving the chances of survival; and racial
determinism itself made the very purest statement of association
between physical quality and a wholeness of moral, intellectual, and
cultural capacity.

Awareness of the need to respond, in some way or another, to
Darwin's work constantly recurs within the essays gathered here.
In reading them we must remember that his originality derived not
from the idea of evolution as such but from the concept of natural
selection as the principal mode of operation. It is no less germane
to bear in mind that the latter can be interpreted in terms of
differential rates of reproduction. Thus it provides the clearest point
of convergence between Darwinian, racial, and eugenic ideas. As
Michael Banton notes: 'In contrast to the pessimism of men like

Gobineau, Darwinists thought that the operation of natural selection would create pure races out of the prevailing diversity; while many of them held that if eugenic measures were adopted biological change could be on the side of human progress.'[14] In *The Descent of Man* itself there are echoes of Wallace's prediction about the extinction of the lower races, and support for selective breeding along lines proposed in Galton's article of 1865 (Selection 2). It has recently been argued with vigour that here in eugenics, if anywhere, we find the core of Darwinism's application to society. 'Whether borrowed from Malthus or not,' writes R. J. Halliday, 'Darwin's simple observation that individual members within a population enjoyed differential reproductive success unavoidably linked the fact of evolution by natural selection to an empirical concern with population dynamics. . . The eugenists were true Darwinians in assimilating the biological problem of survival to the social problem of reproduction.'[15]

The relevance of all this to the varying worth of populations viewed as racial entities is patent enough. Less immediately obvious, perhaps, is the fact that comparisons were being made not merely between but also within societies. Eugenists worried not only over competition from what was distinctively alien but also over gradations of value inside their own stock. All too often the domestic proletariat was found as disturbingly prolific as any foreign horde. Most pertinent here is the fact that some such dualism was roughly reflected in racial thinking at large. Nineteenth-century Europeans conceived readily enough of race in terms of colour, but significant also for an understanding of their anxieties is the frequency with which they focused on the subtler racial distinctions deemed to exist within the ranks of white men themselves. Each of these two areas is of importance; so too are the links between them.

British attitudes towards stocks of darker hue were naturally affected by such dramatic events of the mid-Victorian period as the Indian Mutiny, the American Civil War, the Jamaican Revolt, and the Second Maori War. From the racial viewpoint India presented some outstandingly delicate problems. These often derived from the now widespread belief in the Aryan ancestry of the white race, with Afghanistan and Northern India as its likely cradle. Did this not suggest some community of origin with certain Indians at least?

The most eligible candidates were the lighter-skinned peoples from
the northern parts of the sub-continent, whose own attitudes to the
caste system showed a consciousness of superiority over the Drav-
idians and other darker types. Many British and Indian commentators found this view convenient, even if its precise implications
for current issues remained on all sides disputable.[16] Where Britons
came closest to unanimity was in their reluctance to allow that
common ancestry implied contemporary equality with men so
strange in custom and so heathen in worship. Even those who
welcomed rule over India as a reunion of parted cousins believed
that the natives had failed to match their own rate of progress in
civilization. The discrepancy was most commonly explained by
observing that Indian conditions had provided only very inadequate
stimuli to upward development. But any hope which reformists
might derive from this approach was threatened by scepticism about
whether such long standing debilitation was now remediable to any
significant extent. Here the environmental argument could merge
into the racialist one, which dwelt on the supposition that in its
ancient homelands the Aryan stock had become weakened and
demoralized through mixture with darker breeds.

Against this background, the Indian Mutiny encouraged those
who wished to emphasize that the racial kinship, if any did indeed
exist, was of the most distant kind. The events of 1857 helped to
render more complex the European's existing stereotype of the
Indian, as one prone above all to docility. Henceforth it would
embrace a clearer image of the potentially treacherous schemer, so
that the perilously inscrutable Oriental might appear increasingly
not only in mongoloid form. Still, even after the Mutiny, Indians
– like yellow men of the East – tended to be associated more readily
with 'barbarism' than with 'savagery'. The latter, and lower, condition was reserved by many primarily for the Negro.

During the late eighteenth and early nineteenth century many
currents of humanitarian feeling had been working to the black
man's advantage. These, as well as economic considerations,
prompted the abolition of the slave trade in 1807 and then of
slaveholding itself throughout British territories in 1833. But there
was also a harsher side to the picture. Abolitionism, in itself, did
not necessitate granting the Blacks any general parity of esteem.

Indeed, throughout the age of Wilberforce there survived quite strongly a literature dismissive of them. Lines of continuity run from David Hume's avowal of 1748 about the Negro's natural inferiority to the more frenetic contempt expressed a century later in Thomas Carlyle's *Occasional Discourse on the Nigger Question*.[17]

By the early 1860s the Negro's condition and potential were being debated particularly within the context of the American Civil War. Its relevance to racial questions was pursued with a passion amply illustrated in the contrasting essays of John Elliot Cairnes and Charles Mackay (Selections 3 & 4). Though the latter's candid advocacy of slavery represented a minority position, his low estimate of Negro capabilities elicited more general sympathy. So too did his condemnation of Northern hypocrisy. Many Victorians saw the Southern planters as decent, free-trading, country gentlemen who, even if mistaken in their possession of slaves, did not deserve persecution by Yankees motivated more by greed than by humane concern.[18] Abolitionists themselves were forced into admitting that President Lincoln's conversion to a policy of emancipation had been belated. Many of them argued indeed that the effective liberation of the Southern Black might come more quickly via the decisions of an independent Confederacy and the natural laws of economics than through any fiat from Northerners who were bent only on exploiting both the races of the South.

What supporters of North and of South tended to have most in common, on each side of the Atlantic, was an unflattering image of the Negro. Even Harriet Beecher Stowe's international best-seller *Uncle Tom's Cabin* (1852) proved, despite its beneficence of intent, a mixed blessing. Its conception of Negro virtue appeared to involve the attribution of an almost mindless simplicity. More generally, mid-Victorians elaborated the stereotype of 'singing Sambo' equipped with 'banjo and bones', to which it was impossible to accord real dignity. Nor did this characterization erase another picture already long engrained in the consciousness of white men everywhere – that of the Negro's vast and barely suppressed appetites for sex and violence. Few British commentators, whatever their stand on the Civil War, doubted that America's Anglo-Saxons, both North and South, were dealing here with men of lesser worth. The Negro who was not actually vicious seemed likely to be, at best,

helpless and in need of paternalistic guidance. Those who, like Mill
and John Bright, joined Cairnes in boldly advocating votes for
freedmen remained a minority in the whole debate. Such radicals
were attacked not only for thus endangering America's 'great
experiment' but also for imperilling the fabric of British political
life. If the newly emancipated slaves were to have the vote on one
side of the Atlantic, what excesses of franchise extension might not
follow upon the other?

Scarcely was the Civil War over than Britain was shaken by news
of the Jamaican Revolt.[19] During October 1865 disturbances at
Morant Bay were quelled by Governor Edward Eyre, in an action
which involved killing over 400 natives. The upshot at home was
vigorous and bitter controversy, in which racial questions were
often to the fore. Those who saw Eyre's reaction as unnecessarily
vicious formed a 'Jamaica Committee', which counted among its
number Mill, Bright, Lyell, Darwin, Spencer, and Huxley. Still, the
great bulk of middle-class opinion seems to have favoured treating
the Governor as hero not murderer. Among his defenders were
Carlyle, Kingsley, Ruskin, Tennyson, and Dickens. The Anthropological Society, to which Eyre belonged, held a public meeting to
explain how his tough reaction accorded with current scientific
estimates of the Negro's inferiority. On 13 November *The Times*
itself thundered that it was 'impossible to eradicate the original
savageness of African blood'.

This sort of approach to Caribbean questions had dominated
Edward Long's famous *History of Jamaica* 90 years before, and
much more recently it had been evident in Anthony Trollope's
account of travel in the West Indies.[20] Mackay's observations on
the 1865 rebellion fall within the same tradition. Even those who
pressed for proceedings against Eyre were often moved to act, as
Huxley himself avowed, through concern for the rule of law rather
than out of any great respect for the Negro. Though a Royal
Commission reported adversely on the Governor's handling of the
affair, it was the Jamaicans themselves who suffered most. The
island lost its elements of self-government, including some limited
provision for black franchise, and came still more directly under
British control as a Crown Colony. James Walvin remarks: 'To read
the response to Morant Bay is to be pitched back a full century and

to imagine that the efforts of the philanthropists to restore the reality of black humanity had been in vain.'[21] The Jamaican uprising had simply played into the hands of those who wished to emphasize that the Negro was not merely different, but also dangerously so.

Such attitudes were still dominant when, during the last two decades of the century, Britain joined in the general 'scramble for Africa'. After 1880, comment Robinson and Gallagher, 'national and racial feelings in Europe, in Egypt, and south Africa were becoming more heated, and liberalism everywhere was on the decline. . . Gladstone's sympathy with oppressed nationalities was hardening into Cromer's distrust of subject races.'[22] Until then nineteenth-century British governments had tended to resist the enlargement of territory overseas. Greater effort had gone into developing altogether more informal modes of influence and into colonizing such Empire as had been acquired earlier, particularly its more sparsely populated areas where issues of native subjugation were secondary. Even so, we can discern during the mid-Victorian years an intensification of that belief in white superiority which the new imperialism soon found so conveniently to hand.

The scramble may have been initiated more through concern for the global balance of political or commercial power than by feelings of racial pride; yet the latter are of central importance to any understanding both of the methods which came to be employed in this vast bout of empire-building and of the justifications which were eventually developed in its defence. Cecil Rhodes was typical even of the lesser entrepreneurs of Empire in holding an idea of dominance that embraced axiomatic assumptions about the natural cultural and intellectual pre-eminence of White over Black. 'In the average European dependency,' writes A. P. Thornton, 'the native races were never admitted to the mental life of their masters. . . This was the true barrier. All other forms of segregation were flimsy compared to it.'[23] Still, there were also some late Victorians for whom the imperial explosion became the object of deeper questioning, and even anxiety. One doubt frequently expressed was whether the racial virtues of Europeans could be permanently sustained in such exotic environments. When Rudyard Kipling referred to the coloured native as 'half-devil and half-child' he revealed elements of fear as well as paternalism; and around the turn of the century speculation on 'the yellow peril' would become commoner not only in Britain but also on the Continent and across the United States.[24]

Historians have not found it hard to accept that even before the late-nineteenth-century drive into Africa there had occurred a significant harshening in British views of non-whites; dispute has centred, rather, upon just why these tougher attitudes developed so rapidly amongst the more articulate sections of Victorian society during the 1860s and 1870s. There is no space here adequately to investigate the proper balance of factors involved, but something at least of their range can be suggested. Clearly the supposedly scientific work of such racial determinists as Knox and Hunt had some part to play, as did – still more importantly – the diffusion of certain versions of social Darwinism. The role of events like the Mutiny and the Jamaican troubles has also been noted. What we need to recognize, in addition, is the potential relevance of those developments within contemporary British society which served to connect considerations of race with those of class.

The sterner attitudes being elaborated in regard to men of colour were not so very different from those which, over many centuries, the British governing classes had taken towards the vast bulk of the home population. In each case, contends Bernard Semmel, the victims were treated 'as thoroughly undisciplined, with a tendency to revert to bestial behaviour, consequently requiring to be kept in order by force, and by occasional but severe flashes of violence; vicious and sly, incapable of telling the truth, naturally lazy and unwilling to work unless under compulsion'.[25] However, by the 1860s, those Britons hitherto so condemned were asserting with growing force the demand for greater equalization of political and economic power. It is arguable that, faced with this challenge, the proponents of social inequality slipped all the more readily into racial rhetoric. Galton, for instance, believed that the lowest classes of civilized man possessed natures not far removed from those of barbarians, and this conviction helps to explain the urgency of his plea for domestic eugenic engineering.

During the last third of the century even those who displayed a more sensitive concern for the plight of the poorest were often tempted to speak of them almost as an alien tribe.[26] According to

V. G. Kiernan: 'Discontented native in the colonies, labour agitator in the mills, were the same serpent in alternate disguises. Much of the talk about the barbarism or darkness of the outer world. . . was a transmuted fear of the masses at home. Equally, sympathy with the lower orders at home, or curiosity about them, might find expression in associations of ideas between them and the benighted heathen far away.'[27] Overall, the advancing spectre of equality prompted many mid-Victorian gentlemen to nurture far greater consciousness of distinctions in status. Philip Mason sees something of this captured in the shift from the world of Surtees to that of Trollope.[28] This enhanced sense of exclusiveness, working against social inferiors at home, seems to have operated more harshly still against the darker stocks beyond. It might no longer be prudent to employ in Manchester the methods of Peterloo, but the majority of the political nation remained eager to condone similar action against the savages of Morant Bay.

These remarks suggest, once more, that mid-Victorian images of race had bearing on distinctions within the ranks of white men as well as, more obviously and powerfully, on issues of colour confrontation. The point is reinforced by consideration of the range of contexts in which one could vaunt the peculiar genius and manifest destiny of Anglo-Saxon stock. The Victorians inherited a tradition of respect for the legacy of Hengist and Horsa, but never before had it been expressed in such distinctively racial terms.[29] One of the hallmarks of such Anglo-Saxonism was flexibility, not to say inconsistency. Its use transcended party political divisions, appealing to radicals like Charles Dilke no less than to conservatives like the third Marquess of Salisbury. No less significantly, the creed was applicable at various levels of geographical generality. It features prominently in the literature of Empire, yet it also had relevance to debate on relations with the United State, on rivalries in Europe, and on tensions within the British Isles themselves.

Knox, who identified himself as a Saxon, had been spurred into publishing *The Races of Men* primarily because of his concern to explain and justify the European revolutionary turmoil of 1848–9. Over the following generation much of the map of Europe was redrawn, and many others – like King and Freeman here – were moved to speculate on the role of race in the recent, and future,

development of the Continent. It was tempting, above all, to examine
the dramatic advance of Bismarck's Germany in this light. Opinion
did vary as to the degree of racial kinship surviving between the
Anglo-Saxon and Teutonic peoples. Yet most Victorian commentators could agree that both stood higher in the ranks of the chosen
than the Latin stocks to the south and the Slavonic hordes to the
east.[30]

It was possible for these broad classifications to co-exist with the
subtler racial distinctions deemed appropriate to the particular
regions of Europe.[31] In the case of Britain, as the samples from
Huxley and Grant Allen illustrate (Selections 7 and 11), much of
the debate centred on the history of interaction between earlier,
Celtic, inhabitants and later Roman, Saxon, Danish, and Norman
migrants. Radical literature of the seventeenth and eighteenth
centuries had often treated 1066 as the most critical date, marking
the point at which honest Saxons had fallen beneath the rule of an
alien aristocracy.[32] This vision of 'the Norman yoke' thus encouraged
an association of racial and class concerns – one similar to that
traced by Léon Poliakov in certain other European countries over
the same span.[33] The theme of ancient Saxon subjugation survived
into the nineteenth century, particularly through such historical
novels as Walter Scott's *Ivanhoe* (1819) and Charles Kingsley's
Hereward the Wake: Last of the English (1866). Nonetheless, the
rhetoric of confrontation between earl and churl seemed lacking
now in much of its earlier political bite. The idea of Saxon dignity
and virtue flourished, but increasingly it would be treated as
reconcilable with positive contributions from the other broadly
Teutonic peoples, including the Normans themselves.

Prominent among those who fared rather less well were the Celts.
Their inferiority to Anglo-Saxon or Teutonic stock was a recurrent
theme in much Victorian writing, especially by historians.[34] The
self-flattering cult of things Germanic had deeply affected Thomas
Arnold's lectures of 1841 as Regius Professor at Oxford; 20 years
later it was similarly apparent in the equivalent addresses delivered
by Kingsley at Cambridge.[35] Carlyle's essays *On Heroes* (1841) and
John Kemble's work on *The Saxons in England* (1849) made
influential contributions to the tradition. During the second half of
the century this promotion of healthy Teutonic pedigree was sus-

tained by such respected chroniclers as Freeman, John Seeley, William Stubbs, and John Green, the author of the enormously popular *Short History of the English People* (1874). L. P. Curtis Jr comments thus upon their perception of inherent contrast between Saxons and Celts: 'The politically mature and emotionally stable, virile and enlightened Saxon yeoman emerged as the heroic archetype immeasurably superior in all respects to the clannish, primitive, excitable and feminine Celt.' He goes on to suggest, more speculatively, that 'This racial and emotional antithesis contained many reassuring features for those respectable Victorians who were apprehensive about the ability of the Anglo-Saxon race and the capacity of their own class to survive the growing menace of democratization, social mobility, and alien or Celtic immigration.'[36] Huxley's more reconciliatory view of English pedigree was offered precisely in response to these divisive currents; and Grant Allen's observations belong to a still stronger reaction against Teutonism – to a counter-movement which, towards the end of the century, became entwined in a more general and self-assertive stirring of Celticist feeling.[37]

This is the context in which to mention, more specifically, some connections between Victorian racial thinking and the question of Ireland. Uncertainty about the very meaning of 'race' was supremely evident in the debates about the degree of affinity linking the Irish to the other inhabitants of Britain. Those who, like Huxley, emphasized the fact, and often the merit, of past blending between these populations were confronted by others keen to dwell on their disparity. Belief in important distinctions between Celt and Saxon was often exploited by the discontented Irish nationalists themselves. Among the English, it encouraged some to advocate that Ireland be simply abandoned to suffer the miseries which would flow from Home Rule; but it helped many more to conclude that the country's destinies should be left in the hands of the fitter breed. Even before the mid-Victorian period an unflattering picture of 'Paddy' and 'Biddy' had become well established in Britain. However, there is much evidence, both literary and pictorial, to suggest that some tendency towards lending these cultural stereotypes a more markedly racial connotation became particularly apparent during the 1860s and 1870s.[38] It was now easier than before to discern in the Irish Celt a backwardness that stemmed less from successive generations of English misrule than from his innate unfitness to enjoy the full fruits of higher civilization.

The result was sometimes startlingly harsh. All racial stereotyping, by its very nature, must strip its victims of individuality. Yet it also runs, at the very least, the risk of proceeding from such depersonalization to a still more alarming dehumanization. Here perhaps the most striking feature of contemporary comment on the Irish was a constant hinting at their resemblance to the ape, whose relevance to racial debate had been so suddenly accentuated by the controversy surrounding Darwin. In 1860, during a visit to Sligo, Kingsley wrote as follows: 'I am haunted by the human chimpanzees I saw along that hundred miles of horrible country. . . . To see white chimpanzees is dreadful; if they were black, one would not feel it so much.'[39] Thus might a white man and a non-white one be together threatened with the loss of their full measure of human dignity.

Today it is easy for us, who live beyond the epoch of Auschwitz, to appreciate readily the ultimately dehumanizing logic implicit in Kingsley's remark. Precisely for this reason, we need to recognize all the more clearly that this was not the conclusion at which he himself aimed.[40] The Rector of Eversley could believe, without conscious hypocrisy, that the Negro's lowliness in nature did not detract from a still deeper equality with all other men, inside the scheme of Christian redemption. Certainly that qualification offered in this life little besides cold comfort to the Blacks of Morant Bay, yet it does remain essential to any truly historical understanding of Kingsley's overall attitude. In the study of nineteenth-century racial ideas at large, broadly similar reservations have repeatedly to be made. It seems, for instance, that the disparagement of alien stocks sometimes began as a mere incidental to the vaunting of quality in the writer's own breed, with little thought about the harsher implications of such distinction. In short, we must avoid remoulding nineteenth-century images of race merely to make them conform better with the categories of a later era.

The mid-Victorians were indeed perplexed about the nature and significance of human diversity, and about the relationship between heredity and environment. Yet, as we have good cause still to know, these are genuinely complicated issues. Mid-Victorian approaches to them were marked more frequently by honest confusion than by calculated cynicism. Even when the conclusions seem most hostile to ideas of common human dignity, it is generally unhelpful to label them 'racialist', at least without scrupulous attention to the anachronistic complications involved. Only in our own century have events compelled a more rigorous sensitivity to the full horrors which can be perpetrated in the name of race, and of racial supremacy. In some of the articles collected here it is easy enough, now, to discern certain portents of the miseries ahead. But hindsight comes cheaper than foresight, especially in this particular field. Thus these mid-Victorian essays about race are best assessed on their own terms, as evidence from an age of relative innocence.

NOTES

1. 'Historical Inevitability', in Isaiah Berlin, *Four Essays on Liberty* (1969), 106.
2. Benjamin Disraeli, *Tancred, or The New Crusade* (Hughenden Edition, 1882), 149.
3. Robert Knox, *The Races of Men: A Fragment* (1850), p. v. The enlarged edition of 1862 is sub-titled *A Philosophical Enquiry into the Influence of Race over the Destinies of Nations.* See also M. D. Biddiss, 'The Politics of Anatomy: Dr Robert Knox and Victorian Racism', *Proceedings of the Royal Society of Medicine*, LXIX, 1976, 245–50.
4. Philip Curtin, *The Image of Africa: British Ideas and Action, 1780–1850* (Madison, 1964), 383.
5. The best discussions are G. W. Stocking Jr, 'What's In A Name?: The Origins of the Royal Anthropological Institute (1837–71)', *Man*, VI, 1971, pp. 369–390; and J. W. Burrow, *Evolution and Society: A Study in Victorian Social Theory* (1966), Chapter 4.
6. See L. Poliakov, *The Aryan Myth: A History of Racist and Nationalist Ideas in Europe* (1974), especially Chapter 9.
7. See D. de Giustino, *Conquest of Mind: Phrenology and Victorian Social Thought* (1975), 68-72; and P. Collins, 'The First Science of Mind', *Times Literary Supplement*, 25 April 1975, pp. 455-6.
8. Speech of 1 February 1849, quoted in H. Odom, 'Generalizations on Race in Nineteenth-Century Physical Anthropology', *Isis*, LVIII, 1967, 9.
9. John S. Haller, *Outcasts from Evolution: Scientific Attitudes of Racial Inferiority, 1859–1900* (Urbana, 1971), 77.
10. For these and related issues see C. C. Gillispie, *Genesis and Geology: A Study in the Relations of Scientific Thought, Natural Theology, and Social Opinion in Great Britain, 1790–1850* (New York, 1959).
11. Charles Darwin, *The Origin of Species by means of Natural Selection, or The Preservation of Favoured Races in the Struggle for Life* (ed. J. W. Burrow, 1968), 108.
12. 'The Persistence of Polygenist Thought in Post-Darwinian Anthropology' in G. W. Stocking Jr, *Race, Culture, and Evolution: Essays in the History of Anthropology* (New York, 1968), 45.

13. Jacques Barzun, *Race: A Study in Superstition* (Revised edition, New York, 1965), 48.

14. Michael Banton, *The Idea of Race* (1977), 89; for the Frenchman's significance see M. D. Biddiss, *Father of Racist Ideology: the Social and Political Thought of Count Gobineau* (1970).

15. R. J. Halliday, 'Social Darwinism: A Definition', *Victorian Studies*, XIV, 1971, 400.

16. See two articles by Joan Leopold: 'British Applications of the Aryan Theory of Race to India, 1850–1870', *English Historical Review*, LXXXIX, 1974, 578–603; and 'The Aryan Theory of Race', *Indian Social and Economic History Review*, VII, 1970, 271–97. Note also C. Bolt, *Victorian Attitudes to Race* (1971), Chapter 5.

17. See 'Of National Character', in *The Philosophical Works of David Hume* (1898), Vol. 3, 252; and, for Carlyle's essay (first published anonymously), *Fraser's Magazine*, L, 1849, 670–9. Relevant issues are well and briefly pursued in J. Walvin, *Black and White: The Negro and English Society, 1555–1945* (1973), especially Chapter 10. Note also the wealth of material on European attitudes contained in W. D. Jordan, *White Over Black: American Attitudes Toward the Negro, 1550–1812* (Baltimore, 1969), Parts 1–3.

18. See Bolt, *op. cit.*, Chapter 2; and D. A. Lorimer, 'The Role of Anti-Slavery Sentiment in English Reactions to the American Civil War', *Historical Journal*, XIX, 1976, 405–20.

19. See B. Semmel, *The Governor Eyre Controversy* (1962); and Bolt, *op. cit.*, Chapter 3.

20. E. Long, *History of Jamaica* (3 vols, 1774); A. Trollope, *The West Indies and the Spanish Main* (1859).

21. See Walvin, *op. cit.*, 172.

22. R. Robinson and J. Gallagher, with A. Denny, *Africa and the Victorians: The Official Mind of Imperialism* (1961), 466–7. See also Robin Hallett's richly rewarding treatment of 'Changing European Attitudes to Africa', in J. E. Flint (ed.), *The Cambridge History of Africa*, Vol. 5 (1976), 458–96.

23. A. P. Thornton, *Doctrines of Imperialism* (New York, 1965), 197–8.

24. For an admirable survey of European attitudes towards the mongoloid stocks see H. Gollwitzer, *Die Gelbe Gefahr: Geschichte eines Schlagworts - Studien zum imperialistischen Denken* (Göttingen, 1962). British perceptions of the 'peril' receive particular attention on pp. 47–67.

25. See Semmel, *op. cit.*, 135.

26. This theme emerges strongly, for instance, within Peter Keating's valuable anthology *Into Unknown England: Selections from the Social Explorers, 1866–1913* (1976).

27. V. G. Kiernan, *The Lords of Human Kind: European Attitudes towards the Outside World in the Imperial Age* (Revised edition, 1972), 330.

28. See Philip Mason, *Prospero's Magic: Some Thoughts on Class and Race* (1962), 18–19. The relevance to racial attitudes of this whole transition has recently been treated, with reference to a remarkably wide range of evidence, by Douglas Lorimer in *Colour, Class, and the Victorians: English Attitudes to the Negro in the Mid-Nineteenth Century* (1978).

29. See R. Horsman, 'Origins of Racial Anglo-Saxonism in Great Britain before 1850', *Journal of the History of Ideas*, XXXVII, 1976, 387–410.

30. Joseph Chamberlain's campaign in the late 1890s for 'Union of the Teutonic Peoples is especially illuminating: see E. Halévy, *Imperialism and the Rise of Labour* (1961), 41–68.

31. Perhaps the most remarkable monument to taxonomic subtlety was left by Dr John Beddoe. He strove to compile, county by county, a detailed physical anthropological record before the railway could further confuse older patterns of distribution. See *The Races of Britain: A Contribution to the Physical Anthropology of Western Europe* (1885; republished in facsimile, 1971).

32. See C. Hill, 'The Norman Yoke', in *Puritanism and Revolution: Studies in Interpretation of the English Revolution of the 17th Century* (1968), 58–125.

33. See Poliakov, *op. cit.*, Part 1, for comparison with Spain, France, Italy, Germany, and Russia.

34. See the useful historiographical outline provided by Asa Briggs's Historical Association pamphlet *Saxons, Normans, and Victorians* (1966).

35. T. Arnold, *Introductory Lectures on Modern History* (1842); C. Kingsley, *The Roman and the Teuton* (1864).

36. L. P. Curtis Jr, *Anglo-Saxons and Celts: A Study of Anti-Irish Prejudice in Victorian England* (Bridgeport, Conn., 1968), 89. The theme of racial response to an alien influx assumes new significance around the turn of the century, within the setting of Jewish migration. See L. P. Gartner, *The Jewish Immigrant in England, 1870–1914* (1960); J. A. Garrard, *The English and Immigration, 1880–1910* (1971); and B. Gainer, *The Alien Invasion: The Origins of the Aliens Act of 1905* (1972). A more general perspective is provided by C. Holmes (ed.), *Immigrants and Minorities in British Society* (1978).

37. See Curtis, *op. cit.*, Chapter 9.

38. This is the central theme of the work by Curtis previously mentioned. Its findings are complemented, from the pictorial angle, by his subsequent study of *Apes and Angels: The Irishman in Victorian Caricature* (1971). For lively criticism of this thesis see S. Gilley, 'English Attitudes to the Irish, 1780–1900', in Holmes, *op. cit.*, 81–110.

39. *Charles Kingsley: His Letters and Memories of his Life* (edited by his wife, 1877), Vol. 2, 107.

40. See 'A Nineteenth-Century Racial Philosophy: Charles Kingsley', in Banton, *op. cit.*, 63–88.

ONE

ALFRED RUSSEL WALLACE (1823–1913)

The Origin of Human Races and the Antiquity of Man deduced from the theory of 'Natural Selection'

Journal of the Anthropological Society
Volume 2, 1864, pp. clviii–clxx

No episode in Victorian science is more famous than Wallace's part in spurring publication of Origin of Species. *In June 1858 Darwin received from his fellow-naturalist a draft paper of truly stunning significance. This showed that Wallace had now arrived quite independently at conclusions about the operation of Natural Selection which coincided broadly with those contained in Darwin's own unpublished sketches from the early 1840s. In July the findings of each were reported to the Linnean Society, and soon Darwin was preparing that fuller 'abstract' of his theory which appeared as* Origin of Species *in November 1859.*

The following paper was read before the Anthropological Society on 1 March 1864. It met with Darwin's approval, though later Wallace would become less confident than he about the explanatory scope of Natural Selection. The essay explores the more distinctively human implications of the selective process, and in doing so it manages to cover many of the major points at issue among those debating racial matters in the generation after 1859. Wallace explains how the new theory renders redundant previous approaches to the question of single or multiple human origins. He tries to harmonize the conflicting views by preferring to talk of 'man' only at the point where 'higher faculties' have developed. What makes humans unique in the organic world is their progression to a state where Natural Selection operates not upon their physical but rather upon their mental and moral condition. Thus the process of diversification in racial physique must belong entirely to the earlier stage, where we find 'the form but hardly the nature of man'. This approach enables Wallace to accept remote common origins while also deploying what is in effect a polygenist argument about the existence and persistence of racial distinctions from the very beginning of properly human history. Moreover the ensuing operation of Natural Selection, now in the context of differential mental and moral development, suggests that these races of men are anything but equal in their fitness to survive. Wallace has no doubt of the superiority, intellectual and physical, of European over other stocks. He also predicts that 'the higher. . . must displace the lower and more degraded races', and envisages this as a process of improvement continuing 'till the world is again inhabited by a single homogeneous race, no individual of which will be inferior to the noblest specimens of existing humanity'. This view of the sheer inevitability of progress towards racial perfection struck most Victorian supporters of eugenics as unduly complacent.

The Anthropological Society itself was far from generally unsympathetic to assertions about racial inequality. But its broadly hostile reception of this paper (see ibid., pp. clxx–clxxxvii) indicated that most members were still reluctant to use Darwinian modes of justification. Relations between Wallace and the Society were henceforth prickly, and in October 1865 he wrote of it to Darwin as 'that bête noire'.

Among the most advanced students of man, there exists a wide difference of opinion on some of the most vital questions respecting his nature and origin. Anthropologists are now, indeed, pretty well agreed that man is not a recent introduction into the earth. All who have studied the question now admit that his antiquity is very great; and that, though we have to some extent ascertained the minimum of time during which he *must* have existed, we have made no approximation towards determining that far greater period during which he *may* have, and probably *has*, existed. We can with tolerable certainty affirm that man must have inhabited the earth a thousand centuries ago, but we cannot assert that he positively did not exist, or that there is any good evidence against his having existed, for a period of a hundred thousand centuries. We know positively that he was contemporaneous with many now extinct animals, and has survived changes of the earth's surface fifty or a hundred times greater than any that have occurred during the historical period; but we cannot place any definite limit to the number of species he may have outlived, or to the amount of terrestrial change he may have witnessed.

But while on this question of man's antiquity there is a very general agreement,—and all are waiting eagerly for fresh evidence to clear up those points which all admit to be full of doubt,—on other and not less obscure and difficult questions a considerable amount of dogmatism is exhibited; doctrines are put forward as established truth, no doubt or hesitation is admitted, and it seems to be supposed that no further evidence is required, or that any new facts can modify our convictions. This is especially the case when we inquire, *Are the various forms under which man now exists primitive, or derived from preexisting forms; in other words, is man of one or many species?* To this question we immediately obtain distinct answers diametrically opposed to each other: the one party positively maintaining that man is a *species* and is essentially *one*—that all differences are but local and temporary variations, produced by the different physical and moral conditions by which he is surrounded; the other party maintaining with equal confidence that man is a genus of *many species*, each of which is practically unchangeable, and has ever been as distinct, or even more distinct, than we now behold them. This difference of opinion is somewhat remarkable, when we consider that both parties are well acquainted with the subject; both use the same vast accumulation of facts; both reject those early traditions of mankind which profess to give an account of his origin; and both declare that they are seeking fearlessly after truth alone.   I believe, however, it will be found to be the old story over again of the shield—gold on one side and silver on the other—about which the knights disputed; each party will persist in looking only at the portion of truth on his own side of the question, and at the error which is mingled with his opponent's doctrine.   It is my wish to show how the two opposing |clix| views can be combined so as to eliminate the error and retain the truth in each, and it is by means of Mr. Darwin's celebrated theory of "Natural Selection" that I hope to do this, and thus to harmonise the conflicting theories of modern anthropologists.

Let us first see what each party has to say for itself.   In favour of the unity of mankind it is argued that there are no races without transitions to others; that every race exhibits within itself variations of colour, of hair, of feature, and of form, to such a degree as to bridge over to a large extent the gap that separates it from other races.   It is asserted that no race is homogeneous; that there is a tendency to vary; that climate, food, and habits produce and render permanent physical peculiarities, which, though slight in the limited periods allowed to our observation, would, in the long ages during which the human race has existed, have sufficed to produce all the differences that now appear.   It is further asserted that the advocates of the opposite theory do not agree among themselves; that some would make three, some five, some fifty or a hundred and fifty species of man; some would have had each species created in pairs, while others require nations to have at once sprung into existence, and that there is no stability or consistency in any doctrine but that of one primitive stock.

The advocates of the original diversity of man, on the other hand, have much to say for themselves.   They argue that proofs of change in man have never been brought forward except to the most trifling amount, while evidence of his permanence meets us everywhere. The Portuguese and Spaniards, settled for two or three centuries in South America, retain their chief physical, mental, and moral characteristics; the Dutch boers at the Cape, and the descendants of the early Dutch settlers in the Moluccas, have not lost the features or the colour of the Germanic races; the Jews, scattered over the world in the most diverse climates, retain the same characteristic lineaments everywhere; the Egyptian sculptures and paintings show us that, for at least 4000 or 5000 years, the strongly contrasted features of the Negro and the Semitic races have remained altogether unchanged; while more recent discoveries prove that, in the case at least of the American aborigines, the mound-buildings of the Mississippi valley, and the dwellers on Brazilian mountains, had still in the very infancy of the human race the same characteristic type of cranial formation that now distinguishes them.

If we endeavour to decide impartially on the merits of this difficult controversy, judging solely by the evidence that each party has brought forward, it certainly seems that the best of the argument is on the side of those who maintain the primitive diversity of man. Their opponents have not been able to refute the permanence of existing races as far back as we can trace them, and have failed to show, in a single case, that at any former epoch the well marked varieties of mankind approximated more closely than they do at the present day. At the same time this is but negative evidence. A condition of immobility for four or five thousand years, does not preclude an advance at an earlier epoch, and—if we can show that there |clx| are causes in nature which would check any further physical change when certain conditions were fulfilled—does not even render such an advance improbable, if there are any general arguments to be adduced in its favour. Such a cause, I believe, does exist, and I shall now endeavour to point out its nature and its mode of operation.

In order to make my argument intelligible, it is necessary for me to explain very briefly the theory of "Natural Selection" promulgated by Mr. Darwin, and the power which it possesses of modifying the forms of animals and plants. The grand feature in the multiplication of organic life is that of close general resemblance, combined with more or less individual variation. The child resembles its parents or ancestors more or less closely in all its peculiarities, deformities, or beauties; it resembles them in general more than it does any other individuals; yet children of the same parents are not all alike, and it often happens that they differ very considerably from their parents and from each other. This is equally true of man, of all animals, and of all plants. Moreover, it is found that individuals do not differ from their parents in certain particulars

only, while in all others they are exact duplicates of them.   They
differ from them and from each other in every particular: in form,
in size, in colour, in the structure of internal as well as of external
organs; in those subtle peculiarities which produce differences of
constitution, as well as in those still more subtle ones which lead
to modifications of mind and character.   In other words, in every
possible way, in every organ and in every function, individuals of
the same stock vary.

Now, health, strength, and long life are the results of a harmony
between the individual and the universe that surrounds it.   Let us
suppose that at any given moment this harmony is perfect.   A
certain animal is exactly fitted to secure its prey, to escape from its
enemies, to resist the inclemencies of the seasons, and to rear a
numerous and healthy offspring.   But a change now takes place.
A series of cold winters, for instance, come on, making food scare,
and bringing an immigration of some other animals to compete with
the former inhabitants of the district.   The new immigrant is swift
of foot, and surpasses its rivals in the pursuit of game; the winter
nights are colder, and require a thicker fur as a protection, and
more nourishing food to keep up the heat of the system.   Our
supposed perfect animal is no longer in harmony with its universe;
it is in danger of dying of cold or of starvation.   But the animal
varies in its offspring.   Some of these are swifter than others—they
still manage to catch food enough; some are hardier and more
thickly furred—they manage in the cold nights to keep warm
enough; the slow, the weak, and the thinly clad soon die off.   Again
and again, in each succeeding generation, the same thing takes
place.   By this natural process, which is so inevitable that it cannot
be conceived not to act, those best adapted to live, live; those least
adapted, die.   It is sometimes said that we have no direct evidence
of the action of this selecting power in nature.   But it seems to me
we have better evidence than even direct observation would be,
because it is more universal, viz., the evidence of necessity.   It
must be so; for, as all wild animals in-|clxi|crease in a geometrical
ratio, while their actual numbers remain on the average stationary,
it follows that as many die annually as are born.   If therefore, we
deny natural selection, it can only be by asserting that in such a
case as I have supposed, the strong, the healthy, the swift, the well
clad, the well organised animals in every respect, have no advantage

over,—do not on the average live longer than the weak, the unhealthy, the slow, the ill-clad, and the imperfectly organised individuals; and this no sane man has yet been found hardy enough to assert.   But this is not all; for the offspring on the average resemble their parents, and the selected portion of each succeeding generation will therefore be stronger, swifter, and more thickly furred than the last; and if this process goes on for thousands of generations, our animal will have again become thoroughly in harmony with the new conditions in which is is placed.   But he will now be a different creature.   He will be not only swifter and stronger, and more furry, he will also probably have changed in colour, in form, perhaps have acquired a longer tail, or differently shaped ears; for it is an ascertained fact, that when one part of an animal is modified, some other parts almost always change as it were in sympathy with it.   Mr. Darwin calls this *"correlation of growth,"* and gives as instances that hairless dogs have imperfect teeth; blue eyed cats are deaf; small feet accompany short beaks in pigeons; and other equally interesting cases.

Grant, therefore, the premises: 1st.   That peculiarities of every kind are more or less hereditary.   2nd.   That the offspring of every animal vary more or less in all parts of their organisation.   3rd. That the universe in which these animals live, is not absolutely invariable;—none of which propositions can be denied; and then consider that the animals in any country (those at least which are not dying out) must at each successive period be brought into harmony with the surrounding conditions; and we have all the elements for a change of form and structure in the animals, keeping exact pace with changes of whatever nature in the surrounding universe.   Such changes must be slow, for the changes in the universe are very slow; but just as these slow changes become important, when we look at results after long periods of action, as we do when we perceive the alterations of the earth's surface during geological epochs; so the parallel changes in animal form become more and more striking according as the time they have been going on is great, as we see when we compare our living animals with those which we disentomb from each successively older geological formation.

This is briefly the theory of "natural selection," which explains the changes in the organic world as being parallel with, and in part dependent on those in the inorganic.   What we now have to inquire is,—Can this theory be applied in any way to the question of the origin of the races of man? or is there anything in human nature that takes him out of the category of those organic existences, over whose successive mutations it has had such powerful sway?

In order to answer these questions, we must consider why it is that "natural selection" acts so powerfully upon animals, and we shall, I |clxii| believe, find that its effect depends mainly upon their self-dependence and individual isolation.   A slight injury, a temporary illness, will often end in death, because it leaves the individual powerless against its enemies.   If a herbivorous animal is a little sick and has not fed well for a day or two, and the herd is then pursued by a beast of prey, our poor invalid inevitably falls a victim.   So in a carnivorous animal the least deficiency of vigour prevents its capturing food, and it soon dies of starvation.   There is, as a general rule, no mutual assistance between adults, which enables them to tide over a period of sickness.   Neither is there any division of labour; each must fulfil *all* the conditions of its existence, and, therefore, "natural selection" keeps all up to a pretty uniform standard.

But in man, as we now behold him, this is different.   He is social and sympathetic.   In the rudest tribes the sick are assisted at least with food; less robust health and vigour than the average does not entail death.   Neither does the want of perfect limbs or other organs produce the same effects as among animals.   Some division of labour takes place; the swiftest hunt, the less active fish, or gather fruits; food is to some extent exchanged or divided.   The action of natural selection is therefore checked; the weaker, the dwarfish, those of less active limbs, or less piercing eyesight, do not suffer the extreme penalty which falls upon animals so defective.

In proportion as these physical characteristics become of less importance, mental and moral qualities will have increasing influence on the well-being of the race.   Capacity for acting in concert, for protection and for the acquisition of food and shelter; sympathy, which leads all in turn to assist each other; the sense of right, which checks depredations upon our fellows; the decrease of the combative and destructive propensities; self-restraint in present appetites; and that intelligent foresight which prepares for the future, are all qualities that from their earliest appearance must have been for the benefit of each community, and would, therefore, have become the subjects of "natural selection." For it is evident that such qualities would be for the well-being of man; would guard him against external enemies, against internal dissensions, and against the effects of inclement seasons and impending famine, more surely than could any merely physical modification. Tribes in which such mental and moral qualities were predominant, would therefore have an advantage in the struggle for existence over other tribes in which they were less developed, would live and maintain their numbers, while the others would decrease and finally succumb.

Again, when any slow changes of physical geography, or of climate, make it necessary for an animal to alter its food, its clothing, or its weapons, it can only do so by a corresponding change in its own bodily structure and internal organisation. If a larger or more powerful beast is to be captured and devoured, as when a carnivorous animal which has hitherto preyed on sheep is obliged from their decreasing numbers to attack buffaloes, it is only the strongest who can hold,—those with most powerful claws, and formidable canine teeth, that can struggle with and overcome such an animal. Natural |clxiii| selection immediately comes into play, and by its action these organs gradually become adapted to their new requirements. But man, under similar circumstances, does not require longer nails or teeth, greater bodily strength or swiftness. He makes sharper spears, or a better bow, or he constructs a cunning pitfall, or combines in a hunting party to circumvent his new prey. The capacities which enable him to do this are what he requires to be strengthened, and these will, therefore, be gradually modified by "natural selection," while the form and structure of his body will remain unchanged. So when a glacial epoch comes on, some animals must acquire warmer fur, or a covering of fat, or else die of cold. Those best clothed by nature are, therefore, preserved by natural selection. Man, under the same circumstances, will make himself warmer clothing, and build better houses; and the necessity of doing this will react upon his mental organisation and social condition—will advance them while his natural body remains naked as before.

When the accustomed food of some animal becomes scarce or totally fails, it can only exist by becoming adapted to a new kind of food, a food perhaps less nourishing and less digestible. "Natural

selection" will now act upon the stomach and intestines, and all
their individual variations will be taken advantage of to modify the
race into harmony with its new food.   In many cases, however, its
is probable that this cannot be done.   The internal organs may not
vary quick enough, and then the animal will decrease in numbers,
and finally become extinct.   But man guards himself from such
accidents by superintending and guiding the operations of nature.
He plants the seed of his most agreeable food, and thus procures a
supply independent of the accidents of varying seasons or natural
extinction.   He domesticates animals which serve him either to
capture food or for food itself, and thus changes of any great extent
in his teeth or digestive organs are rendered unnecessary.   Man,
too, has everywhere the use of fire, and by its means can render
palatable a variety of animal and vegetable substances, which he
could hardly otherwise make use of, and thus obtains for himself
a supply of food far more varied and abundant than that which any
animal can command.

Thus man, by the mere capacity of clothing himself, and making
weapons and tools, has taken away from nature that power of
changing the external form and structure which she exercises over
all other animals.   As the competing races by which they are
surrounded, the climate, the vegetation, or the animals which serve
them for food, are slowly changing, they must undergo a corresponding change in their structure, habits, and constitution, to keep
them in harmony with the new conditions—to enable them to live
and maintain their numbers.   But man does this by means of his
intellect alone; which enables him with an unchanged body still to
keep in harmony with the changing universe.

From the time, therefore, when the social and sympathetic feelings
came into active operation, and the intellectual and moral faculties
became fairly developed, man would cease to be influenced by
"natural selection" in his physical form and structure; as an |clxiv|
animal he would remain almost stationary; the changes of the
surrounding universe would cease to have upon him that powerful
modifying effect which it exercises over other parts of the organic
world.   But from the moment that his body became stationary, his
mind would become subject to those very influences from which his
body had escaped; every slight variation in his mental and moral
nature which should enable him better to guard against adverse

circumstances, and combine for mutual comfort and protection, would be preserved and accumulated; the better and higher specimens or our race would therefore increase and spread, the lower and more brutal would give way and successively die out, and that rapid advancement of mental organisation would occur, which has raised the very lowest races of man so far above the brutes, (although differing so little from some of them in physical structure), and, in conjunction with scarcely perceptible modifications of form, has developed the wonderful intellect of the Germanic races.

But from the time when this mental and moral advance commenced, and man's physical character became fixed and immutable, a new series of causes would come into action, and take part in his mental growth. The diverse aspects of nature would now make themselves felt, and profoundly influence the character of the primitive man.

When the power that had hitherto modified the body, transferred its action to the mind, then races would advance and become improved merely by the harsh discipline of a sterile soil and inclement seasons. Under their influence, a hardier, a more provident, and a more social race would be developed, than in those regions where the earth produces a perennial supply of vegetable food, and where neither foresight nor ingenuity are required to prepare for the rigours of winter. And is it not the fact that in all ages, and in every quarter of the globe, the inhabitants of temperate have been superior to those of tropical countries? All the great invasions and displacements of races have been from North to South, rather than the reverse; and we have no record of there ever having existed, any more than there exists to-day, a solitary instance of an indigenous inter-tropical civilisation. The Mexican civilisation and government came from the North, and, as well as the Peruvian, was established, not in the rich tropical plains, but on the lofty and sterile plateaux of the Andes. The religion and civilisation of Ceylon were introduced from North India; the successive conquerors of the Indian peninsula came from the North-west, and it was the bold and adventurous tribes of the North that overran and infused new life into Southern Europe.

It is the same great law of *"the preservation of favoured races in the struggle for life,"* which leads to the inevitable extinction of all |clxv| those low and mentally undeveloped populations with which Europeans come in contact. The red Indian in North America, and in Brazil; the Tasmanian, Australian and New Zealander in the southern hemisphere, die out, not from any one special cause, but from the inevitable effects of an unequal mental and physical struggle. The intellectual and moral, as well as the physical qualities of the European are superior; the same powers and capacities which have made him rise in a few centuries from the condition of the wandering savage with a scanty and stationary population to his present state of culture and advancement, with a greater average longevity, a greater average strength, and a capacity of more rapid increase,—enable him when in contact with the savage man, to conquer in the struggle for existence, and to increase at his expense, just as the more favourable increase at the expense of the less favourable varieties in the animal and vegetable kingdoms, just as the weeds of Europe overrun North America and Australia, extinguishing native productions by the inherent vigour of their organisation, and by their greater capacity for existence and multiplication.

If these views are correct; if in proportion as man's social, moral and intellectual faculties became developed, his physical structure would cease to be affected by the operation of "natural selection," we have a most important clue to the origin of races.   For it will follow, that those striking and constant peculiarities which mark the great divisions of mankind, could not have been produced and rendered permanent after the action of this power had become transferred from physical to mental variations.   They must, therefore, have existed since the very infancy of the race; they must have originated at a period when man was gregarious, but scarcely social, with a mind perceptive but not reflective, ere any sense of *right* or feelings of *sympathy* had been developed in him.

By a powerful effort of the imagination, it is just possible to perceive him at that early epoch existing as a single homogeneous race without the faculty of speech, and probably inhabiting some tropical region.   He would be still subject, like the rest of the organic world, to the action of "natural selection," which would retain his physical form and constitution in harmony with the surrounding universe.   He must have been even then a dominant race, spreading widely over the warmer regions of the earth as it then existed, and, in agreement with what we see in the case of other dominant species, gradually becoming modified in accordance with local conditions.   As he ranged farther from his original home, and became exposed to greater extremes of climate, to greater changes of food, and had to contend with new enemies, organic and inorganic, useful variations in his constitution would be selected and rendered permanent, and would, on the principle of "correlation of growth", be accompanied |clxvi| by corresponding external physical changes.   Thus arose those striking characteristics and special modifications which still distinguish the chief races of mankind. The red, black, yellow, or blushing white skin; the straight, the curly, the woolly hair; the scanty or abundant beard; the straight or oblique eyes; the various forms of the pelvis, the cranium, and other parts of the skeleton.

But while these changes had been going on, his mental development had correspondingly advanced, and had now reached that condition in which it began powerfully to influence his whole existence, and would therefore, become subject to the irresistible action of "natural selection."   This action would rapidly give the ascendancy to mind: speech would probably now be first developed, leading to a still further advance of the mental faculties, and from that moment man as regards his physical form would remain almost stationary.   The art of making weapons, division of labour, anticipation of the future, restraint of the appetites, moral, social and sympathetic feelings, would now have a preponderating influence on his well being, and would therefore be that part of his nature on which "natural selection" would most powerfully act; and we should thus have explained that wonderful persistence of mere physical characteristics, which is the stumbling-block of those who advocate the unity of mankind.

We are now, therefore, enabled to harmonise the conflicting views of anthropologists on this subject.   Man may have been, indeed I believe must have been, once a homogeneous race; but it was at a period of which we have as yet discovered no remains, at a period so remote in his history, that he had not yet acquired that wonderfully developed brain, the organ of the mind, which now, even in his lowest examples, raises him far above the highest brutes;—at a period when he had the form but hardly the nature of man, when he neither possessed human speech, nor those sympathetic and moral feelings which in a greater or less degree everywhere now distinguish the race. Just in proportion as these truly human faculties became developed in him would his physical features become fixed and permanent, because the latter would be of less importance to his well being; he would be kept in harmony with the slowly changing universe around him, by an advance in mind, rather than by a change in body. If, therefore, we are of opinion that he was not really man till these higher faculties were developed, we may fairly assert that there were many originally distinct races of men; while, if we think that a being like us in form and structure, but with mental faculties scarcely raised above the brute, must still be considered to have been human, we are fully entitled to maintain the common origin of all mankind.

These considerations, it will be seen, enable us to place the origin of man at a much more remote geological epoch than has yet been thought possible. He may even have lived in the Eocene or Miocene period, when not a single mammal possessed the same form as any existing species. For, in the long series of ages during which the forms of these primeval mammals were being slowly specialised into those now inhabiting the earth, the power which acted to modify them would |clxvii| only affect the mental organisation of man. His brain alone would have increased in size and complexity and his cranium have undergone corresponding changes of form, while the whole structure of lower animals was being changed. This will enable us to understand how the fossil crania of Denise and Engis agree so closely with existing forms, although they undoubtedly existed in company with large mammalia now extinct. The Neanderthal skull may be a specimen of one of the lowest races then existing, just as the Australians are the lowest of our modern epoch. We have no reason to suppose that mind and brain and skull-modification, could go on quicker than that of the other parts of the organisation, and we must, therefore, look back very far in the past to find man in that early condition in which his mind was not sufficiently developed to remove his body from the modifying influence of external conditions, and the cumulative action of "natural selection." I believe, therefore, that there is no *à priori* reason against our finding the remains of man or his works, in the middle or later tertiary deposits. The absence of all such remains in the European beds of this age has little weight, because as we go further back in time, it is natural to suppose that man's distribution over the surface of the earth was less universal than at present. Besides, Europe was in a great measure submerged during the tertiary epoch, and though its scattered islands may have been uninhabited by man, it by no means follows that he did not at the same time exist in warm or tropical continents.   If geologists can point out to us the most extensive land in the warmer regions of the earth, which has not been submerged since eocene or miocene times, it is there that we may expect to find some traces of the very early progenitors of man.   It is there that we may trace back the gradually decreasing brain of former races, till we come to a time when the body also, begins materially to differ.   Then we shall have reached the starting point of the human family.   Before that period, he had not mind enough to preserve his body from change, and would, therefore, have been subject to the same comparatively rapid modifications of form as the other mammals.

If the views I have here endeavoured to sustain have any foundation, they give us a new argument for placing man apart, as not only the head and culminating point of the grand series of organic nature, but as in some degree a new and distinct order of being.   From those infinitely remote ages, when the first rudiments of organic life appeared upon the earth, every plant, and every animal has been subject to one great law of physical change.   As the earth has gone through its grand cycles of geological, climatal and organic progress, every form of life has been subject to its irresistible action, and has been continually, but imperceptibly moulded into such new shapes as would preserve their harmony with the ever changing universe.   No living thing could escape this law of its being; none could remain unchanged and live, amid the universal change around it.

At length, however, there came into existence a being in whom that subtle force we term *mind*, became of greater importance than his mere bodily structure.   Though with a naked and unprotected |clxviii| body, *this* gave him clothing against the varying inclemencies of the seasons.   Though unable to compete with the deer in swiftness, or with the wild bull in strength, *this* gave him weapons with which to capture or overcome both.   Though less capable than most other animals of living on the herbs and the fruits that unaided nature supplies, this wonderful faculty taught him to govern and direct nature to his own benefit, and make her produce food for him

when and where he pleased.   From the moment when the first skin
was used as a covering, when the first rude spear was formed to
assist in the chase, the first seed sown or shoot planted, a grand
revolution was effected in nature, a revolution which in all the
previous ages of the earth's history had had no parallel, for a being
had arisen who was no longer necessarily subject to change with the
changing universe—a being who was in some degree superior to
nature, inasmuch, as he knew how to control and regulate her
action, and could keep himself in harmony with her, not by a change
in body, but by an advance of mind.

Here, then, we see the true grandeur and dignity of man.   On
this view of his special attributes, we may admit that even those
who claim for him a position as an order, a class, or a sub-kingdom
by himself, have some reason on their side.   He is, indeed, a being
apart, since he is not influenced by the great laws which irresistibly
modify all other organic beings.   Nay more; this victory which he
has gained for himself gives him a directing influence over other
existences.   Man has not only escaped "natural selection" himself,
but he actually is able to take away some of that power from nature
which, before his appearance, she universally exercised.   We can
anticipate the time when the earth will produce only cultivated
plants and domestic animals; when man's selection shall have
supplanted "natural selection"; and when the ocean will be the only
domain in which that power can be exerted, which for countless
cycles of ages ruled supreme over all the earth.

Briefly to recapitulate the argument;—in two distinct ways has
man escaped the influence of those laws which have produced
unceasing change in the animal world.   By his superior intellect
he is enabled to provide himself with clothing and weapons, and by
cultivating the soil to obtain a constant supply of congenial food.
This renders it unnecessary for his body, like those of the the lower
animals, to be modified in accordance with changing conditions—to
gain a warmer natural covering, to acquire more powerful teeth or
claws, or to become adapted to obtain and digest new kinds of food,
as circumstances may require.   By his superior sympathetic and
moral feelings, he becomes fitted for the social state; he ceases to
plunder the weak and helpless of his tribe; he shares the game which
he has caught with less active or less fortunate hunters, or exchanges
it for weapons which even the sick or the deformed can fashion; he

saves the sick and wounded from death; and thus the power which leads to the rigid destruction of all animals who cannot in every respect help themselves, is prevented from acting on him.

This power is "natural selection"; and, as by no other means can |clxix| it be shewn that individual variations can ever become accumulated and rendered permanent so as to form well-marked races, it follows that the differences we now behold in mankind must have been produced before he became possessed of a human intellect or human sympathies.   This view also renders possible, or even requires, the existence of man at a comparatively remote geological epoch.   For, during the long periods in which other animals have been undergoing modification in their whole structure to such an amount as to constitute distinct genera and families, man's *body* will have remained generically, or even specifically, the same, while his *head* and *brain* alone will have undergone modification equal to theirs.   We can thus understand how it is that, judging from the head and brain, Professor Owen places man in a distinct sub-class of mammalia, while, as regards the rest of his body, there is the closest anatomical resemblance to that of the anthropoid apes, "every tooth, every bone, strictly homologous—which makes the determination of the difference between *Homo* and *Pithecus* the anatomist's difficulty."   The present theory fully recognises and accounts for these facts; and we may perhaps claim as corroborative of its truth, that it neither requires us to depreciate the intellectual chasm which separates man from the apes, nor refuses full recognition of the striking resemblances to them which exist in other parts of its structure.

In concluding this brief sketch of a great subject, I would point out its bearing upon the future of the human race.   If my conclusions are just, it must inevitably follow that the higher—the more intellectual and moral—must displace the lower and more degraded races; and the power of "natural selection", still acting on his mental organisation, must ever lead to the more perfect adaptation of man's higher faculties to the conditions of surrounding nature, and to the exigencies of the social state.   While his external form will probably ever remain unchanged, except in the development of that perfect beauty which results from a healthy and well organised body, refined and ennobled by the highest intellectual faculties and sympathetic emotions, his mental constitution may continue to advance and improve till the world is again inhabited by a single homogeneous race, no individual of which will be inferior to the noblest specimens of existing humanity.   Each one will then work out his own happiness in relation to that of his fellows; perfect freedom of action will be maintained, since the well balanced moral faculties will never permit any one to transgress on the equal freedom of others; restrictive laws will not be wanted, for each man will be guided by the best of laws; a thorough appreciation of the rights, and a perfect sympathy with the feelings, of all about him; compulsory government will have died away as unnecessary (for every man will know how to govern himself), and will be replaced by voluntary associations for all beneficial public purposes; the passions and animal propensities will be restrained within those limits which most conduce to happiness; and mankind will have at length discovered |clxx| that it was only required of them to develop the capacities of their higher nature, in order to convert this earth, which had so long been the theatre of their unbridled passions, and the scene of unimaginable misery, into as bright a paradise as ever haunted the dreams of seer or poet.*

---

* The general idea and argument of this paper I believe to be new.   It was, however, the perusal of Mr. Herbert Spencer's works, especially *Social Statics*, that suggested it to me, and at the same time furnished me with some of the applications.

TWO

FRANCIS GALTON (1822–1911)

Hereditary Talent and Character

Macmillan's Magazine
Volume 12, 1865, pp. 318–27

Galton, a younger cousin of Darwin, was perhaps the greatest polymath of his time. Of all his works none brought him more renown than Hereditary Genius *(1869). Here he sought to demonstrate that certain mental characteristics, and intelligence especially, were inherited in the same way as physical attributes. His Preface opened thus: 'The idea of investigating the subject of hereditary genius occurred to me during the course of a purely ethnological inquiry, into the mental peculiarities of different races.' Galton's preliminary thoughts on the subject had been marshalled in two identically titled articles for* Macmillan's Magazine *(June and August 1865), of which Darwin wrote approvingly. The second of these, reprinted below, provides a helpful early summary of his views about the need for eugenic policies in Europe and beyond. Galton believes in the existence of a clear and heritable hierarchy of physical and mental talent both within and between races. He hints that those who are best endowed among the higher stocks must strive to retain dominance over inferiors of their own kind as well as over members of other races. For Galton this dominance is inseparable from questions of differential breeding rates. Early in the essay he suggests that there is nothing too difficult about causing the inferior elements within a population to disappear inside a few generations. However, he is already less sanguine than Wallace about a* laissez-faire *approach towards any racial improvement. Galton certainly thought it possible to breed a race mentally and morally much superior to anything known in the contemporary world, but equally he had no doubt that conscious direction was essential to any effective eugenic campaign. Concerted effort was required to counteract the one great drawback to civilization which he identified towards the end of the essay. This was its tendency to diminish the rigour with which Natural Selection should operate, and thereby to disturb proper patterns of hierarchy.*

I have shown, in my previous paper, that intellectual capacity is so largely transmitted by descent that, out of every hundred sons of men distinguished in the open professions, no less than eight are found to have rivalled their fathers in eminence.   It must be recollected that success of this kind implies the simultaneous inheritance of many points of character, in addition to mere intellectual capacity.   A man must inherit good health, a love of mental work, a strong purpose, and considerable ambition, in order to achieve successes of the high order of which we are speaking.   The deficiency of any one of these qualities would certainly be injurious, and probably be fatal to his chance of obtaining great distinction.   But more than this: the proportion we have arrived at takes |319| no account whatever of one-half of the hereditary influences that form the nature of the child.   My particular method of inquiry did not admit of regard being paid to the influences transmitted by the mother, whether they had strengthened or weakened those transmitted by the father.   Lastly, though the talent and character of both of the parents might, in any particular case, be of a remarkably noble order, and thoroughly congenial, yet they would necessarily have such mongrel antecedents that it would be absurd to expect their children to invariably equal them in their natural endowments.   The law of atavism prevents it.   When we estimate at its true importance this accumulation of impediments in the way of the son of a distinguished father rivalling his parent—the mother being selected, as it were, at haphazard—we cannot but feel amazed at the number of instances in which a successful rivalship has occurred.   Eight per cent. is as large a proportion as could have been expected on the most stringent hypothesis of hereditary transmission.   No one, I think, can doubt, from the facts and analogies I have brought forward, that, if talented men were mated with talented women, of the same mental and physical characters as themselves, generation after generation, we might produce a highly-bred human race, with no more tendency to revert to meaner ancestral types than is shown by our long-established breeds of race-horses and fox-hounds.

It may be said that, even granting the validity of my arguments, it would be impossible to carry their indications into practical effect.   For instance, if we divided the rising generation into two castes, A and B, of which A was selected for natural gifts, and B was the refuse, then, supposing marriage was confined within the pale of the caste to which each individual belonged, it might be objected that we should simply differentiate our race—that we should create a good and bad caste, but we should not improve the race as a whole.   I reply that this is by no means the necessary result.   There remains another very important law to be brought into play.   Any agency, however indirect, that would somewhat hasten the marriages in caste A, and retard those in caste B, would result in a larger proportion of children being born to A than to B, and would end by wholly eliminating B, and replacing it by A.

Let us take a definite case, in order to give precision to our ideas.   We will suppose the population to be, in the first instance, stationary; A and B to be equal in numbers; and the children of each married-pair who survive to maturity to be rather more than 2½ in the case of A, and rather less than 1½ in the case of B. This no extravagant hypothesis.   Half the population of the British Isles are born of mothers under the age of thirty years.

The result in the first generation would be that the total population would be unchanged, but that only one-third part of it would consist of the children of B.   In the second generation, the descendants of B would be reduced to two-ninths of their original numbers, but the total population would begin to increase, owing to the greater preponderance of the prolific caste A.   At this point the law of natural selection would powerfully assist in the substitution of caste A for caste B, by pressing heavily on the minority of weakly and incapable men.

The customs that affect the direction and date of marriages are already numerous.   In many families, marriages between cousins are discouraged and checked.   Marriages, in other respects appropriate, are very commonly deferred, through prudential considerations.   If it was generally felt that intermarriages between A and B were as unadvisable as they are supposed to be between cousins, and that marriages in A ought to be hastened, on the ground of prudential considerations, while those in B ought to be discouraged and retarded, then, I believe, we should have agencies amply sufficient to eliminate B in a few generations.

I hence conclude that the improvement of the breed of mankind is no |320| insuperable difficulty.   If everybody were to agree on the improvement of the race of man being a matter of the very utmost importance, and if the theory of the hereditary transmission of qualities in men was as thoroughly understood as it is in the case of our domestic animals, I see no absurdity in supposing that, in some way or other, the improvement would be carried into effect.

It remains for me in the present article to show that hereditary influence is as clearly marked in mental aptitudes as in general intellectual power.   I will then enter into some of the considerations which my views on hereditary talent and character naturally suggest.

I will first quote a few of those cases in which characteristics have been inherited that clearly depend on peculiarities of organization.   Prosper Lucas was among our earliest encyclopaedists on this subject.   It is distinctly shown by him, and agreed to by others, such as Mr. G. Lewes, that predisposition to any form of disease, or any malformation, may become an inheritance.   Thus disease of the heart is hereditary; so are tubercles in the lungs; so also are diseases of the brain, of the liver, and of the kidney; so are diseases of the eye and of the ear.   General maladies are equally inheritable, as gout and madness.   Longevity on the one hand, and premature deaths on the other, go by descent.   If we consider a class of peculiarities, more recondite in their origin than these, we shall still find the law of inheritance to hold good.   A morbid susceptibility to contagious disease, or to the poisonous effects of opium, or of calomel, and an aversion to the taste of meat, are all found to be inherited.   So is a craving for drink, or for gambling, strong sexual passion, a proclivity to pauperism, to crimes of violence, and to crimes of fraud.

There are certain marked types of character, justly associated with marked types of feature and of temperament.   We hold, axiomatically, that the latter are inherited (the case being too notorious, and too consistent with the analogy afforded by brute animals, to render argument necessary), and we therefore infer the same of the former.   For instance, the face of the combatant is square, coarse, and heavily jawed.   It differs from that of the ascetic, the voluptuary, the dreamer, and the charlatan.

Still more strongly marked than these, are the typical features and characters of different races of men.   The Mongolians, Jews, Negroes, Gipsies, and American Indians; severally propagate their kinds; and each kind differs in character and intellect, as well as in

colour and shape, from the other four.   They, and a vast number
of other races, form a class of instances worthy of close investigation,
in which peculiarities of character are invariably transmitted from
the parents to the offspring.

In founding argument on the innate character of different races,
it is necessary to bear in mind the exceeding docility of man.   His
mental habits in mature life are the creatures of social discipline,
as well as of inborn aptitudes, and it is impossible to ascertain what
is due to the latter alone, except by observing several individuals
of the same race, reared under various influences, and noting the
peculiarities of character that invariably assert themselves.   But,
even when we have imposed these restrictions to check a hasty and
imaginative conclusion, we find there remain abundant data to
prove an astonishing diversity in the natural characteristics of
different races.   It will be sufficient for our purpose if we fix our
attention upon the peculiarities of one or two of them.

The race of the American Indians is spread over an enormous
area, and through every climate; for it reaches from the frozen
regions of the North, through the equator, down to the inclement
regions of the South.   It exists in thousands of disconnected
communities, speaking nearly as many different languages.   It has
been subjected to a strange variety of political influences, such as
its own despotisms in Peru, Mexico, Natchez, and Bogota, and its
|321| numerous republics, large and small.   Members of the race
have been conquered and ruled by military adventures from Spain
and Portugal; others have been subjugated to Jesuitical rule;
numerous settlements have been made by strangers on its soil; and,
finally, the north of the continent has been colonized by European
races.   Excellent observers have watched the American Indians
under all these influences, and their almost unanimous conclusion
is as follows:—

The race is divided into many varieties, but it has fundamentally
the same character throughout the whole of America.   The men,
and in a less degree the women, are naturally cold, melancholic,
patient, and taciturn.   A father, mother, and their children, are
said to live together in a hut, like persons assembled by accident,
not tied by affection.   The youths treat their parents with neglect,
and often with such harshness and insolence as to horrify Europeans
who have witnessed their conduct.   The mothers have been seen

to commit infanticide without the slightest discomposure, and numerous savage tribes have died out in consequence of this practice. The American Indians are eminently non-gregarious. They nourish a sullen reserve, and show little sympathy with each other, even when in great distress. The Spaniards had to enforce the common duties of humanity by positive laws. They are strangely taciturn. When not engaged in action they will sit whole days in one posture without opening their lips, and wrapped up in their narrow thoughts. They usually march in Indian file, that is to say, in a long line, at some distance from each other, without exchanging a word. They keep the same profound silence in rowing a canoe, unless they happen to be excited by some extraneous cause. On the other hand, their patriotism and local attachments are strong, and they have an astonishing sense of personal dignity. The nature of the American Indians appears to contain the minimum of affectionate and social qualities compatible with the continuance of their race.

Here, then, is a well-marked type of character, that formerly prevailed over a large part of the globe, with which other equally marked types of character in other regions are strongly contrasted. Take, for instance, the typical West African Negro. He is more unlike the Red man in his mind than in his body. Their characters are almost opposite, one to the other. The Red man has great patience, great reticence, great dignity, and no passion; the Negro has strong impulsive passions, and neither patience, reticence, nor dignity. He is warm-hearted, loving towards his master's children, and idolised by the children in return. He is eminently gregarious, for he is always jabbering, quarrelling, tom-tom-ing, or dancing. He is remarkably domestic, and he is endowed with such constitutional vigour, and is so prolific, that his race is irrepressible.

The Hindu, the Arab, the Mongol, the Teuton, and very many more, have each of them their peculiar characters. We have not space to analyse them on this occasion; but, whatever they are, they are transmitted, generation after generation, as truly as their physical forms.

What is true for the entire race is equally true for its varieties. If we were to select persons who were born with a type of character that we desired to intensify,—suppose it was one that approached to some ideal standard of perfection—and if we compelled marriage within the limits of the society so selected, generation after generation; there can be no doubt that the offspring would ultimately be born with the qualities we sought, as surely as if we had been breeding for physical features, and not for intellect or disposition.

Our natural constitution seems to bear as direct and stringent a relation to that of our forefathers as any other physical effect does to its cause.   Our bodies, minds, and capabilities of development have been derived from them.   Everything we possess at our birth is a heritage from our ancestors.

Can we hand anything down to our children, that we have fairly won by |322| our own independent exertions?   Will our children be born with more virtuous dispositions, if we ourselves have acquired virtuous habits?   Or are we no more than passive transmitters of a nature we have received, and which we have no power to modify?   There are but a few instances in which habit even seems to be inherited.   The chief among them are such as those of dogs being born excellent pointers; of the attachment to man shown by dogs; and of the fear of man, rapidly learnt and established among the birds of newly-discovered islands.   But all of these admit of being accounted for on other grounds than the hereditary transmission of habits.   Pointing is, in some faint degree, a natural disposition of all dogs.   Breeders have gradually improved upon it, and created the race we now possess.   There is nothing to show that the reason why dogs are born staunch pointers is that their parents had been broken into acquiring an artificial habit.   So as regards the fondness of dogs for man.   It is inherent to a great extent in the genus.   The dingo, or wild dog of Australia, is attached to the man who has caught him when a puppy, and clings to him even although he is turned adrift to hunt for his own living.   This quality in dogs is made more intense by the custom of selection. The savage dogs are lost or killed; the tame ones are kept and bred from.   Lastly, as regards the birds.   As soon as any of their flock has learned to fear, I presume that its frightened movements on the approach of man form a language that is rapidly and unerringly understood by the rest, old or young; and that, after a few repetitions of the signal, man becomes an object of well-remembered mistrust.   Moreover, just as natural selection has been shown to encourage love of man in domestic dogs, so it tends to encourage fear of man in all wild animals—the tamer varieties perishing owing to their misplaced confidence, and the wilder ones continuing their breed.

If we examine the question from the opposite side, a list of life-long habits in the parents might be adduced which leave no per-ceptible trace on their descendants.   I cannot ascertain that the son of an old soldier learns his drill more quickly than the son of an artizan.   I am assured that the sons of fishermen, whose ancestors have pursued the same calling time out of mind, are just as sea-sick as the sons of landsmen when they first go to sea. I cannot discover that the castes of India show signs of being naturally endowed with special aptitudes.   If the habits of an individual are transmitted to his descendants, it is, as Darwin says, in a very small degree, and is hardly, if at all, traceable.

We shall therefore take an approximately correct view of the origin of our life, if we consider our own embryos to have sprung immediately from those embryos whence our parents were developed, and these from the embryos of *their* parents, and so on for ever. We should in this way look on the nature of mankind, and perhaps on that of the whole animated creation, as one continuous system, ever pushing out new branches in all directions, that variously interlace, and that bud into separate lives at every point of interlacement.

This simile does not at all express the popular notion of life. Most persons seem to have a vague idea that a new element, specially fashioned in heaven, and not transmitted by simple descent, is introduced into the body of every newly-born infant.   Such a notion is unfitted to stand upon any scientific basis with which we are acquainted.   It is impossible it should be true, unless there exists some property or quality in man that is not transmissible by descent.   But the terms *talent* and *character* are exhaustive: they include the whole of man's spiritual nature so far as we are able to understand it.   No other class of qualities is known to exist, that we might suppose to have been interpolated from on high.   More-over, the idea is improbable from *à priori* considerations, because there is no other instance in which creative power operates under our own observation at the |323| present day, except it may be in the freedom in action of our own wills.   Wherever else we turn our eyes, we see nothing but law and order, and effect following cause.

But though, when we look back to our ancestors, the embryos of our progenitors may be conceived to have been developed, in each generation, immediately from the one that preceded it, yet we cannot take so restricted a view when we look forward. The interval that separates the full-grown animal from its embryo is too important to be disregarded. It is in this interval that Darwin's law of natural selection comes into play; and those conditions are entered into, which affect, we know not how, the "individual variation" of the offspring. I mean those that cause dissimilarity among brothers and sisters who are born successively, while twins, produced simultaneously, are often almost identical. If it were possible that embryos should descend directly from embryos, there might be developments in every direction, and the world would be filled with monstrosities. But this is not the order of nature. It is her fiat that the natural tendencies of animals should never disaccord long and widely with the conditions under which they are placed. Every animal before it is of an age to bear offspring, has to undergo frequent stern examinations before the board of nature, under the law of natural selection; where to be "plucked" is not necessarily disgrace, but is certainly death. Never let it be forgotten that man, as a reasonable being, has the privilege of not being helpless under the tyranny of uncongenial requirements, but that he can, and that he does, modify the subjects in which nature examines him, and that he has considerable power in settling beforehand the relative importance in the examination that shall be assigned to each separate subject.

It becomes a question of great interest how far moral monstrosities admit of being bred. Is there any obvious law that assigns a limit to the propagation of supremely vicious or extremely virtuous natures? In strength, agility, and other physical qualities, Darwin's law of natural selection acts with unimpassioned, merciless severity. The weakly die in the battle for life; the stronger and more capable individuals are alone permitted to survive, and to bequeath their constitutional vigour to future generations. Is there any corresponding rule in respect to moral character? I believe there is, and I have already hinted at it when speaking of the American Indians. I am prepared to maintain that its action by insuring a certain fundamental unity in the quality of the affections, enables men and the higher order of animals to sympathise in some degree with each other, and also, that this law forms the broad basis of our religious sentiments.

Animal life, in all but the very lowest classes, depends on at least one, and, more commonly, on all of the four following principles:—There must be affection, and it must be of four kinds: sexual, parental, filial, and social. The absolute deficiency of any one of these would be a serious hindrance, if not a bar to the continuance of any race. Those who possessed all of them, in the strongest measure, would, speaking generally, have an advantage in the struggle for existence. Without sexual affection, there would be no marriages, and no children; without parental affection, the children would be abandoned; without filial affection, they would stray and perish; and, without the social, each individual would be single-handed against rivals who were capable of banding themselves into tribes. Affection for others as well as for self, is therefore a necessary part of animal character. Disinterestedness is as essential to a brute's well-being as selfishness. No animal lives for itself alone, but also, at least occasionally, for its parent, its mate, its offspring, or its fellow. Companionship is frequently more grateful to an animal than abundant food. The safety of her young is considered by many a mother as a paramount object to her own. The passion for a mate is equally strong. The gregarious bird posts itself during its turn of duty as watchman on a tree, |324| by the side of the feeding flock. Its zeal to serve the common cause exceeds its care to attend to its own interests. Extreme selfishness is not a common vice. Narrow thoughts of self by no means absorb the minds of ordinary men; they occupy a secondary position in the thoughts of the more noble and generous of our race. A large part of an Englishman's life is devoted to others, or to the furtherance of general ideas, and not to directly personal ends. The Jesuit toils for his order, not for himself. Many plan for that which they can never live to see   At the hour of death they are still planning. An incompleted will, which might work unfairness among those who would succeed to the property of a dying man, harasses his mind. Personal obligations of all sorts press as heavily as in the fulness of health, although the touch of death is known to be on the point of cancelling them. It is so with animals. A dog's thoughts are towards his master, even when he suffers the extremest pain. His mind is largely filled at all times with sentiments of affection. But disinterested feelings are more necessary to man than to any other animal, because of the long period of his dependent childhood, and also because of his great social needs, due to his physical helplessness.   Darwin's law of natural selection would therefore be expected to develop these sentiments among men, even among the lowest barbarians, to a greater degree than among animals.

I believe that our religious sentiments spring primarily from these four sources.   The institution of celibacy is an open acknowledgment that the theistic and human affections are more or less convertible; I mean that by starving the one class the other becomes more intense and absorbing.   In savages, the theistic sentiment is chiefly, if not wholly, absent.   I would refer my readers, who may hesitate in accepting this assertion, to the recently published work of my friend Sir John Lubbock, "Prehistoric Times," p. 467—472, where the reports of travellers on the religion of savages are very ably and fairly collated.   The theistic sentiment is secondary, not primary. It becomes developed within us under the influence or reflection and reason.   All evidence tends to show that man is directed to the contemplation and love of God by instincts that he shares with the whole animal world, and that primarily appeal to the love of his neighbour.

Moral monsters are born among Englishmen, even at the present day; and, when they are betrayed by their acts, the law puts them out of the way, by the prison or the gallows, and so prevents them from continuing their breed. Townley, the murderer, is an instance in point.   He behaved with decorum and propriety; he was perfectly well-conducted to the gaol officials, and he corresponded with his mother in a style that was certainly flippant, but was not generally considered to be insane.   However, with all this reasonableness of disposition, he could not be brought to see that he had done anything particularly wrong in murdering the girl that was disinclined to marry him.   He was thoroughly consistent in his disregard for life, because, when his own existence became wearisome, he ended it with perfect coolness, by jumping from an upper staircase   It is a notable fact that a man without a conscience, like Townley, should be able to mix in English society for years, just like other people.

How enormous is the compass of the scale of human character, which reaches from dispositions like those we have just described, to that of a Socrates!   How various are the intermediate types of character that commonly fall under everybody's notice, and how differently are the principles of virtue measured out to different natures!   We can clearly observe the extreme diversity of character in children.   Some are naturally generous and open, others mean and tricky; some are warm and loving, others cold and heartless; some are meek and patient, others obstinate and self-asserting; some few have the tempers of angels, and at least as many have the tempers of devils.   In the |325| same way, as I showed in my previous paper, that by selecting men and women of rare and similar talent, and mating them together, generation after generation, an extraordinary gifted race might be developed, so a yet more rigid selection, having regard to their moral nature, would, I believe, result in a no less marked improvement of their natural disposition.

Let us consider an instance in which different social influences have modified the inborn dispositions of a nation.   The North American people has been bred from the most restless and combative class of Europe.   Whenever, during the last ten or twelve genera-tions, a political or religious party has suffered defeat, its prominent members, whether they were the best, or only the noisiest, have been apt to emigrate to America, as a refuge from persecution. Men fled to America for conscience' sake, and for that of unappre-ciated patriotism.   Every scheming knave, and every brutal ruffian, who feared the arm of the law, also turned his eyes in the same direction.   Peasants and artizans, whose spirit rebelled against the tyranny of society and the monotony of their daily life, and men of a higher position, who chafed under conventional restraints, all yearned towards America.   Thus the dispositions of the parents of the American people have been exceedingly varied, and usually extreme, either for good or for evil.   But in one respect they almost universally agreed.   Every head of an emigrant family brought with him a restless character, and a spirit apt to rebel.   If we estimate the moral nature of Americans from their present social state, we shall find it to be just what we might have expected from such a parentage.   They are enterprising, defiant, and touchy; impatient of authority; furious politicians; very tolerant of fraud and violence; possessing much high and generous spirit, and some true religious feeling, but strongly addicted to cant.

We have seen that the law of natural selection develops disinterested affection of a varied character even in animals and barbarian man.   Is the same law different in its requirements when acting on civilised man?   It is no doubt more favourable on the whole to civilized progress, but we must not expect to find as yet many marked signs of its action.   As a matter of history, our Anglo-Saxon civilization is only skin-deep.   It is but eight hundred years, or twenty-six generations, since the Conquest, and the ancestors of the large majority of Englishmen were the merest boors at a much later date than that.   It is said that among the heads of noble houses of England there can barely be found one that has a right to claim the sixteen quarterings—that is to say, whose great-great-grandparents were, all of them (sixteen in number), entitled to carry arms. Generally the nobility of a family is represented by only a few slender rills among a multiplicity of non-noble sources.

The most notable quality that the requirements of civilization have hitherto bred in us, living as we do in a rigorous climate and on a naturally barren soil, is the instinct of continuous steady labour.   This is alone possessed by civilized races, and it is possessed in a far greater degree by the feeblest individuals among them than by the most able-bodied savages.   Unless a man can work hard and regularly in England, he becomes an outcast.   If he only works by fits and starts he has not a chance of competition with steady workmen.   An artizan who has variable impulses, and wayward moods, is almost sure to end in intemperance and ruin.   In short, men who are born with wild and irregular dispositions, even though they contain much that is truly noble, are alien to the spirit of a civilized country, and they and their breed are eliminated from it by the law of selection.   On the other hand, a wild, untameable restlessness is innate with savages.   I have collected numerous instances where children of a low race have been separated at an early age from their parents, and reared as part of a settler's family, quite apart from their own people.   Yet, after years of civilized ways, in some fit of passion, or under |326| some craving, like that of a bird about to emigrate, they have abandoned their home, flung away their dress, and sought their countrymen in the bush, among whom they have subsequently been found living in contented barbarism, without a vestige of their gentle nurture.   This is eminently the case with the Australians, and I have heard of many others in South Africa.   There are also numerous instances in England where the restless nature of gipsy half-blood asserts itself with irresistible force.

Another difference, which may either be due to natural selection or to original difference of race, is the fact that savages seem incapable of progress after the first few years of their life.   The average children of all races are much on a par.   Occasionally, those of the lower races are more precocious than the Anglo-Saxons; as a brute beast of a few weeks old is certainly more apt and forward than a child of the same age.   But, as the years go by, the higher races continue to progress, while the lower ones gradually stop. They remain children in mind, with the passions of grown men. Eminent genius commonly asserts itself in tender years, but it continues long to develop.   The highest minds in the highest race seem to have been those who had the longest boyhood.   It is not those who were little men in early youth who have succeeded.   Here I may remark that, in the great mortality that besets the children of our poor, those who are members of precocious families, and who are therefore able to help in earning wages at a very early age, have a marked advantage over their competitors.   They, on the whole, live, and breed their like, while the others die.   But, if this sort of precocity be unfavourable to a race—if it be generally followed by an early arrest of development, and by a premature old age—then modern industrial civilization, in encouraging precocious varieties of men, deteriorates the breed.

Besides these three points of difference—endurance of steady labour, tameness of disposition, and prolonged development—I know of none that very markedly distinguishes the nature of the lower classes of civilized man from that of barbarians.   In the excitement of a pillaged town the English soldier is just as brutal as the savage.   Gentle manners seem, under those circumstances, to have been a mere gloss thrown by education over a barbarous nature.   One of the effect of civilization is to diminish the rigour of the application of the law of natural selection.   It preserves weakly lives, that would have perished in barbarous lands.   The sickly children of a wealthy family have a better chance of living and rearing offspring than the stalwart children of a poor one.   As with the body, so with the mind.   Poverty is more adverse to early marriages than is natural bad temper, or inferiority of intellect. In civilized society, money interposes her aegis between the law of

natural selection and very many of its rightful victims. Scrofula
and madness are naturalised among us by wealth; short-sightedness
is becoming so. There seems no limit to the morbific tendencies
of body or mind that might accumulate in a land where the law of
primogeniture was general, and where riches were more esteemed
than personal qualities. Neither is there any known limit to the
intellectual and moral grandeur of nature that might be introduced
into aristocratical families, if their representatives, who have such
rare privilege in winning wives that please them best, should
invariably, generation after generation, marry with a view of
transmitting those noble qualities to their descendants. Inferior
blood in the representative of a family might be eliminated from it
in a few generations. The share that a man retains in the constitution of his remote descendants is inconceivably small. The father
transmits, on an average, one-half of his nature, the grandfather
one-fourth, the great-grandfather one-eighth; the share decreasing
step by step, in a geometrical ratio, with great rapidity. Thus the
man who claims descent from a Norman baron, who accompanied
William the Conqueror twenty-six generations ago, has so minute
a share of that baron's influence in his |327| constitution, that, if
he weighs fourteen stone, the part of him which may be ascribed
to the baron (supposing, of course, there have been no additional
lines of relationship) is only one-fiftieth of a grain in weight—an
amount ludicrously disproportioned to the value popularly ascribed
to ancient descent. As a stroke of policy, I question if the head
of a great family, or a prince, would not give more strength to his
position, by marrying a wife who would bear him talented sons,
than one who would merely bring him the support of high family
connexions.

With the few but not insignificant exceptions we have specified
above, we are still barbarians in our nature, and we show it in a
thousand ways. The children who dabble and dig in the dirt have
inherited the instincts of untold generations of barbarian forefathers,
who dug with their nails for a large fraction of their lives. Our
ancestors were grubbing by the hour, each day, to get at the roots
they chiefly lived upon. They had to grub out pitfalls for their
game, holes for their palisades and hut-poles, hiding-places, and
ovens. Man became a digging animal by nature; and so we see the
delicately-reared children of our era very ready to revert to primeval

habits.   Instinct breaks out in them, just as it does in the silk-haired, boudoir-nurtured spaniel, with a ribbon round its neck, that runs away from the endearments of its mistress, to sniff and revel in some road-side mess of carrion.

It is a common theme of moralists of many creeds, that man is born with an imperfect nature.   He has lofty aspirations, but there is a weakness in his disposition that incapacitates him from carrying his nobler purposes into effect.   He sees that some particular course of action is his duty, and should be his delight; but his inclinations are fickle and base, and do not conform to his better judgment. The whole moral nature of man is tainted with sin, which prevents him from doing the things he knows to be right.

I venture to offer an explanation of this apparent anomaly, which seems perfectly satisfactory from a scientific point of view.   It is neither more nor less than that the development of our nature, under Darwin's law of natural selection, has not yet overtaken the development of our religious civilization.   Man was barbarous but yesterday, and therefore it is not to be expected that the natural aptitudes of his race should already have become moulded into accordance with his very recent advance.   We men of the present centuries are like animals suddenly transplanted among new conditions of climate and of food: our instincts fail us under the altered circumstances.

My theory is confirmed by the fact that the members of old civilizations are far less sensible than those newly converted from barbarism of their nature being inadequate to their moral needs. The conscience of a negro is aghast at his own wild, impulsive nature, and is easily stirred by a preacher, but it is scarcely possible to ruffle the self-complacency of a steady-going Chinaman.

The sense of original sin would show, according to my theory, not that man was fallen from a high estate, but that he was rapidly rising from a low one.   It would therefore confirm the conclusion that has been arrived at by every independent line of ethnological research—that our forefathers were utter savages from the beginning; and, that after myriads of years of barbarism, our race has but very recently grown to be civilized and religious.

THREE

JOHN ELLIOT CAIRNES (1823–75)

The Negro Suffrage

Macmillan's Magazine
Volume 12, 1865, pp. 334–43

Cairnes, an Irish economist and associate of J. S. Mill, made his name with The Slave Power. *This book was published in 1862, four years before its author's election to the Chair of Political Economy at University College, London. It constituted probably the most influential pro-Northern treatise to appear in Britain during the American Civil War. As the conflict developed Cairnes became increasingly convinced of the need for a particularly speedy post-war grant of full citizenship to the Negro. He feared that otherwise the South, even if defeated on the battlefield, might well win the peace. This is the theme of the following essay which, having been written in July and published in August 1865, dates from the first critical months of the Reconstruction period. In it Cairnes upholds the classic position of the radical 'negrophiles'. He argues against the view that Negroes are inherently unfitted for political life, and suggests that any apparent incapacity among them is traceable primarily to their recent condition of enslavement. If the franchise is to be qualified by reference to some educational test then this should be applied regardless of colour and should not take effect until the Negro has been given adequate opportunities for schooling. Cairnes stresses that the black man's exclusion from voting is particularly unjust because 'under the electoral laws of the Southern States as in force up to the present time, the most ignorant and lawless population to be found in any country making pretence to civilization are already invested with political power'. He suggests that this is an important point*

of distinction between the current American and British contro-
versies about wider enfranchisement. Even so, Cairnes's argument
was clearly very relevant to the debates which culminated in the
Derby ministry's Reform Act of 1867.

Since the French Revolution, no political work of equal importance with that now in progress in the restored Union has been laid upon the energies of any nation. It may be questioned if even the reconstruction of society in France after the disruption of 1789 involved issues so radical as that which now tasks the resources of American statesmanship; for, as Tocqueville has shown, the great revolution of the eighteenth century, sweeping and destructive as it seemed, was in its essence rather a realization and acceleration of social and political tendencies already in operation than their overthrow and reversal; whereas, in order that anything durable should be effected for the South—which is, in other words, to say, in order that a society be there established harmonious in its character and tendencies with the larger political body of which it forms a part—nothing short of a positive reversal of the preexisting social and political conditions of those states will be adequate. The forces of slave society, growing steadily more definitive from the foundation of the Union down to 1860, culminated in the rebellion, and have now been crushed by its defeat: the problem for the Unionists is to prevent their resuscitation, and at the same time to lay the foundation of a society of opposite quality, fitted to form a constituent element in a free and democratic nation.

Of the causes which shall determine the character of the new structure, obviously the most important of all is the place assigned in it to the negro. Shall the negro, now that he is emancipated, be admitted at once to the full prerogatives of citizenship, or is he to remain a mere sojourner on sufferance in the great Republic which he has assisted to save? Such is the question which the work of reconstruction has now brought to the foreground of American politics. Up to the present the main armies of the great parties have perhaps scarcely realized in all the fulness of its importance the issue proposed to them. But between the advanced posts on either side some sharp skirmishing has for some time been going on—the prelude, obviously, to a serious struggle. On the one hand the conservative section, the section which opposed the emancipation of the negro, is, as might be expected, still more opposed to the concession to him of political rights; but, on the other hand, in support of his claims there stands the same party which has befriended him hitherto—the party which |335| has, so far, been uniformly successful in impressing its idea, on the course of this revolution.   Surrounded with the *prestige* of accomplished emancipation, led by Mr. Sumner in the Senate, and by Mr. Wendell Phillips on the platform, the advanced Republican party has already inscribed on its banner the words, "Negro Suffrage," demanding, as the one effectual security for all that has been gained, that the coloured race shall, with the white man, have equal possession of every political right.   "Our duty to-day," said Mr. Phillips, on a recent occasion, "is to announce our purpose at least gallantly to struggle that no state shall come back to the Union unless she brings back a constitution which knows no distinction of race.   It is no matter whether the suffrage is limited by property, whether it is limited by intelligence, whether it is limited by age, or by any other condition: the sole thing which it must not be limited by to-day is the colour of a man's skin."

The policy here announced will not, improbably, shock the conservative suceptibilities of even liberal politicians here,   While we in England are hesitating about extending the franchise to a select number of the educated artisans of our towns, here is a proposition to enfranchise at a stroke a whole race of men, but yesterday enslaved, but yesterday excluded by law not alone from political training, but from every means of enlightenment.   It would seem to be a dictate of the most ordinary prudence that time should be given to the newly-emancipated to acquire some experience in personal freedom before investing them with political power.   Some such reflection as this is what will occur to almost every Englishman on hearing of the proposal to confer the suffrage on the negroes; yet, in truth, it has little bearing on the question now agitated in the United States.   That question is not as to the expediency of admitting poor and ignorant persons to the franchise, but as to the justice of making colour a test of poverty and ignorance.   For it must not be forgotten that, under the electoral laws of the Southern States as in force up to the present time, the most ignorant and lawless population to be found in any country making pretence to civilization are already invested with political power; and the practical question accordingly is, not whether a high or whether any electoral qualification shall be adopted (on this point the views of Mr. Sumner and Mr. Phillips might possibly be found not to differ so widely from that of moderate politicians here as the latter may imagine) but whether—the electoral qualification being what it is—a special exception from its operation shall be made against a particular class—a class distinguished from others, not by anything indicative of unfitness for political functions, but by a mere ethnological mark. It is, in short against the principle of caste in politics that the radical party in the United States has now taken its stand. It seems to the present writer that, in doing this, they have been guided by true political wisdom: and he now proposes—the subject having as yet received little attention in this country—to state for English readers what seem to him the conclusive and irresistible grounds of the radical case.

In approaching the question of the negro suffrage, one encounters the assumption, made with so much confidence by reasoners of a different race, of the inherent unfitness of the negro for political life. The shape of his skull, the prominence of his lower jaw, the size and hardness of his pelvis, indicate, say these reasoners, closer relationship with the chimpanzee than is consistent with the effective discharge of the duties of citizenship. With such anatomical peculiarities, he must be incapable of understanding his own interest, or of voting for the representative best fitted to promote it. He must therefore be excluded from the sphere of politics, and by consequence from all the opportunities of improvement which the sphere of politics opens. Montaigne thought, as we have been lately reminded, that it was assigning rather too great value to conjectures concerning witchcraft, |336| to burn human beings alive on such grounds. Whether to consign a whole race to perpetual serfdom be as serious a step as the burning alive of a small proportion of each successive generation, it is unnecessary to determine; but this at least we may say, that the adoption of either course on grounds no stronger than the prosecutors of witches could formerly, or the advocates of negro subjection can now, adduce, argues, to say the least, very remarkable confidence in the value of conjectural speculation. It would argue this even were there no facts to rebut such *à priori* guesses; but, in truth, such facts abound. To give a few examples: the race which, under all the disadvantages of African slavery, produced Toussaint L'Ouverture, the Haytian patriot and hero; which produced Benjamin Banneker, the negro astronomer, distinguished enough to attract the attention of Jefferson and to elicit compliments from Condorcet; which produced William Crafts, the African explorer, the eloquent defender of the humanity of his race, and now the leading merchant and reformer in the kingdom of Dahomey; which produced Frederick Douglass and Sella Martin, now too well known in this country to need characterization here; which produced Robert Small, who, but the other day, with no help but that rendered him by a few brother slaves, carried a vessel out of Charleston from under the eyes of his masters and past the guns of Fort Sumter; which produced—to give another recent instance—the scholar who lately obtained a double-first degree at the University of Toronto—this race must, I think, be admitted to have furnished credentials entitling it, at all events, to a fair stage without favour in the struggle for political existence.

These are isolated examples, and may be regarded as exceptional. Recent events have greatly enlarged our experience, and given us some evidence of what the average negro is capable of. It is a noteworthy fact, that, just in proportion as, with the progress of the Northern arms, the Northern people have extended their observation of the negro, their estimate of his character has risen; this estimate being highest with those who have been brought into closest and most frequent contact with him. All the prognostications of his detractors have been falsified; all the hopes of his friends have been more than fulfilled. Even in that quality in which it was supposed that his weakness was most conspicuous, that quality which his previous mode of life was certainly well fitted to eradicate—courage—he has proved himself on many a well-contested field a match for his white antagonist—he has shown himself, as R. W. Emerson is reported to have said, "the natural soldier of the Republic;" and generals, who in the first years of the war spurned negroes from their divisions, eagerly welcomed them ere its close. On the other hand, the negro has exhibited valuable civic virtues which are wholly foreign to the men who formed the staple of the late Southern armies—the hereditary border ruffians and filibusters of the South. Take one illustration. "The negroes," says the able correspondent of the *Daily News*, in a recent letter, "show a great capacity for passive resistance, and a good deal of ability in peaceful agitation. At the recent election in the eastern counties of Virginia, where they were not allowed to vote at the polls, they assembled, and, after offering their ballots to the proper officers, as a sort of protest, and being refused, quietly deposited them, and registered their votes in their own meeting-houses. This course will most likely be generally followed in North Carolina also, and everywhere else that Mr. Johnson's plan of reconstruction is adopted." Considering the past of the negroes, will any one deny that such proceedings indicate a very remarkable aptitude for taking part in the working of democratic institutions?

But in truth the consideration of race is almost irrelevant to the question we are discussing. The bulk of the freed-men who are now demanding admission to citizenship in the United States have, it must never be forgotten, quite as much Anglo-Saxon as African blood in |337| their veins. In the opinion of men familiar with the South, three-fourths of this recently emancipated population of the Southern States are composed of mulattoes, quadroons, sexteroons, octoroons, and others with a still smaller proportion of negro blood. "It is indeed a rare thing," says Mr. M. D. Conway, "to see a really black man; and such a negro passing through the streets, as I have generally observed, would attract attention and comment." The truth is, the great majority of the freedmen of the South are not negroes, but Anglo-Africans. Now, considering the part which mixed races have taken in carrying civilization thus far, may it not be possible that this one should bring to our future development some new human force—some element of value? At all events it is scarcely, one would say, for the United States to close against a people so derived, on grounds of mere ethnological presumption, the doors of political advancement.

So much for à priori considerations. But it is not here that we shall find the strength of the negroe's case: that rests upon the special character of the work to be done, and his fitness as an instrument in its accomplishment. The grand danger besetting the South is a return to the state of things which has passed away—a quiet resumption of authority by the old leaders, or men imbued with their spirit, issuing in the re-establishment in substance of what the Federal Government has abolished in form. The cause of independence is, no doubt, utterly lost; but the cause for the sake of which independence was desired—the cause which, when in the last throes of the Confederacy the choice had to be made, was deliberately preferred to independence—the cause of slavery—is not yet absolutely hopeless. The thing to be apprehended is that the old slave-holding class, seeing that the war game is up, will seek to recover by policy what has been lost in the appeal to force—will once more grasp at the reins of power; and, acquiescing formally in the restored authority of the Union and even in the emancipation decrees, proceed to set up again, under a slightly modified form, the social system which has just been pulled down.   This is what the *ci-devant* slaveholders will assuredly attempt, and it is but too certain that they will find a ready support in this policy from the bulk of the white population, in whom the caste feeling under the exasperation of the war, as some horrible cruelties recently perpetrated in the Southern States on defenceless negroes only too clearly show, has acquired increased fierceness.   Already in Tennessee, in Mississippi, in Arkansas—wherever the movement for reconstruction has commenced—things are sliding into this groove.   "Widely known Southern gentlemen"—some of them the framers and movers of secession ordinances—convene meetings, acknowledge themselves "whipped," declare their respect for the government which has so handsomely performed that operation, express their confidence in its "magnanimity," and prepare with the utmost coolness, as a matter of course, to resume under the Union the leadership which they have just vacated under the Confederacy. . . . |338| Here is the danger which threatens.   Now what securities have been devised by the Government of the United States against its realization?

Up to the present time, and apart from the measure which forms the subject of the present paper, three securities have been adopted or proposed:—The oath of allegiance, the exceptions in the amnesty, and the emancipation decrees to be ratified by the Constitutional Amendment. To any one who has appreciated the character of the danger, the inadequacy of such safeguards must be apparent. As regards the oath of allegiance, it is already evident that it will not present the slightest obstacle to the return to political power of the most embittered enemy of the Union, of the most fanatical believer in the rights of human bondage. . . The exceptions in the amnesty, give the Government a hold on most of the prominent men, and, were the spirit of disaffection to the new order of things confined to these, the provision might be a valuable security.   But this notoriously is far from being the case: that feeling pervades nearly the whole of the Southern white population.   Baffled in their political aims, and smarting from defeat, they still cling to their social ideal, and cherish the hope of setting up again, if not in its former completeness, at least in some form, their beloved institu-

tion—at the worst, of rendering impossible the policy of emancipation, and making good their oft-repeated prediction of the
unfitness of the negro for freedom.

Lastly, there are the emancipation decrees, to be converted, as
we may assume will be the case, through the requisite vote of the
States, into a constitutional law.   Now let us consider |339| what
amount of security this expedient, in the absence of any further
measures than those which we have just considered, contains for
the practical freedom of the negro.   The effect of the Constitutional
Amendment, supposing it to be passed, will be to abolish throughout
the Union slavery and involuntary servitude except in punishment
of crimes.   So long as the Federal Government retains its hold on
the revolted States, we may fairly assume that this provision will
be carried into operation in its plain sense.   But reconstruction of
the Union under the Constitution means restoration of State rights;
and State rights once restored, it will be for the State, not the
Federal, authorities to give effect to the new law.   With a view to
the future, therefore, the practical question is—What will be the
interpretation placed on the Constitutional Amendment by the new
State authorities?

It will be observed that the prohibition in the proposed amendment is qualified by an exception.   Involuntary servitude is pro-
hibited "*except* in punishment of crimes."   But what is a
"crime"?   The determination of this point belongs, under the
Constitution, not to Congress, but to the legislature of each State.
What, then, is to prevent any State legislature from designating as
a "crime" any act it pleases, thereby qualifying for involuntary
servitude all persons against whom such act can be proved?   A
State, for example, may declare vagrancy a "crime", and then
proceed to award slavery as the punishment of vagrants.   This, in
fact, is what the State legislature of Western Tennessee has just
done.   In a bill which lately passed the House of Representatives
in that State, it is, among other things of a like tendency, provided,
that vagrancy in "free persons of colour" be punished with impris-
onment, and that on failure to pay the jail fees "the culprit may be
hired out to the highest bidder after due notice."   The Tennesseean
legislators have even gone further than this.   "The twelfth section
applies the poor laws affecting white people to the free people of
colour, *and adds a proviso* for the rendition to other countries and

states of the poor and indigent people of colour"—in fact a fugitive slave law.

The conditions justifying in law a return of the negroes to slavery having been settled, there will be clearly no difficulty in producing those conditions in fact. In the present chaotic condition of the South, it is plain that, even with the best disposition on the part of the people, a large amount of vagrancy is inevitable. With the actual feeling which exists—with the foregone conclusion on the part of the depositaries of power, that the experiment of freedom shall fail—it will be strange indeed, supposing they are to have their way uncontrolled, if vagrancy should not shortly be coextensive with the whole coloured population. It is only necessary that landholders should for a time refuse the negroes work (which, with the "mean whites" at hand and just now coerced to industry by hunger, they may easily without much inconvenience do); or offer it on terms incompatible with human existence.

Already recourse has been had to both these expedients. From a correspondent of the *New York World*—not a paper likely to twist facts to favour the negro—we learn that "a number of those who were slaveholders refuse to employ negroes, and have driven many of them off, the excuse being that they cannot feed them. This may be true," adds the writer, "in some cases, but in others we suspect it proceeds from different motives." Virginia furnishes an example of the other expedient. The rate of wages for negroes has been fixed by a combination of masters in that State at five dollars a month—less than one-third the rate paid a few years since by those same masters to each other for the hire of the same negroes. In South Carolina, as appears from a letter from the Charleston correspondent of the *New York Times*, a still more effectual plan has been adopted, or at all events has been proposed, namely, that payment of wages to the freedman should be postponed until the whole work of the harvest is completed. "How can they |340| expect to get compensation," writes this Charleston economist, "before they perform the labour? and the labour is not performed till the crops are gathered." With this spirit prevailing, and power monopolised by the class whom it animates, it is pretty evident that vagrancy must ere long be the condition of the bulk of the negroes. Thus legally qualified for servitude, what is to prevent, and that at no distant date—the Constitutional Amendment notwithstanding—a wholesale return of the oppressed race to the bondage from which they have scarce escaped?

These fears are no vague fancies: they are but too well founded in experience. An example is at hand which ought not to be lost on the people of the Free States—the example of West Indian emancipation. It is usual with those in this country amongst whom traditions of West Indian slavery are still cherished, to speak of that experiment as a "failure." In fact, as recent evidence places beyond doubt, emancipation in the West Indies has been a remarkable success—a success that is to say, judged, not by the gains of a small planter class, already ere the experiment was launched hopelessly plunged in debt, and with estates impoverished through the exhausting effects of a century of slave cultivation, but by the well-being of the bulk of the inhabitants.* This result, however, has not been achieved without a struggle in which difficulties have been encountered quite analogous to those which beset the revolution we are now witnessing in the Southern States. The following passage, from Mr. Edward Bean Underhill's work, will give an idea of the obstacles with which the cause of emancipation had there to contend:—

"The House of Assembly at the time of emancipation possessed the fullest powers to remedy and defect in that great measure. But it abused its powers. Instead of enacting laws calculated to elevate and benefit the people, it pursued a contrary course. By an Ejectment Act it gave the planters the right to turn out the enfranchised peasantry, without regard to sex or age, at a week's notice, from the homes in which they had been born and bred; to root up their provision grounds, and to cut down their fruit trees, which gave them both shelter and food; in order that, through dread of the consequences of refusal, the negroes might be driven to work on the planters' own terms. . . . Driven from his cabin on the estate by the harsh treatment of his former master, the free labourer had to build a cottage for himself. Immediately the custom on shingles

---

* I make this statement notwithstanding reports lately received of severe and widespread distress among the negroes in Jamaica. That distress is referred by those best acquainted with the island to causes mainly of a temporary kind—principally to a protracted drought occurring at the moment when the people were already suffering from the commercial effects of the American Civil War. . . . [*Editor's Note*: The Jamaican Revolt occurred a mere two months after the appearance of this article.]

for the roof to shelter his family from the seasons was more than
doubled; while the duty on staves and hoops for sugar hogsheads,
the planters' property, was greatly reduced.   And when the houses
were built, they were assessed at a rate which in some parishes bore
so heavily on the occupants as to lead to the abandonment of their
dwellings for shanties of mud and boughs.... Some proprietors at
|341| emancipation drove their labourers from the estates.... One...
swore that he would not allow a nigger to live within three miles
of his house.   If the House of Assembly has had any policy in its
treatment of the labouring classes, it has been a 'policy of alienation.'   Only the perpetual interposition of the English government
has prevented the enfranchised negro from being reduced to the
condition of a serf by the selfish partisan legislation of the Jamaica
planters.... As slaves, the people never were instructed in husban-
dry, or in the general cultivation of the soil; as free men, the
Legislature has utterly neglected them, and they have had to learn
as they could the commonest processes of agriculture.   No attempt
has been made to provide a fitting education for them.... Speaking
of this feature of Jamaica legislation, Earl Grey, writing in 1853,
says:—'The Statute Book of the island for the last six years presents
nearly a blank, as regards laws calculated to improve the condition
of the population, and to raise them in the scale of civilization.' "

Here is a picture in miniature of the dangers now threatening the
experiment of emancipation in the Southern States, with this difference, that the exasperation of the Jamaica planters was a mild
sentiment compared with that which is now felt by the defeated
Confederates; and with this further difference, that, the Union once
reconstructed, and State rights once recognised, there will be in
America no Imperial Government to interpose its shield between
the negroes and their enraged masters.   In presence of these
dangers, I agree with the Abolitionists that there is need of a policy
of "Thorough."   The heart of the evil is the monopoly of power
possessed by the dominant caste; and nothing which stops short of
breaking that monopoly will reach the evil in its vital source.   To
constitute protectors of the negroes' freedom the very men who
have just been defeated in a desperate conspiracy to render their
bondage perpetual, would indeed be a bitter jest.   Plainly, there is
but one adequate remedy—the freedmen must be made the guardians
of their own rights.

Our inquiry has thus led us to the conclusion that the policy of negro enfranchisement is dictated by political necessity as the only means of saving the revolution. Is there anything in its practical consequences from which we should recoil? Let us for a moment regard the policy of the Republicans under this aspect; and consider what the questions are on which the negro, supposing him to be admitted to the suffrage, will be called upon to decide. They will for some time be chiefly such questions as the following:—Shall the negroes be allowed to live and maintain themselve in the States where they have been born and reared? Shall they be permitted to enter into legal marriage? Shall negro parents be allowed the same rights over their children as are enjoyed by other people? Shall negroes have access to the public schools? Shall the evidence of negroes be received in the courts of justice? Shall they be permitted to make their contracts for the commodity in which they deal—their labour—with the same freedom as is accorded to other men? In a word, shall the negroes be admitted to the same rights and privileges under the law—to the same opportunities of improvement and advancement—as other inhabitants of the same country enjoy? Now, such being the character of the |342| political questions on which for some time the negro in his capacity as a voter would be called upon to pronounce, it may fairly be asked, Where would be the practical danger of admitting him to the franchise? Every honest friend of liberty at least will admit that such questions should be answered in the affirmative, and it is quite certain that this is the sense in which they would be answered by the negro. It is scarcely less certain that they would be answered in the opposite sense by the caste now dominant in the South; and these questions, be it remembered, are the master questions of Southern policy—the questions which in their determination will fix for good or evil the future character and direction of Southern development. It would seem strange statesmanship which, in laying the bases of a new social system, should exclude from participation in the task just those artificers the soundness of whose work may be most entirely trusted.

Of course the time will come when, questions of primary right and justice being settled, questions of a more complicated character will come up for solution; and lack of instruction in any class of the community will then doubtless be felt as an evil. This forms a good reason for adopting an educational test; but, as has been already explained, it is altogether beside the question involved in the present agitation. The advocates of negro suffrage are quite content to accept an educational test, they only stipulate for two conditions—that it shall be impartially applied, and that, in order to [achieve] this, time be given to the negroes to qualify themselves for undergoing it. The second condition is no less necessary than the first. It may be true that the negroes are now the least educated portion of the Southern population. But why are they so? Notoriously because, by the deliberate policy of their masters, they have been excluded by law from all the opportunities of education which are open to other members of the community; and shall it be permitted to these same masters to make the ignorance they have themselves produced the ground for perpetuating the bondage of the race whom they have so deeply injured? It is surely, then, not without good reason—reason founded on the plainest rules of justice—that the friends of the negro stipulate that in applying the educational test, time shall be allowed to render the conditions fair. Meanwhile, as has just been shown, no practical mischief is likely to arise from his ignorance; the questions first coming on for settlement being of that simple kind on which his instincts are certain to keep him right.

There is a further aspect of this case which may recommend itself even to those who decline to be swayed by arguments of mere humanity and justice. As Mr. Sumner has eloquently insisted, slavery and rebellion are in the Union but different sides of the same fact. Without slavery, the people of the South have no reason for disaffection, and loyalty is a matter of course: with slavery, loyalty is simply impossible, because slavery, in its nature antagonistic to freedom, must in a free community act as a centrifugal force, and tend to separation. It is a corollary from this teaching that the race which forms the best security for freedom forms also the best security for the Union. As the negroes are the only large portion of the Southern population that can be trusted to support democracy and freedom, so they are the only one whose loyalty is to be absolutely trusted. They cannot falter in their allegiance to this cause without treason to themselves: their safety for the present, their hopes for the future, are alike bound up with the Northern alliance. Here, then, is the firm anchorage at which the vessel of the State may ride in safety; here, if anywhere, is the rock on which to found in the South the Union cause.   The slaveholders, wise in their generation, proposed to make the enslaved negro the corner-stone of their empire. Let the freemen of the North not despise the teaching of an enemy.   The corner-stone the negro is still, let us hope, destined to be, but the negro in freedom.

|343| The Union has been saved, and in the work of salvation the negro has borne his part, no less by his submission, patience, and forbearance, than by his gallantry on the field of battle.   How different from the part expected from him even by those who judged not unkindly!   Jefferson, thinking of him, and reflecting that God was just, trembled for his country.   Longfellow, looking forward with prophetic vision to the long-impending struggle, could see in the negro only an instrument of vengeance, and a cause of ruin:—

"There is a poor blind Sampson in the land,
    Shorn of his strength and bound in bars of steel,
Who may, in some grim revel, raise his hand
    And shake the pillars of the common weal—
Till the great temple of our liberties
A shapeless mass of wreck and ruin lies."

The hour of grim revel at length came, and the American Sampson raised his hand, but for a purpose far different from that which the poet dreaded—not to shake, but to stay up the tottering temple of American liberties—that temple in which he had only received insult and unutterable wrong.   Was the Christian maxim ever so illustrated before?

In the foregoing remarks I have abstained entirely from reference to the constitutional question.   I have done so deliberately, because I do not believe that it is by constitutional considerations that the policy of the Union will be governed in the present crisis.   Constitutional arguments in times of revolution can only be regarded as convenient fictions to allure the weak, or perhaps as feints to mask the movements which shall really determine the battle; but they are not themselves the effective forces; and there is now, surely, revolution in America.   If the President is competent to take from a white man the right to vote, because the safety of the Republic requires it, may he not for the same reason confer that right upon

a black man?   Necessity—in legal parlance, "The War Power"—is,
for either exercise of authority, the sole justification.   If that plea
be valid for one, it would seem that it is valid for every step.

FOUR

CHARLES MACKAY (1814–89)

The Negro and the Negrophilists

Blackwood's Edinburgh Magazine
Volume 99, 1866, pp. 581–97

In Mackay's piece, first published anonymously, we see every argument of Cairnes inverted. Its author was a prolific writer, among whose early novels we find the significantly titled Long-beard, or the Revolt of the Saxons *(1841). He worked for* The Illustrated London News *from 1852 to 1859, and reached the height of his influence between 1862 and 1865 when acting as* The Times' *special correspondent in New York. This latter appointment was symptomatic of the paper's support for the South in the Civil War, but ultimately even Printing House Square became disconcerted by the extremeness of Mackay's partisanship. The Times promoted the Confederates' cause because it saw them as oppressed country gentlemen, and sympathized with their stand on States' rights and the preservation of free trade. However, despite its notorious lapse of 1 January 1863 into a biblical justification of the South's 'peculiar institution', the paper was not generally committed to any defence of slavery itself. So long as Mackay stressed such things as the elements of cant in the North's belated conversion to distinctively abolitionist war aims there was little cause for friction between himself and his employers. Disagreement came, rather, because of his keenness to enter unreservedly into justifications of slavery by reference to the severity of the Negro's innate inferiority.*

By 1866 Mackay was alarmed not only at Cairnes's sort of approach towards Reconstruction in the United States but also at the campaign being waged against Governor Eyre's tough hand-

ling of the Jamaican Revolt. The vigorous essay presented here provides us with that image of the Negro which is archetypal within much nineteenth-century racial polemic. Mackay even resorts to the pseudo-humanitarian argument that Blacks will always fare better and more happily within the security of slavery than under the strain of freedom. He contends that, even though slaveholding is now surely doomed, good statesmanship must continue to take account of the reality of racial repugnance. This exists, at one level, between Anglo-Saxon and Irishman; but it must affect still more deeply the dealings between white and black men. According to Mackay, the 'negrophilists' stand condemned of naivety and hypocrisy alike. He asks whether the Yankee is not merely using the Negro to punish the Southern secessionists, and whether any inhabitant of Britain would wish to treat Negroes as his equals if he found four million of them living as his neighbours.

The two foremost nations in the world are suffering at this moment from a moral malady, which the Americans, with more force than elegance, call "nigger on the brain." This disease, it may be remarked, does not attack either nations or individuals that are not of Anglo-Saxon stock, or who profess the Roman Catholic religion, but prevails almost exclusively among English-speaking people and Protestants. It scarcely affects Frenchmen, and leaves Spaniards, Portuguese, Italians, and Roman Catholic Irishmen wholly untouched. In England the imperfectly educated and untravelled crowds who delight in the peculiar Christianity of the Rev. Messrs Stiggins and Chadband, aided by the politicians of the conventicle and of the ultra radical school, who, if not at heart republicans, would Americanise the institutions of Great Britain to the utmost extent compatible with the existence of the monarchy, are up in arms to defend the Jamaica negro, not alone as "a man and a brother," but as something more sacred than a European, and as standing in even a tenderer relation than brotherhood to men of white skins. Knowing little or nothing of the character and capabilities of the negro race, except by hearsay—living in a country where a full-blooded Ethiopian is as rare as a black swan, where from January to December even a mulatto is seldom seen, and where, in consequence of this unfamiliarity, no antipathy of race is excited, as in the West Indies and the United States—these philanthropists, who have been well named malignant in the results, though probably not in the motives, of their teaching, have for the last three months been beside themselves with an excess of what they may themselves consider to be Christian charity, but which to other eyes looks marvellously like unchristian malevolence and theological rancour. Weekly or daily they invoke the vengeance of the law against Governor Eyre, who, in a moment of extreme peril to the small European and white community of which, as well as of the blacks and mulattoes, he was the chief magistrate, presumed to think that the means adequate to suppress a political rebellion of white malcontents, unexasperated by antipathies of race and colour, were not altogether sufficient to stamp out a "Jacquerie" of black peasants, thirsting for the blood of their social superiors, and indulging in such eccentric atrocities as the chopping-up of white magistrates and landowners into little bits, and the commission of other horrors which the tongue refuses to name and the pen to write. In America the same class of persons—whose love for the negro is theological rather than humanitarian, and who promulgate the theory without understanding the truths of ethnology which point to a different conclusion, that "God made of one blood all the nations of the earth"—a class comprising preachers, professional lecturers, salaried philanthropists, and weak-minded women, who are equally at home under the ministrations of the Rev. Mr Treacle, or of the Rev. Mr Brimstone, together with the philosophers and the strong-minded women, who are too strong-minded to attend either church or chapel, and all the multitude of theorists who would abolish slavery even at the cost of abolishing the negro—have for the last four years been hounding on their countrymen to mutual slaughter. They have not only thought, but said, with Mr Zachariah Chandler, Senator for Michigan, that the Union "was not worth a *cuss* without blood-letting," and with Mr Wen-|582|dell Phillips that it would be better to exterminate the whole Southern people, and colonise the land afresh, rather than suffer such a wrong as negro slavery to be tenderly treated or gradually abolished.   The sacred name of human liberty has been in their mouths, while in their hearts there has been little but an unappeasable desire for the aggrandisement of their political party, and the creation of a central despotism at Washington, sufficiently powerful to make the United States—*vice* Great Britain and France, deposed and relegated to the second rank—the arbiter of peace and war, and controller of the destinies of Christendom.   At this hour the malady rages as virulently as ever.   Peace has been nominally restored over the unhappy South, but the moral pest of negrophilism prevents the reconstruction—in fact as well as in theory, in heart as well as in law—of the great union of free white people, which it was the main and only legitimate object of the war to accomplish.   The money cost of the war, even if diminished by two-thirds, would have been enough to purchase the peaceable, gradual, and safe manumission of every slave in the United States; but the sword, in setting them free by violence, has not only cost the conquerors and the conquered half a million of white lives, but diminished the number of the negroes to little more than half of what they were before the outbreak of hostilities—diminished them by neglect, hunger, fever, smallpox, and misery, as well as by the multitudinous casualties of the camp and the battle-field.   The sword also, that never in the long-run

settles any great moral or social question, has accompanied the gift
of freedom to the sad remnant of the blacks, with the calamitous
addendum of ruin to their late masters and employers, and present
starvation to themselves, with the prospect, but too clearly and
palpably defined, of worse evils yet in store for the weaker of the
two races.

It has been said that no man ever gained, after long and persistent
struggles, the thing which he earnestly desired, without making the
melancholy discovery that Fate or Providence had attached some
condition to the triumph which deprived it of some portion of its
value, or lessened its charm and glory.   They snatch the golden
bowl, filled with the intoxicating liquor of success, and they find a
drop of gall, if not of poison, in the draught, and pass it from their
lips, if not untasted, unenjoyed.   The victorious North is at present
in this condition.   A vast majority of its people did not care a cent
for the abolition of slavery on the day when the South inaugurated
the war by the attack on Fort Sumter: many devoutly wished that
a "nigger" had never been introduced into the country; and as many
more, with Mr Lincoln at their head, would have rejoiced exceedingly
if the whole race could have been retransported to their native
Africa, or shovelled into Central America, to live or die as chance
might determine.   These people, aiding the abolitionists in their
unnatural war against their white brother, not for the sake of the
negro, but for the sake of the Union—the great and only object of
American reverence and idolatry—have had their triumph.   And
with the triumph has come the Nemesis, the black shadow of whose
avenging hand creeps over the morning sky, and threatens ere noon
to darken the whole hemisphere.   In liberating the negroes by the
sword, the North has itself become a slave.   It is bound, like a
Siamese twin, to the side of the "irrepressible nigger."   Like the
unhappy fisherman in the Arabian tale, it has liberated the dusky
genie from the vase in which he was enclosed with the seal of
Solomon upon the lid; and the dark vapour and smoke is assuming
a form that is ominous alike of the |583| power and the inclination
to do mischief.   Contrary to the prediction of the South, the war
proved that cotton was *not* king.   The peace, if peace that state
of things can be called which prevails over the cotton States, proves
but too conclusively the advent to power of another and less
agreeable monarch.   The negro, notwithstanding his misery and

degradation, is the master of the situation and ruler of the hour; and Messrs Charles Sumner, Thaddeus Steven, and Wendell Phillips, are the ministers who do his high behests, and retard, by their acerb agitation, the real pacification of men's minds, and the much-needed reorganisation of the industry of their country.   The "nigger" stops the way to peace, improvement, and occupation, and bids fair to stop it until the periodical election of a new Congress may enable the representatives of the South to take that share in the legislation of the Union, from which they are now excluded by a tyrannical faction that usurps the functions of a majority.   By a defect in an unelastic constitution that snapped asunder at the first strain, the President, unlike the constitutional monarch of Great Britain, or the governors of the British Colonies, has no power to dismiss a legislature that has ceased to represent the opinions of the country, or that thwarts systematically the whole policy of the executive. In consequence of this defect, the President and the Congress are at open war.   Neither can coerce or get rid of the other until the ordinary term of their service expires.   Thus there is a dead-lock, with the negro in the key-hole, and two years must at least elapse before he can be got out of it.   In these two years no one can say what evils may not arise to convulse the country, and rekindle the smouldering embers of civil and servile strife.

But is the negro worth all the trouble, anxiety, bloodshed, and misery which his wrongs or his rights have produced, and are producing?   Is it possible for the European races, Anglo-Saxon, Teutonic, or Celtic, to live in peace and amity with the African, in any country where the whites and blacks are equal, or nearly equal, in point of numbers, and especially, as in Jamaica and South Carolina, where the blacks are in the majority, unless the whites control and govern?   These are questions which indirectly concern England, which painfully and directly concern America, and upon which the course of events in the United States, during the last four years, has thrown a lurid light; questions which the writer has studied both in the Northern and the Southern States, and on which he may claim to speak from large personal experience.   Perhaps during the next four years events may be still more startling to the preconceived notions of English and American philanthropists. White pauperism is a difficult problem to deal with, as most Englishmen know, if Americans do not.   Black pauperism, if such be the result of the American war, may perhaps be far less easy of solution, and prove even more deplorable a business than the war from which it emanated.

***

|585| However unanimous the British and European public, who only know of the negro by hearsay, may be in its detestation of slavery, no such unanimity exists in America, where the negro is but known too well   The great city of New York, the real and only metropolis of America, was before and up to the close of the war intensely pro-slavery, and ninety-nine hun-|586|dredths of its working and trading classes would rejoice if not a negro were left among them.   Mr Fernando Wood, late Mayor of New York, has repeatedly declared that he could at any time call a public meeting, to which admission should be free and without tickets, in which resolutions in favour of slavery could be carried by an overwhelming majority.   Even the late Mr Cobden, than whom no sincerer opponent of slavery ever existed, confessed that his views upon the question of the sudden emancipation of the slaves, and the real condition of the negroes, had been greatly modified by a visit to the South.   At an early period of the civil war, Mr Lincoln, aware that there was a negro question as well as a slavery question, emphatically declared that he had neither the wish nor the right to abolish slavery; and as emphatically told the free negroes, through a deputation which sought his advice, that Africa or Central America was better suited for them than any portion of the United States, North or South. Mr Seward, the author of the famous prediction that the contest between North and South on the slavery question was "irrepressible," was no sooner involved in the heavy as well as intricate responsibilities of office than he too became prudent, and would have been glad to compromise with the South for the perpetuation of slavery within its then existing limits, provided the South would have agreed to its non-extension into any new territories.   And before English abolitionists and humanitarians condemn the Americans for their past willingness to tolerate slavery within certain limits, and their present unwillingness, in spite of laws and acts of Congress, to elevate the negroes to political and social equality with the white race, it might be as well if they would ask themselves whether, if, unhappily for Great Britain and Ireland, there were four millions of negroes within the compass of their isles, they too

might not be less willing to confess than they are now that the
negro is a full brother, fit to take a seat in Parliament or on the
bench of justice, to be made a bishop, a peer, or an ambassador, or
to intermarry with the fair daughters of our landed or commercial
aristocracy.

The introduction of the African race into America seems to have
been a great calamity to all concerned—to white as well as to
black. America profited for a while by the importation; but the
penalty she paid during the late civil war, and which she will yet
have to pay before the account, either in blood or money, is settled,
is far more than enough to overbalance all the gains by the rice,
cotton, and sugar trade which negro labour develops, were they
trebled or quadrupled. The war is supposed to have freed the
negroes. Will peace, when restored, in fact as well as in name,
enable the freedmen to live in happiness, to increase and multiply,
and perform those proper functions of the good citizen which are
expected of the whites—the functions of steady labour, of thrift,
or prudent forethought—all of which are necessary, not alone for
the advancement in civilisation of any race of men, but for the
prevention of its relapse into partial or complete barbarism? This
is the question which weighs heavily upon the minds of all the true
statesmen in America at this moment, though it may be lightly
estimated by women and preachers, and have no terrors for rabid
theorists who act and speak as if they would rather that the heavens
should crack, and chaos come again, than that their private notions
of abstract justice should not become the law both of man and
nature.

In answering this and other dependent questions, we have to
consider what the negro is in his native Africa; what he was in
bondage |587| prior to his enforced emancipation in the Southern
States of the Union; what he is in freedom when left to himself, as
in Hayti; what he is in freedom shared with the whites, as in
Jamaica; and what he is in the Northern States of America and in
Canada, where he suffers under social ban and political exclusion.
Fair, impartial, and unprejudiced answers to these questions may
have no weight with the theorists, either of the press, the debating
club, or the pulpit; but they cannot but have an influence upon the
minds of statesmen and men of sense and business, who are content
to live under natural conditions, and make the best of them, without

grieving that neither Great Britain nor America is Utopia or Barataria; or imagining, in their insolent and blasphemous conceit, that they are wiser than the Almighty, and able to eradicate evils and contradictions from a world in which He has permitted them to exist.

It will be admitted, that in his native Africa the negro has never emerged out of primitive barbarism.   He is not, it is true, of the fiercest order of savages who delight in bloodshed and the chase, but a pastoral and agricultural savage of a milder type, though addicted to wild and gloomy superstitions, and having no idea of a God, though strong ideas of a devil.   He worships a Fetish or Mumbo Jumbo, offers human sacrifices, sells his own race into slavery, and makes the females of his family, who are very superior to the males, do all the drudgery of the little agriculture he understands or desires, while he delivers himself up to sloth and such base animal indulgences as his nature prompts.   Civilisation has never been promoted or understood by him in the slightest degree.   There have been various forms of high civilisation in China, Japan, India, Persia, and Arabia. There have been Phenician, Assyrian, and Egyptian states and monarchies, in which art, science, and literature have been cultivated, and in which philosophy—not to be shamed by that of modern times—has shed its beneficent light upon the darkness of the ages.   Greece, Carthage, Rome, have shown what civilising energy and intellect they possessed; and that if they originated in barbarism, they grew rapidly out of it by the innate virtue of their blood.   The great Caucasian stock, spreading from Asia westwards and southwards, has peopled Europe, America, and Australia with bold enterprising and progressive men, and founded states and empires that, by their superior brilliancy, cast into shadow the most splendid achievements of the monarchies and people of old.   But during this time the negro has done nothing. In all the record of history, from Moses downwards, the negro has been the same.   He has remained in Africa, fastened like a limpet to his rock, and given no sign of improvement in the long interval, or shown the least capacity for self-advancement.   He is as unchanged as the beaver, the bee, and the monkey.   As he was four thousand years ago, so he is now.   Had he not been discovered by the European races, and forcibly removed from his own *habitat*, like the horse, to be made available as a labourer in a country which knew him not, he never of his own accord would have sought his fortune, or been impressed with the remotest desire of seeking it elsewhere than in his own tropical fields and jungles.

But when transplanted into the New World, and subjected to the control of white men, and to the influences of their civilisation, the negro race develops many useful qualities. If a native of Africa, and taken violently from his home to be sold into slavery, the negro reconciles himself to his fate, because slavery is an African institution, and his own chiefs and kings are slave-dealers and slave-owners, |588| and treat their human chattels with far greater barbarity than the whites were ever known to be guilty of. When born in America, and scarcely knowing anything of Africa, he takes his condition as a matter of course; and in the second or third generation at farthest, becomes not only a valuable but a contented member of society. The experience of the Southern States showed for two hundred years, under British rule, and afterwards under the Republican Government, that, so far from being miserable, morose, and dangerous in slavery, the negro enjoyed all the pleasures that his easy and docile nature placed within his reach. If he received kind treatment, which he generally did, he loved his master, and would have done anything in his power to serve him. As regards his physical condition, he was far better provided for than the agricultural labourer of Russia, Poland, Germany, and some parts of the south of England. He lived in a good hut or cottage, received medical treatment in infancy, old age, and ill health, at the expense of his master; saw his children provided for, without an extra tax on his own exertions, or any diminution of his usual comforts, and was enabled to provide for the supply of the luxuries which negroes as well as white men crave, by many little indulgences and perquisites which are not placed in the way of his free white compeer in Europe. He was allowed to keep poultry, to feed them on his master's corn, and sell the eggs and the chickens for his own advantage. With the money he purchased tobacco for himself and ribbons for his wife. He was permitted to hunt in the drains, gulleys, and shallow waters for terrapin and the other varieties of land turtle and tortoise, which he himself would not eat on any condition, but which were a great luxury and dainty to his master, to whom he sold them at an established price. The whole of this was gain to the negro. In old age he was provided for more abundantly than any white pauper in England; for slavery, it should be remembered, contained a Poor Law within itself.   Society in this respect, as in others, despotic upon all matters within the sphere of its influence, frowned down the slave-owner who allowed his worn-out labourers in their senility or sickness to be otherwise than tenderly and liberally provided for.   In this condition, with all its disadvantages—and, it may be conceded, with all its outrages against the rights of a man to be his own proprietor—though the negro may have been made a slave, he ceased to be a savage.   If the fears of his master—fears which the late war in America proved to have been singularly unfounded—denied him the privilege of education, and the use of those admirable tools of education too commonly considered to be education in themselves—namely, reading, writing, and arithmetic—he was, at all events, instructed in the religion of Christ; his only chance, according to some, of that heavenly beatitude, which others believe to be the inheritance of the whole human race. Those who are ultra-Christian in this respect, will doubtless acknowledge, however much they abhor slavery, that the Christian slave in the South was in a better condition, with all the wrongs and hardships attendant upon his lot, than the free savage, who possesses his own huts and his own labour, but does not possess his own soul.   But the question need not be placed upon this basis.   It may be made to rest upon a lower and more worldly platform.   In slavery, up to the outbreak of the great civil war, the negro race multiplied exceedingly.   In many States their numbers were fast encroaching upon those of the whites; and in South Carolina they actually, from small beginnings, had become the majority.   Had they suffered from want, from ill-treatment, from neglect, from disease, or |589| from uncongenial circumstances—had the iron of oppression, to use a current phrase, "entered into their souls"—had the keen competition for existence, and the cares and sorrows attendant upon it, among more responsible and in some respects more unhappy human beings, weighed heavily upon their minds and bodies,—it is not probably that their numbers would have increased so steadily and so rapidly, but highly probable that they would have as steadily diminished.

If we turn from the condition of the negro in slavery to his condition in freedom, and estimate his physical, his moral, his social, and religious advantages, a very different picture presents itself.

The state of Hayti, in which he as jealously excludes the white man
from political power as the white man excluded him in South
Carolina, is well known.   From being one of the richest, it has
become one of the poorest islands of that teeming climate.   Production has decreased; the lands are relapsing into aboriginal wilderness; the negro, content with little, basks in the sun, as careless
and about as nude as the hog; and what little Christianity he once
understood is replaced by the frightful superstition of Obeah, which
the race brought with them from their native Africa, and which no
Christian teaching suffices to eradicate.   He is not quite so bad in
Jamaica, where a leaven of white men purifies the black mass, and
keeps it from total putrefaction.   But even in this lovely island,
where he lives side by side with a white minority, able to deny him
social privilege and companionship, but unable to deprive him of
political rights and legal equality, we find that, although his numbers
increase, his usefulness to himself and to society diminishes.   His
wants are few, the climate suits him, and he dislikes labour.   The
land either goes untilled, or is so partially cultivated as to give him
only the pumpkin, which is the prime necessity of his life.   The
ruin of Jamaica as a colony that added largely to the wealth of the
world, is too old and familiar a story to need repetition.   The facts
are known, and so distasteful to the great bulk of the thinking
people of England, that if the United States desired to buy the island
outright, it is likely that most of us would think a hundred pounds
a liberal offer for so barren an acquisition.   And although there is
much religion (so called) among the negroes in Jamaica—though
they believe the Saviour of the world to have been a black man, and
though they sing Christian hymns with a fervour that springs more
from musical imitativeness and love of melody than from piety or
comprehension of the sentiments inculcated—their religion has so
little root in their nature that "Obeahism" lives in their hearts,
while Christianity only dwells on their lips.   This frightful superstition of their African ancestors, with its cruel, disgusting, and
obscene rites, defies all the vigilance of the magistracy and all the
efforts of the clergy to root it out.   It would be easy to expatiate
upon this subject, and to pile proof upon proof of the degeneracy
of the negro when left to his own governance, or, as in Jamaica,
when his numbers are such, compared with the whites, as to give
him the preponderance.   The world has rung with the fearful story

of his doings in St Domingo, and might have rung once more, with a story even more hideous, four months ago, in this very island of Jamaica, had it not been for the severity and promptitude—technically illegal perhaps in the case of Gordon, but in its general results highly beneficial to blacks and whites—which were displayed by Governor Eyre in the suppression of a war of races, and the condign and speedy punishment of the aggressors. And here it may be observed, *en passant*, that our English philanthropists of the malig- |590| nant type were grossly deceived by the "sensation" headings of the 'New York Herald,' which was one of the first journals in America to record the circumstances. "THE GROUND CUMBERED WITH THE SLAIN," "EIGHT MILES OF DEAD BODIES," were captions designed for American, not for European purposes—prepense exaggerations after the true American manner, and intended by the pro-slavery and anti-negro party to alarm the abolitionists and black republicans, lest the gift of too much freedom to a semi-barbarous race in the South should cause a black Jacquerie in the cotton districts, and perhaps extend its ravages to the border and northern States. "Behold," it was said, "the baleful effects of abolition! England, that first set the pernicious example of setting the negro free, and that sent its emissaries to stir up civil war in our own happy land on behalf of the 'nigger,' begins to see the error of her ways, and makes short, sharp, and decisive work of her black *protégé* as soon as he becomes troublesome. We too perhaps may have to imitate her example at no distant day, if we are stupid enough to pamper, the 'nigger' and give him a vote." But our English black republicans, unaware either of the exaggeration or its motives, were deluded, as they usually are when a negro is concerned, and made ample use of the fabulous "eight miles of dead bodies" in their denunciations of Mr Eyre. Even to his day the phrase does good service in their cowardly cause, and gives force to the invective which they never weary in directing against a man who, in the service of any other government than that of England, would have received the thanks and the encouragement of his superiors, if not reward and promotion.

Philosophy may talk as it will of the natural equality of the whole human race; but there is an instinct in man as well as in animals—an instinct which, if it cannot argue, can act—and in the long-run often proves itself stronger than the most faultless reasoning.

There *is* an antipathy of race, against which all argument is
powerless.   Even in our own little isles, where we are all white,
there is a repugnance between the Irish and the Anglo-Saxon, and
vice versa, which defies analysis and logic, and which prevails
among the same races when transplanted to America.   The antipathy of the Anglo-Saxon against people of a different colour from
his own springs, in the first place, from a desire to rule and to
possess.   The savage aborigines of every continent and island which
he has invaded in order to colonise and retain the land, have been
invariably persecuted with relentless ferocity.   The Red man has
all but disappeared from the United States.   At the census of 1860
it was found that no more than 300,000 of the race that once
possessed the continent, remained on Federal territory between the
Atlantic and the Pacific—about as large a population, if all collected
together in one spot, as would about equal that of the city Baltimore.   The race was too proud, too wild, too independent, too lazy,
and in all respects too worthless, to be enslaved.   As the Red man
could not be made to work, the Anglo-Saxons resolved to exterminate
him, and they have all but accomplished their purpose.   Similar
results have grown out of similar causes in South Africa, Australia,
and New Zealand.   Philosophy, humanity, Christianity, all are alike
impotent to stay the inevitable catastrophe.   The inferior race
provokes aggression, even when the superior would gladly do no
more than banish it beyond the boundaries of civilisation; and at
every provocation the aggressors suffer infinitely more than the
superior race which repels and punishes them.   The Anglo-Saxon
farmer and the Anglo-Saxon missionary have different ideas upon
the subject; but it is the ideas of the |591| farmer and not of the
missionary which ultimately prevail; and the rifle of the one settles
a question, which all the piety and all the logic of the other is unable
to take out of the Court of Brute Force into the higher Court of
Reason. In the Northern States of America, in which slavery was
unprofitable, and in many of which, Massachusetts among the
number, care was taken to sell the slaves to Southern planters before
the formal abolition of slavery within their territories, the antagonism and antipathy to the negro has never been so strong as
against the Red man. At all events, the free negro in the cold North,
where he could find no unoccupied land on which he could squat
and grow pumpkins, was compelled either to work, to die, or to go

South, with the certainty of slavery if he took the last alternative. A few chose to turn their faces southwards and take all the risks of slavery. The great bulk of them, however, remained in the North; and while population was scanty, and was not continually reinforced by such swarms of Irishmen and Germans as have poured into the country from European ports for the last sixteen years, found occupations as coachmen, barbers, and waiters.   Twenty years ago the negroes all but monopolised these avocations in the Northern and Middle States.   But the copious immigration of Irish and Germans has wrought a change in these respects.   Five millions of white labourers having come into the country, the weaker and less intelligent race, unable to compete with them, has as usual gone to the wall.   The Irish have all but driven the negroes out of the position of waiters and coachmen; and the Germans have rapidly superseded them as barbers.   Year by year the negroes have been squeezed out of their former place; and all avocations have been closed against them, except those of the porter, the night-man, the whitewasher, and the chimney-sweep.   In the first business—where nothing is wanted but strong arms and a strong back—the Irishman, in all the great cities and ports of the Atlantic, is fast taking the lead; and the poor negro has no resource but the lowest paid and most offensive avocations, like those of the sweep and the dust-man.   And even from these he bids fair to be driven by white competition, when there will be nothing left for him but pauperism, the grave, or emigration.   Black pauperism neither the Yankees nor the men of the South will tolerate, so that the choice left for the poor negro is but a dreary one.   In the meanwhile death is coming to the relief of his unhappy race.   In 1860, prior to the civil war, it was proved by the decennial returns of the census that, notwithstanding all the accessions to the free negro population of the North derived from the influx of runaway slaves, and the operation of what it was then the fashion to call the Underground Railway, the births did not equal the deaths, nor the influx of Southern negroes keep up the numbers of the race.   The cold of the climate, poverty, disease, dejection—all combined to thin their numbers, and point to the day, distant perhaps, but certain to come, when the negro would be as rare in the Northern States of America as he is in Europe.

It is constantly urged by those who have much zeal and little knowledge that, low as may be the mental condition of the negro in his natural state, it may be greatly improved by education. There is no doubt that negroes can be educated, if by education be meant that they can be taught to read, to write, and to master the fundamental rules of arithmetic.   There is no doubt also that they are highly imitative, and after going to church or chapel learn to preach after a fashion, delightful to black men and women, but to no one else.   But if by education be meant the use of reading, writing, and arithmetic as tools of |592| knowledge, as instruments of progress, and the development of truth; and that by any amount of education a Plato, a Socrates, a Bacon, a Newton, a Shakespeare, a Mendelssohn, a Rubens, a Watt, a Humboldt, or a Canova, can arise among the black race,—it is incumbent upon those who make such a claim on the negro's behalf to give some little proof of the faith that is in them.   Did anybody ever hear of a negro mathematician, of a negro engineer, of a negro architect, of a negro painter, of a negro political economist, of a negro poet, or even of a negro musician—using the word in the sense of a creator of melody and harmony?   It is no more possible, by means of education, to confer upon the negro the mental vigour of the white man, than it is, by means of education, to elevate the white man into angelic perfection.   Nature, which fixed the limits of the white man's mind, fixed those also of the black; and no training, no example, can cultivate the lower animal into the higher.   It is true that to a certain extent the negro can be improved by admixture of blood with the white race.   The mulatto is generally more intelligent than the full-blooded negro, and the quadroon and octoroon make still further advances in the scale of humanity; but even this intermixture of blood can only be carried to a definable limit.   Nature is inexorable in punishing infractions of her laws. The white and the black may intermarry, but the decree of ultimate barrenness is the penalty pronounced upon the hybrid race—a penalty that is certain to be exacted in the fourth generation.   After that time the unnatural plant dies out, and nature vidicates her own intention to suffer no permanent amalgamation.   As a pure black the negro may live and multiply, but not otherwise.   And as a pure black his history is the same in all ages.   Left to himself, and without white control and guidance, he forgets the lessons he has learnt, and slides rapidly back to his original barbarism.

The faction in the North that, for a political purpose, and the retention of power in its own hands, desires to neutralise or swamp the votes of the Southern whites by conferring the fullest political franchise upon the ignorant blacks, has no real love for the race it professes a desire to elevate.   Its policy is inspired not by affection for the negro, but by democratic hatred for the former master of slaves, whom it considers—and perhaps not altogether erroneously—to be of necessity an aristocrat.   But the great bulk of the American people, even in Massachusetts, treat the negro with aversion.   Ultra-democratic in political theory, they become social aristocrats whenever it becomes a question of race and colour.   The white man in New England, *quoad* the black man, is as much of an aristocrat in heart and feeling as any Duke of Broadacres is in England, *quoad* his footman or his shoe-black.   The negro is in no State of the Union a full citizen, in right of his manhood, as the white man is.   In some States he is absolutely excluded from all political right and privilege, simply and solely because he is black. In others he is allowed a vote if he have a certain money qualification not necessary in the white man's case.   In most, if not all, of what were once called the "free States," he is excluded from the jury-box.   In none of the States has a black man ever been elected to a judgeship, a governorship, or a senatorship, or been chosen as a representative of the people in Congress or the local legislature. There was never a black clerk in the Custom-House or the Post-Office, or even a black keeper of a lighthouse, of all which appointments the Government of the day possess the patronage.   Black men in New England, New York, the Middle States, and the Far West, must not show themselves in boxes at the theatres, |593| and in some cities they must not ride in the omnibuses.   It has been found impossible to prohibit them from travelling by the rail, but on many lines there is a negro-car, reserved exclusively for the use of these coloured pariahs.   A recent case—that of a very respectable and worthy negro, who keeps a restaurant and ice-cream saloon at New Brighton, in Staten Island—shows a still more unworthy mode of oppression against the race.   This "coloured gentleman," one of the aristocracy of his people, was travelling, during the heats of last summer, in a car on one of the New York railways, when he had occasion, as his white companions had, to go to the ice-pitcher for a drink of water.   The conductor in charge of the train forbade his drinking. The water was for white people, not for blacks. It was thought apparently that the touch of a negro's lips would be pollution to the tin can from which others drank, and that the stain could not be washed out, any more than that on Lady Macbeth's hand, by all the water of the ocean. This negro, though unable to read or write, had influence enough with some one who could, to procure the publication of a statement of the case in some of the newspapers; but all the satisfaction he got from the railway officials whose conduct he impugned was the assertion, that he had been very generously treated in being allowed a seat in the car; and that the next time he attempted to travel on that line, he would either be excluded altogether, put into the cattle-truck, or locked up by himself. In some of the Western States, Indiana among the number, a negro is not allowed to settle, or even to enter without satisfactory proof to the proper authorities at the frontier, or the nearest town to it, that he only intends to pass through, and that he has money enough to pay his way while he remains in the prohibited territory. In all menial offices, the negro is not only tolerated but approved of; but if he presume to step out of his sphere and claim either social or political fellowship with the dominant race, he speedily finds to his sorrow that he has made a mistake. The 'Tribune,' edited very ably, zealously, and honestly by Mr Horace Greeley, and the 'Independent,' a religious paper lately edited by the Rev. Henry Ward Beecher, and now by the Rev. Theodore Tilton, may each, to the full scope of their will, knowledge, and earnestness, advocate the cause of the negro—assert his complete social and political, as well as legal equality with the white man—and maintain, as the latter once did, that the blood of the white race would be greatly improved by an admixture with that of the black; but if either of those influential editors ventured to carry his preaching into practice so far as to employ a black compositor in his composing-rooms, or a black pressman at his printing-presses, the whole of his white workmen would immediately strike work and leave the premises, even though the ruin of their employers might be the result. The same principles that lead workmen in England and Scotland to establish trades-unions, lead the working classes in America to combine against the negro. They not only despise and look down upon him as an inferior, on account of his colour, but they dread his competition in the labour-market; for they know that his necessities—and, it may be added, the smaller number of his wants—render him willing to work for smaller wages than the whites.   The newly-arrived Irish—as well as those of older standing, who have no means of living but by the comparatively unskilled labour of their hands, and with whom, in consequence, the negroes come into more intimate competition than with any other class—are for this reason particularly hostile to the "niggers," or, as they mostly pronounce the word, the "naygurs."   During the anti-conscription riots |594| in New York in the summer of 1863, this animosity of the Irish against the negroes was frightfully exhibited.   Poor inoffensive black men, unaware of the commotion, and quietly passing along the streets in the exercise of their ordinary business, were bruised and beaten to death, stoned to death, shot, stabbed, and hung to lamp-posts, amid the exultations of a fiendish multitude, nine-tenths of whom were Irishmen and Irishwomen. If the rioters had had a leader—which they fortunately had not—or had such leader possessed the art of directing and organising the populace, there is much reason to believe that the antagonism of race—of which cool philosophers in their closets, and hot preachers in their pulpits, sometimes deny the existence—would have received another proof of its vitality as horrible as that of St Domingo, and with the added shame, that the aggressors were the stronger, and not the weaker race.   So ineradicable is the feeling, that many eminent native-born Americans, who hate the Irish politically as much as they dislike the negroes socially, were sorry that the riots did not extend all over the country, in order, as they said, that every Irishman in America might have killed a nigger, and been hung for it.

There have been slave-owners in the South as conscientiously convinced as any abolitionist or black republican in the North that slavery was a crime; and who proved their faith by their works, and emancipated their slaves, either during their own lives, or by express testamentary order after their death.   Among others, the celebrated Virginian, John Randolph of Roanoke, by his will freed his four hundred slaves, and left sufficient money to purchase a tract of sixteen thousand acres of fine arable land in Ohio, to be divided among the four hundred in farms of forty acres each.   The well-meant experiment ended in failure and disaster.   The white farmers of the district disapproved of the importation of so many black men into their neighbourhood; and the negroes, left to their own guidance, became very bad agriculturists. They found it pleasanter to smoke than to plough, to snooze than to dig. Idle, thriftless, improvident, and careless of the morrow, they speedily reduced themselves to poverty. They did not even see the necessity, or at all events they did not act upon it, of saving from the harvest of one year the seed necessary for that of the next. In less than three years more than one-half of them were sold out by the foreclosures of the mortgages they had effected on their farms, and within ten years not a single negro proprietor remained out of the four hundred. The benevolence of John Randolph was wasted, and his great scheme of practical charity came to nought, partly on account of the antagonism of the non-slaveholding whites, and partly on account of the natural incapacity of the negro to till the soil except upon compulsion.

A more recent instance that occurred within a year in Philadelphia—the City of Brotherly Love, the home and hotbed of American humanitarianism, and of many other "isms" that have charms for people who think they are immeasurably wiser and better than all the rest of the human race—will show how deeply rooted are the prejudices entertained against the black race by those who would on no account enslave, or suffer others to enslave, a negro. A respectable mulatto, possessing some of the virtues of thrift, prudence, and industry, inherited along with his white blood, was owner of a lot of two acres in the close vicinity of the city. He turned his ground into a market-garden; and from the produce of potatoes, cabbages, tomatoes, and other vegetables, managed to support himself and family. By degrees the city grew up around his garden, |595| and in process of time the municipality found it necessary to cut a street directly through the property. Houses sprang up on every side; his garden was destroyed, and he was no longer able to make the produce of the severed portions pay for his time and labour. Under the circumstances, he was advised, as the ground was valuable for building purposes, to borrow money upon it, and erect houses. In an evil hour he acted upon the suggestion, and borrowed money at the current rate of 7 per cent. But when his houses were completed, he found that no one would tenant them. It was too degrading for any respectable white man to have a black man for his landlord. As a last resource, to find means to pay the interest on his loan, he reduced the rents below the usual average, and succeeded in letting a few of them to the lowest order of Irish emigrants. These very speedily gave the place a disreputable character; and, what perhaps was quite as bad, they obstinately refused to pay any rent. The result was, after a short time, that the mortgagees entered into possession, cleared out the bad Irish tenants, and handed over to the poor mulatto the value of the property, after settlement of the mortgage bonds, to begin the world afresh.

Were it necessary, scores, if not hundreds, of instances as strong as these could be cited to show the social ban and excommunication under which the free negro labours whenever he attempts to enter into competition or close companionship with the whites, but from which the negro did not suffer when in bondage to his master. "I am very much attached to my horse," said an ex-slave-owner, "but if the animal could speak, and insisted upon sleeping in my parlour or library, instead of in the stable, I am very certain that my attachment would speedily change into aversion. So it is with the negro. Europeans do not understand him: we of the South do. In his place, and under control, we respect, and often have a sincere regard for him. He is useful, faithful, and affectionate. He lies and steals, it is true, and would be lazy if he durst; but a kindly despotism corrects some of his evil, and brings out all his good, qualities. But in freedom, he is, with rare exceptions, as useless to himself as to society, and will end by becoming a public nuisance."

These opinions may be due to prejudice, but American statesmen and British philanthropists—the one interested practically, and the other theoretically, in the subject—will do well to study the facts of daily occurrence in the United States which bear on the condition of the freed negroes. Will these men, so lately slaves, and still so ignorant of the responsibilities and the duties of freedom, consent, as white men do, to work for wages? and will they conscientiously and faithfully earn the wages for which they work? Upon the answer which Time shall give to these questions depends not alone the status, but the fate of the negro in America. If Time reply in the affirmative, the political rights which spiteful abolitionists would bestow upon him in the South, and withhold from him in the North, will follow in due course. The honest, hard-working man will enjoy the privilege of a vote, irrespective of his colour; though whether the black man will ever achieve his social equality with the white, which bitter Northern clergymen and philosophers, and silly spinsters, talk so much about, but never vindicate by their practice or example, is a matter of much less importance, and on which it is scarcely worth while even to speculate.   At present the aspect of the negro labour question is not favourable.   The freed slaves look, for the most part, upon field-labour with distaste, and associate it with the taskmaster from whose clutches they have been delivered.   They flock into |596| the great cities, which they seem greatly to prefer to the rice-swamp, the cotton-field, and the sugar-press, by their labour in which they added to the wealth of the world, and seek employment as coach-drivers, lockmen, and waiters—all very useful avocations, no doubt, but the exercise of which adds nothing to the national resources.   Washington swarms with them, Baltimore is encumbered with them, Richmond brims over with them, Charleston and New Orleans are at their wit's end to know what to do with them.   Were it only the young and ablebodied of both sexes who pressed upon the resources of these cities, the evil, though flagrant, might admit of alleviation, if not of thorough remedy; but when the aged and infirm, and the helpless children of this unhappy race, deprived by the course of war of the protection on which they relied, and in the absence of which they have nothing to depend upon but the charity of white people, who know them not, and who, themselves ruined by the sword and the torch of an unholy conflict, have too little left for their own support to have anything to bestow upon the race whose status was the pretext of strife, the case becomes one of all but hopeless difficulty, perplexity, and misery. To these people liberty and the grave speedily become one and the same blessing.   Typhus and smallpox aggravated by filth and famine, make short work of the black man, and relieve overburdened charity of a task, which charity may have the will, but has not the means or the power, to perform.   It has been calculated that at least five hundred thousand white men lost their lives in the late war for the preservation of a Union, that is not worth a straw if it be not a union of heart, interest, and mutual respect; and that at least twice, if not three times, that number of black men, women, and children, have been sacrificed, not in the battle-field and the trenches merely, but in the swamp, the jungle, the hospital, and the back slums of crowded cities, where they have miserably perished—in freedom, it is true, but in the freedom of kindly death and the hospitable grave.

One thing is clear, slavery is gone—gone at one great blow, gone forever, not to be revived, either in form or in spirit, banished from the minds of all English-speaking people—and restricted to Spain and Brazil, among Christian nations, where it exists with diminished vitality, and is sentenced, there can be no reasonable doubt, to be destroyed, when the hour is ripe for the consummation.   But if the fact of the death of slavery in the South be clear, it is equally clear, in view of the necessities both of the Southern and the Northern people, and of the interests of the whole civilised world, that the free negro must conform himself to the great and paramount law of civilisation.   Like the white man, he must work or die.   He cannot be allowed to lounge about great cities, doing nothing but beg.   He cannot be permitted to possess Southern lands, and suffer them to go out of profitable cultivation.   He cannot be suffered to breed up a race of paupers to prey on the industry of better men. He cannot be tolerated to form hotbeds of filth and fever in the great cities, nor to become either a moral or a physical burden upon the community.   Those who know most of the negro, who under- stand his character best, and who have the greatest liking for him, as the only agricultural labourer who can thrive amid the malaria of the rice-fields, or the heats of the cotton plantations, declare that his wants are so few that he will not work systematically for wages, but that he will cultivate a little patch for bare subsistence, squatting upon other men's lands.   It is not probable that the Southern land- |597| owners will consent to be thus overrun and dispossessed by a prolific race of black paupers, or that if the negroes, not being purchasers of land, shall take forcible possession of it, a new war between white and black in the South will not be the result.   If a system of apprenticeship to labour, or some modified form of serfdom, such as that recommended by General Banks for Louisiana, be not established, there will only be two modes left to settle the stupendous difficulty.   The first is that which has been adopted with regard to the aborigines of America—EXTERMINATION, gradual but sure.   The second is the establishment of a POOR-LAW that shall act upon the fundamental and essential axiom, that no strong, able-bodied man is entitled to live upon the charity of the community, that he who would eat

must work, that labour is a sacred duty; and that any man, whatever
his race or colour, unable or unwilling to support himself except by
beggary and vagrancy, or by breach of the eighth commandment,
shall be held to labour, whether he like it or not; and that if the
nature of the negro is such that many thousands, or hundreds of
thousands, of them be found throughout the South in this condition,
unable to appreciate or turn to account the freedom too suddenly
thrown upon them, such thousands, or hundreds of thousands, or
millions, whatever their numbers may be, shall in their several
parishes and townships, and by the strong arm of the recognised
authorities—civil, if the refractory paupers be few; military, if they
are many—be organised into labour companies, and compelled to
earn their subsistence.   The question under any aspect is one that
threatens to try men's souls before it receives a final and satisfactory
solution.   In the meanwhile the indications are but too palpable,
that the sudden abolition of slavery is no boon to the slave, but a
disruption of old ties, fraught with evil consequences to all concerned,
and most of all to the unhappy negroes.

FIVE

JOHN WILLIAM JACKSON (1809–71)

Race in Legislation and Political Economy

Anthropological Review
Volume 4, 1866, pp. 113–35

This essay was published unsigned. Some have attributed it to Dr James Hunt, President of the Anthropological Society. But the evidence for this is less substantial than that favouring authorship by Jackson, another regular contributor to the Anthropological Review. *The two men were in broad agreement about the operation in society of racial determinants, yet the style of presentation here adopted is more typically that of Jackson. Indeed, we find the paper listed as Jackson's own in his widow's preface to his final work on* Man Contemplated Physically, Morally, Intellectually, and Spiritually *published in 1875. The author, largely self-educated, had made most of his modest living by lecturing on mesmerism and practising phrenology. Particularly interesting is his treatise of 1863 on* Ethnology and Phrenology as an Aid to the Historian. *His shorter essays on the contemporary relevance of race included surveys of the Irish Question (Anthropological Review, Vol. 7, 1869) and the Franco-Prussian War (Journal of the Anthropological Institute, Vol. 1, 1871–2). The Crimean struggle had been similarly treated in a book on* The Peoples of Europe and the War in the East *(1854).*

In the following paper Jackson expounds the general principles lying behind the racial explanations of history, society, and politics so amply used throughout these works. His central aim is to refute the kind of criticism levelled against such determinism by the school of J. S. Mill. In condemning Mill's refusal to allow that many important diversities of conduct and character must be explained essentially in terms of racial differentiation and hierarchy, the essay raises many issues vital to debate upon the relative significance of nature and nurture. Jackson incorporates a wide range of historical and geographical reference, and concludes by warning against Mill's simplistic advocacy of Negro enfranchisement in the United States.

"Of all vulgar modes of escaping from the consideration of the effect of social and moral influences on the human mind, the most vulgar is that of attributing the diversities of conduct and character to inherent natural differences."—MILL, *Principles of Political Economy*.

It is a most mistaken idea that Anthropology is purely speculative and abstract.   It is, on the contrary, more intimately related than any other branch of science to the sympathies of humanity, and we may add, the utilities and requirements of society.   It enters into every question connected with religion, government, commerce, and culture, which are all more or less affected by racial endowment and proclivity.   This, however, is a comparatively new idea, on which the statesman and the legislator are yet scarcely prepared to act, and to which the theologian manifests not merely indifference, but repugnance.   Practically, indeed, the element of race has not yet obtained recognition, as one of the underlying conditions and modifying forms of civilisation.   We must not blame the world for this.   Scientific Anthropology is a thing of yesterday; nor is the study of it yet sufficiently advanced to justify its believers in claiming the reverent attention of duly cultured minds to their hastily formed conclusions.   They must be content to wait and work, sowing the seed of truth to-day, that mankind may reap its golden harvest on some far off to-morrow.   In the meantime, however, its advocates will only be performing a proper duty in occasionally enforcing its claims on the attention of our more advanced thinkers, preparatory, let us trust, to their full recognition by the general voice of civilised society.

In this endeavour to commend Anthropology to more general acceptance, we must not hide from ourselves that two great schools are, on principle, decidedly opposed to our pretensions.   These two |114| influential parties, while differing widely from each other on many other points, at least cordially agree in discarding and even denouncing the truths of Anthropology.   They do so because these truths are directly opposed to their cardinal principle of absolute and original equality among mankind.   The parties to which we refer are the orthodox, and more especially the evangelical body, in religion, and the ultra-liberal and democratic party in politics.   The former proceed on the traditions of Eden and the Flood, and on the assertion, that of one blood God made all the nations of the earth; the latter base their notions on certain metaphysical assumptions and abstract ideas of political right and social justice, as innocent of scientific data, that is, of the fact as it is in nature, as the wildest of the theological figments which set Exeter Hall in periodical commotion, at the never-failing anniversaries of missionary enterprise.

We fear that it is in vain to argue with the religious portion of our opponents.   People whose opinions are based on dogma possess a fortress not easily assailed by reason.   They know in what they believe, and from the vantage ground of a supernatural revelation can afford to laugh at the indications of history and the deductions of science.   They are persuaded themselves, and they have persuaded a very large section of society, that one religion, their own, will do for all mankind to the end of time.   And society believes them, or, at all events, is too ignorant or too busy to oppose this tremendous assumption.   And so we subscribe a million a year, and send out good men and true into all climes, it may be truly said, in denial of the past and defiance of the present.

Our political opponents are not exactly persons of this stamp. They do not profess any particular faith in written records.   They are not prepared to enthrone an eastern myth on the denial of modern science.   They do not intentionally prefer dogma to fact. Opposed to an hereditary aristocracy in the body politic, they are prone to deny the wider and more-enduring aristocracy of race. Believers in the omnipotence of circumstances, they refuse to recognise the aids or the obstacles of inherent endowment.   To them, humanity is one from the educational stand-point, as it is also one to the theologians from the creational stand-point.   The latter assert that a Negro or a Mongol will make as good a Christian as the most finely-developed Caucasian, and the former equally affirm that, with proper training, he will make as good a citizen, as skilful a craftsman, as fine an artist, and as able a poet or philosopher.   We do not mean to say that the latter put their conclusions exactly into these words.   They dare not.   The plain practical good sense of society would prove too much for them were they to do so.   But their assertions, as far as they mean |115| anything, imply this, and are indeed mere idle rhodomontade, if they do not.

And here, perhaps some of our Anthropological friends may be of opinion, that in seriously opposing such absurdities, we are guilty of the folly of the worthy Knight of La Mancha, when he ran a tilt at the windmills.   But in truth these absurdities, from their wide acceptance, are gradually becoming productive of very grave consequences.   The stupendous claims of the Romish hierarchy to the sacerdotal supremacy of the world, are based on the prior assumption of a possible unity among all nations in religious belief and practice, and on the mundane and unending mission of Papal Christianity. The atrocities of the Spaniards in Peru and Mexico were but the dark conclusions, wrought out by the logic of events, from these startling premises.   The wars of the reformation were humanity's assertion of its right to differ,—were, in short, the counter-proclamation of the Teuton in opposition to the claims of the Roman. The watchwords of modern revolution, "liberty, equality and fraternity," more especially the two latter, together with all the absurdities and impossibilities of communism, are but the sinister yet legitimate progeny of the principle of primal and organic equality.   The mischief of such views, indeed, is not and cannot be confined to the sphere of speculation.   They of necessity invade the field of action, where thought ultimates itself in deeds.   They influence most of the colonial enterprises of modern times; and they were at the foundation of the recent civil war in America, and underlie not only the claim of the freedmen to the suffrage, but all the contemplated horrors and abominations of miscegenation.

We have, in a previous paper on Race in History*, already touched on some of the errors of one of the schools to which we have been alluding, that of the Political Economists and Legislative Reformers.   But, in doing so, we confined our remarks almost wholly to the works of one of the youngest of its disciples, the historian Buckle.   But he was only an echo of his masters, Jeremy Bentham and John Stuart Mill, as they are but a continuation of Helvetius and the French Encyclopedists, who were again but a far-off reverberation of Democritus and Epicurus.   There is a terrible tyranny in ideas.   Your principles, even though they be the most fallacious assumptions, will ultimate themselves in legitimate conclusions sooner or later.   John Stuart Mill cannot help claiming the suffrage for the Negro—and the woman.   Such conclusions are

* [*Editor's Note*: also published anonymously in the *Anthropological Review*, Vol. 3, 1865.]

the inevitable result of the premises whence he started.   And had
he paused at such a *reductio ad absurdum* his school would not.
That school, as we have said, dates from the remotest antiquity.
The omnipotence of circumstances |116| and the natal equality of
mankind are not new doctrines.   They are simply materialism, and
the philosphy of the external ultimated.   He who starts from
atoms, guided by chance, must end in absolute democracy, that is,
in racial and individual equality.   It is simply the completion of
the circle, from chaos to chaos.

It need scarcely be said that such a school can only exist in words
or upon paper, for it is in direct contradiction to fact.   Nature is
a grand hierarchy of cosmic and telluric organisms.   Her suns rule
their subordinate planets, surrounded again by their subject satel-
lites.   The vegetable and animal kingdoms are a succession of
organic stages, separated, as Swedenborg would say, by "discrete
degrees."   While at the very apex of this pyramid of form and
function, we find regal man, the virtual king of the earthly
sphere.   And are we to suppose that this hierarchical arrangement
ceases here; that there are no innate and hereditarily transmissible
diversities among men?   Reason as well as fact revolts at so absurd
a conclusion.   Had we, from our limited geographical range, experience only of one race, we might most legitimately conclude there
were others in the distance,—a conclusion now adequately substan-
tiated by geographical discovery.   But John Stuart Mill cannot see
this. His intellectual prepossessions are too strong for such a grasp
of veracity.   His mind is so filled with the *idola* of Codification
and Political Economy, that he cannot see the simple yet unspeakably
important facts of Anthropology.

Let not these remarks on Mr. Mill be misunderstood.   He is the
last man to intentionally maintain an untruth.   Privileged to own
one of the clearest and most logically constituted heads, and we
may add, one of the noblest hearts in Christendom, he unites the
deductive power of the race whence he descends, and we may add,
of the school to which he belongs, with somewhat of their infirmity,
in the too facile rejection or assumption of premises.   No man
marches more carefully from the major to the minor; the process,
in such hands at least, is unerring.   But, alas for the major.   It
may be the sublimest of truths, an axiom on which the universe
could repose unshaken for eternity, or, as in the present case, a

fallacy so transparent, that the simplest cabin-boy, on his homeward voyage, would see its infantile absurdity.

The rejection of truth is perilous, perhaps we might say fatal, to all men. But it must prove especially so to the priesthood of intellect,—to those sages and philosophers, who as legislators, political economists, historians, and men of science, endeavour to explain the truth and the right to others; for when the shepherds go astray, it is no wonder that the flock generally follow. To write of men, and to legislate for men, while rejecting the science of man, is certainly a most extra-|117|ordinary and by no means commendable procedure. And yet it was that of Jeremy Bentham and Thomas Henry Buckle, and is that of John Stuart Mill. The first drew up a code, or shall we say, laid down the principles of codification in the abstract—ignoring diversity of race. The second wrote his otherwise admirable history, and the last has given us the principles of Political Economy, together with sundry treatises on Liberty and Representative Government, not only ignoring, but directly and almost offensively denying the great truth of racial diversity. Ignoring the fact in nature, that men differ in the relative proportion of their passions, affections, sentiments and faculties. Ignoring what is patent, not only to the Anthropologist, but to the soldier, the sailor, and the man of business, that the races of mankind differ in the force of their propensities, in the strength of their sympathies, in the power of their principles, in the accuracy of their perceptions, and in the clearness and the vigour of their thoughts. Ignoring not only the conclusions of the man of science, but the practical experience of all widely-travelled persons, that there are distinctly marked Ethnic diversities, in virtue of which the grander divisions of mankind differ in the persistence of their will, in their power to resist temptation, in their susceptibility to impulse, in their ability for work, and in their innate capacity for literature, science and art. And ignoring therefore what the experience of ages has demonstrated, and what the true wisdom of the present would dictate, the necessity for a diversity of religion and government corresponding to this diversity of race, whereby the formal institutions of a people are brought into harmony with their mental constitution.

These are severe remarks. Let not their spirit be misunderstood. It is because we respect their advocates, that we are so harsh in our judgment of the doctrines.   Error is formidable in proportion to the ability, and, we may add, the virtue of those who hold it.   The fallacies of men like Bentham, Mill, and Buckle, cannot be harmless.   Such minds cast the halo of their glory around even their grossest errors, and just in proportion as we revere them for the good which they have accomplished, must we be stern in our opposition to the evil of which they are unintentionally the authors.   Of such it may be truly said, "if their light be darkness, how great is that darkness!"   If their views be founded on error, how widely diffused must that error be!   It is the very greatness of the men that necessitates our more serious antagonism to their fallacies.   They are too powerful, too influential, to allow us to pass over their mistakes in silence.   The voice which has been oracular for the truth, becomes doubly formidable when employed as the trumpet-blast of error.

In the history of Philosophy, in so far as we can be said to possess |118| anything deserving of the name, nothing is more remarkable than the power of the schools.   Like religious sects, they take the individual helplessly captive, and lead him whithersoever they will. They close his eyes to one phase of truth, and they open them to another.   Nor does any amount of talent or attainment appear to constitute an adequate safeguard against this despotism.   It only makes the individual a more or less apt instrument for the acceptance and promulgation of their doctrines.   He is obviously the organ of a greater power, that sees beyond him, and uses him for a grander purpose, than anything of which he is conscious.   This is the case with Mr. Mill.   It was equally so with Jeremy Bentham.   They are the organs of negation.   In reality, the champions of matter *versus* spirit.   It is their vocation to proclaim the weight and value of *quantity* as opposed to quality.   They ignore the ONE.   They enthrone the *many*.   They do not stand alone in this.   They have not only a large following, but they have had many able precursors, and they have many powerful coadjutors.   They represent the spirit of the age.   Their works are simply Protestantism, logically ulti- mated in the political sphere.   Fourier went beyond them, and carried it into the social, where it eventuated in communism.   Let it not be supposed that in saying this, we pass a judgment of condemnation upon these truly great and deservedly illustrious men.   Their cause is perfectly legitimate.   It represents one of the two great poles of universal truth.   But it is only one pole, and that not the *positive*.   These are rather daring assertions.   We know it, and must now proceed to their confirmation.

It was a grand saying, that all minds are either Platonic or Aristotelean, subjective or objective, spiritual or material in their essential character and tendencies.   This, however, is only saying that men must obey the laws of polarity, the most gifted and earnest being generally the most strongly pronounced in their proclivities. But it is not only men as individuals, but men collectively, who have to obey these laws, and so manifest the spirit of the ages. In a sense, as was shown in some former numbers of this Journal, the entire movement of humanity, in the North-western march of civilisation throughout the historic period, was, intellectually speaking, a descent from the highly spiritualised theosophy of the Orient to the thoroughly-materialised science of the Occident. Now it is this movement in its ultimates, which is represented by Mr. Mill. As we have said, it is a great and legitimate movement, and even in its extremes, deserves to have such a champion to stand up for it.   As the protest of reason against dogma in religion, as the testimony of *à posteriori* fact against *à priori* assumption in philosophy, and as the claim of the rights of the many against the tyranny of the few in |119| politics, it was a great and noble cause, deserving of all honour and worthy of all success.   But when, overstepping these boundaries, it proceeds with its political logic to the denial of inconvenient facts, it is no longer a legitimate movement, but, on the contrary, one demanding strenuous opposition, and deserving utter and shameful defeat.   It has reached this stage in the hands of Mr. Mill and his coadjutors.   They deny the facts of race, and hence our opposition.

We thus see that this great movement is in conflict with itself. Its several sections are no longer in harmony with each other.   Its religion and its politics are at war with its science.   We have arrived at the beginning of the end.   In the fervour of religious propagandism, it demands one faith for all mankind.   And in its enthusiasm for liberty, it proclaims that all men may be politically free, when they have been adequately educated.   In attempting to maintain these stupendous assumptions, it does not condescend to investigate observed facts; but meets the testimony of travellers, and the conclusions of Anthropologists by the annunciation of abstract principles, in reality by a process of *à priori* reasoning, as opposed to the evidence of *à posteriori* experience.   By the dread compulsion of a false position, it is driven to the desparate alternative of ignoring nature and denying phenomena.   It does so, because nature and her phenomena are opposed to its conclusions. Again, we admit these are very severe remarks.   But they only express the simple truth, and hence our reason for their publication.

We make our appeal to nature.   Let us hear what she has to say.   The earth, at her different zones of latitude and longitude, or shall we say in other language, on her several areas, has specially characterised types, vegetable and animal, bestial and human. These specialities are obviously not accidental.   They are transmissible and enduring, and far antedate all history.   The law of distribution is yet beyond us; but it is evident that there is such a law, for we see its effects.   And we see them in the human sphere as distinctly as in any other.   The men of one Ethnic area are not to be confounded with the men of another.   Nor are these distinctions simply physical and organic, they extend also to habits and capacities.   We know that this is denied by Mr. Mill and his school.   But such denial necessitates the rejection of history as well as of science; for history is conclusive as to racial diversity, its annals being in truth but a record of the result of that diversity. For example, to affirm that a Negro is in every way as good a man as an European, is to deny the historic testimony of five thousand years, seeing that in all that time no Negro nation has ever, either with or without assistance, reached the civilisation, again and again achieved in the great centres of Caucasian |120| culture.   To say after this that Negro communities *might* have done so, is simply to beg the question, and take for granted the very thing in dispute.   They have not done so, even with the tuition of Egypt and the example of Carthage; and if our inquiry is to be conducted on *à posteriori* principles of investigation, we must accept the fact of their non-civilisation as in so far conclusive of their incapacity. They have been tried and found wanting.   But this historic evidence is corroborated by their organic inferiority.   The comparative anatomist agrees with the historian in placing them on a lower level than the European.   And the phrenologist agrees with the comparative anatomist.   We know that Mr. Mill does not believe in phrenology, nor we presume in physiognomy.   He cannot.   Either the one or the other would dissipate his day-dream of racial equality within an hour of its acceptance.   The inferior character of the Negro is as distinctly stamped on his organisation as on his destiny, and only minds blinded by the *idola* of preconceived ideas could fail to see the one as well as the other, and to find in both unmistakeable evidence of the Negro's lower position in the scale of being.

Similar remarks may be made on the Mongolian races of Eastern Asia.   Their structure, while superior to that of the Negro, is inferior to that of the European.   It is less developed.   As the type of the Negro is fœtal, that of the Mongol is infantile.   And in strict accordance with this we find that their government, literature and art are infantile also.   They are beardless children, whose life is a task, and whose chief virtue consists in unquestioning obedience.   Were Mr. Mill an anthropologist, we might point out to him the very important physiological fact, that an immemorial civilisation has utterly failed to Caucasianise either the Chinese or Japanese, they being still as essentially Mongolian as the rudest nomad of the northern steppes.   But he would place no value on such a fact.   It could have no significance from his standpoint. Form and function are to him matters of as much indifference as colour, which he avowedly ignores.   He cannot understand why a Chinaman, under adequately favourable circumstances, should not become as good a sculptor as Phidias, or as inspired a poet as Shakespeare.   And the reason why he cannot understand this is, that he ignores the racial element in humanity; in other words, he allows his *preconceived* idea of aboriginal unity and essential equality to dominate all structural evidence of diversity, and all historical evidence of inequality.   This we know is equivalent to saying that his mind is not open to the truth when nature is the witness, and her testimony is opposed to his cherished ideas and favourite speculations.   A severe sentence to pass on England's greatest living logician.   But it is out of his own mouth we convict him.   It is on the evidence afforded by his own works that we pronounce his condemnation.

|121| Now let it be distinctly understood that we say this of Mr. Mill only in his representative character, as the chief of a rather extreme school of political economists.   As an individual, no living man has a greater regard for veracity.   Even in his gravest errors he is perfectly honest, and when blinded to the truth by his deepest

prejudices, feels fully persuaded that he is simply consistent in maintaining a principle. Moreover, it should be remembered that he does not stand alone in ignoring racial diversity. His views, however erroneous, are not individual crotchets, but the well considered and avowed opinions of a large and influential school of thinkers, and as such deserving of the most respectful consideration, even from anthropologists, who so clearly see the egregious fallacies on which they rest. We must not blame men for differing from us. It is our business to provide them with such evidence, as shall suffice to produce a conviction of the truth, and if we fail in this, the fault is not theirs but ours.

What then is the gravamen of our charge against Mr. Mill and his friends? And we reply the unwarranted application of experiences, obtained only from the European race, to the whole of humanity. And as an accompaniment of this, the substitution of art in the place of nature in the process of legislation. As already remarked, these errors are due to the preponderance of abstract ideas over concrete experience. They result from that process of hasty and incautious generalisation, against which Francis of Verulam especially warned his followers. Because certain kinds of government, and certain processes in legislation, have proved successful in Europe, it is at once concluded, that they are abstractedly right and good, and should with all convenient speed be applied to every other family of man. And as these governments are representative and this legislation has been senatorial, it is supposed that such forms and modes of transacting matters gubernatorial, must be the acme of perfection in the way of example, and to which, therefore, the rule of all peoples should be made to gradually approximate, the only consideration being, the kind and degree of culture they may have previously undergone in the way of preparation. Of innate fitness or unfitness, of organic aptitude or inaptitude, these sages of the closet know nothing. Of hereditarily transmissible types of body and mind they are happily ignorant. For ineradicable proclivities, they have a sovereign contempt. "*Racial* specialities" they hold to be a figment of the anthropological imagination, and for which they would substitute "*educational* differences". To their view, races, or as they would say, nations are what circumstances have made them, and consequently alter the circumstances, and in due time you change the race! As already remarked, the logic is sound, but the premises are faulty.   They are so, because they fail to take an important element |122| of the problem into account, we mean the subject-matter on which the circumstances are supposed to operate.

Let us see indeed for what such logic would suffice, were the premises obtained from another ethnic area.   Asia has been immemorially the seat of despotism.   Its idea of authority is essentially unitary.   Its codes, in so far as they have grown, are the cumulative result of the successive edicts of absolute sovereigns.   But in their grand outlines and fundamental principles, they were the products of a single legislator, some divinely inspired Menu, Moses, or Mohammed, who derived his authority not from without but within, not from the people but from God, and whose short but effective preamble was "thus saith the Lord."   Now whether under Assyrian or Saracen, this was doubtless esteemed the better way.   But conceive of its application to Greek, or Roman, or Teuton, above all to these same Anglo-Saxon free-thinking political economists themselves!   Again we must remind Mr. Mill that there is a religion and a government, a literature and an art, which is specially adapted not only to the ontward circumstances but to the inherent and innate qualities of each of the grander divisions of mankind.

In these illustrations we have hitherto purposely omitted any allusion to the more savage races, all quite susceptible of civilisation according to the principles of Mr. Mill, who will not admit that the Australian, the Andaman islander, and the Hottentot labour under any *inherent* incapacity for attaining to the highest culture of ancient Greece or modern Europe!   Their present inferiority is an accident, due to a combination of unfavourable circumstances. They might have been the foremost men of all this world but for certain untoward influences.   To say anything about the Andaman head and the Hottentot brain is only "a vulgar mode of escaping from the consideration of the effect of *social* and *moral* influences on the human mind!"   Now anthropologists do not deny the power of social and moral influences, but they affirm that in conjunction with these the organic conditions and the transmissible mental constitution of their human subject-matter must also be taken into account.   This Mr. Mill denies, and hence his errors, both theoretical and practical, which we must now proceed to examine in detail.

In his otherwise excellent treatise on "Representative Government," Mr. Mill speaks of savage people and civilised people, and of the means by which the former may be gradually raised to the condition of the latter. Of the possibility of this process he has not the smallest misgiving. The idea that there are *savage races* adapted by structure and temperament, by habit of body and constitution of mind for the savage state, has obviously never occurred to him. He thinks a savage tribe |123| is like an ignorant individual, in want only of education, simply that and nothing more. It is the same with his idea of civilised races. He clearly thinks they might be absolutely savage. Taking the past upon trust, like a true closet-scholar putting unquestioning faith in his *books*, he closes his eyes to the present. Having read certain vague traditions about the ancestors of the Greeks and Romans, French and English having once been in a savage state, it has never occurred to him to test the accuracy of this statement, by looking round upon the world of to-day, to see if there be such a phenomenon as a really savage people of Caucasian type. We can readily understand that such a procedure would be in opposition to all his established habitudes of mind, and of this we do not complain. Only to say that such a thinker will prove a very unsafe guide as to the government of any race save his own.

In the same work he speaks of the arrestment of certain civilised nations at the stage of a paternal despotism, instancing the Egyptians and Chinese, with whom he contrasts the far more free and progressive Jews. The stagnation of the former he attributes to the strength of their institutions, which would not break down to permit of national growth, while the unorganised institution of the prophets among the latter people, by ensuring a greater degree of liberty, permitted also of more effective progress. All which is, no doubt, quite true. But then it is not the whole truth, only that, indeed, which lies on the surface. It does not tell us *why* the institutions of the one people were so restrictive and those of the other so comparatively elastic. This, as every anthropologist knows, must be sought in diversity of race—in the ethnic fact that the Chinese are a Mongolic people, and that the higher castes of Egypt were clogged by a numerically preponderant mass of African aborigines; while the Jews, and we may add the Phoenicians, were the most vigorously constituted of all the Asiatic Caucasians, and, indeed, present so many European elements in their national character, that the perfect purity of their oriental descent is still open to considerable suspicion.   But of all this Mr. Mill and his school know nothing, and want to know nothing; and while obtaining full credit with the yet more ignorant public for being very profound, are in point of fact childishly superficial in their habitual treatment of this and all similar topics.   They stop short at effects, and mistaking these for causes, think they have exhausted a subject, of which in truth they have scarcely broken the surface.

Mr. Mill's rejection of race, like the errors of all decisive minds, is thorough.   It pervades his entire system.   Hence he treats even of slavery without an allusion to this important element.   Thus he speaks of the facility with which slaves, when manumitted, assumed the position and discharged the duties of freemen among the Greeks and |124| Romans, which he attributes to the existence of an industrious class who were neither slaves or slave-owners.   Now there is no doubt that this was a very favourable circumstance, but what would it have availed if the freedmen had differed from their owners and the industrious middle-class, as the Negros of the States do from the Caucasian population around them?   The learned freedmen of Rome were often, racially speaking of as good blood as their masters.   And there is no doubt that even the Helots did not differ from the Spartans more than the Anglo-Saxons from the Normans.   Under such circumstances, the individual emancipation of superior slaves, is perfectly easy, nor is there the least wonder that the well-educated among them at once assumed a respectable and recognised position in society.   Nor with such conditions is there ultimately any insuperable difficulty in the emancipation of the whole class, either gradually, as throughout south-western Europe during the middle ages, or even suddenly as in Russia and Hungary in our own day, by an imperial edict or by a senatorial decree.   The absorption of such liberated bondsmen, into the class of freemen, is comparatively easy, because their inferiority is simply social and not organic.   But it is quite otherwise, where the inferiority is stamped upon the organisation, and where consequently the freedman and his children's children to the remotest generation, bear indelible traces of their descent from the servile cast.

Now again we say that the deservedly illustrious name of John Stuart Mill, ought not to cover the grave errors into which he has been led on this subject by his unwise rejection of the racial element, a rejection which by enabling him to speak of slavery in the abstract, has permitted him to confound the purely domestic institution of the better days of Greece and Rome, with the grosser chatteldom of negro slavery in our own times. This, for instance, is his portraiture of the slave proper:—

"A slave properly so called, is a being who has not learnt to help himself. He is, no doubt, one step in advance of the savage. He has not the first lesson of political society still to acquire. He has learnt to obey. But what he obeys is only a direct command. It is the characteristic of *born* slaves to be incapable of conforming their conduct to a rule or law. They can only do what they are ordered, and only when they are ordered to do it. If a man whom they fear is standing over them and threatening them with punishment, they obey; but when his back is turned, the work remains undone. The motive determining them must appeal not to their interests but to their instincts; immediate hope or immediate terror."

Now it need scarcely be said that this is a picture of negro slavery, and that, too, in its very worst form, that of the recently imported African savage working on a plantation. Here again it is obvious that |125| Mr. Mill has been misled by the undue predominance of abstract ideas over concrete experience. His "slave" is, in reality, an abstraction covering the immense gulph which separates a Plato, who was once sold as a slave by the order of the elder Dionysius of Syracuse, from a Congo negro. Assuredly, with all his subservience to ideas and his indifference to facts, Mr. Mill must know that the Greek or Circassian slave of a Turkish emir is a very different being from the woolly haired and thick-lipped Ethiopian, who occupies a yet lower servile position in the same household. Though equally slaves, as being bought with a price, they are yet inherently and essentially wide as the poles asunder, as their rude and ignorant but nevertheless practical master clearly perceives. History informs us that the Mamelukes of Egypt were all purchased slaves from the Caucasus. Does Mr. Mill think their ranks could have been as well recruited from the countries south of the Sahara? But there is no need for multiplying instances. The man who does not know that the social condition of the slave, both during his serfdom and after his manumission, is largely influenced by his racial relationship to, or difference from, his master, has yet, not only his anthropology but his history to acquire.

Closely connected with his deficiencies and misconceptions on the subject of slavery, and originating doubtless in the same fundamental error, is the omission by Mr. Mill of any allusion to hybridism, as an obstruction to the formation and maintenance of a stable government. It is, of course, quite legitimate in *logic*, for the man who does not believe in race, to deny or ignore the existence of half-castes. But, unfortunately, nature will not so ignore them, as Mexico and the South American republics have found to their cost. Where the parental elements are very diverse, the hybrid is himself a fermenting monstrosity. He is ever a more or less chaotic compound. He is in conflict with himself, and but too often exhibits the vices of both parents without the virtues of either. He is a blot on creation, the product of a sin against nature, whom she hastens with all possible expedition to reduce to annihilation. He is not in healthful equilibrium, either mental or physical, and consequently cannot conduce to the stability of anything else. He is ever oscillating between his paternal and maternal proclivities. His very instincts are perverted. He unites the baseness of the negro with the aspirations of the European; and while the creature of ungovernable appetite, longs for that liberty which is only compatible with self-command. Such are the many-coloured many-featured "curs" that abound in most of the colonial populations of modern times, produced, as we have said, by our having overstepped the boundaries of nature in the mixture of races.

Now in any work on Liberty and Representative Government, it |126| surely behoved the writer to take such an element as this into account. And the fact that he has not done so, renders these otherwise admirable productions of Mr. Mill of very inferior value, even in reference to the very subject which they profess to eluci-date. Judging by the time-honoured examples of Egypt and India, the only safe procedure with such a population of hybrids, is the institution and rigid maintenance of caste, to which, under such circumstances, things naturally tend, as we see among our trans-atlantic brethren at the present day. It was, perhaps in part, for the want of this regulation in adequate force, that Carthage ulti-mately succumbed to Rome; for while splendid Numidian cavalry undoubtedly helped Hannibal to some of his early victories, the mingled mobs at home contributed yet more effectually to his final defeat.

And thus we are brought to the great question of political and individual liberty contemplated from the ethnic stand-point. Now it need scarcely be said even to the tyro in anthropology that this is pre-eminently a question of race as well as culture, while Mr. John Stuart Mill treats of it throughout as simply a matter of collective educational preparation. Liberty and slavery are with him equally the possibility of all peoples. That the higher races are inherently more qualified for both political and individual liberty than the lower, he ignores in one place and denies by implication in another. In this he is quite consistent. It is an unavoidable corollary from the premiss of equality, but then, as already remarked, this premiss is itself an assumption of which those most familiar with anthropological science have the most doubt.

Were it not that we are steeled by habit to such proceedings, it might, perhaps, prove matter for grave reflection, that in the midst of our inductive era a school of thinkers can still be found, who independently of all detailed examination of the fact, dare to make the great affirmation of racial equality. That the religious world should do this does not surprise us. It is an accordance with the mediæval proclivities of theological thought. But it is otherwise with Mr. Mill and his followers, of whom, but for their uninquiring subservience to preconceived ideas, we might expect better things. Only think what this affirmation implies. Nothing less than a detailed knowledge of the passional impulses, the moral principles, and the intellectual faculties of all the various divisions of mankind. Why, the collective information of all the Anthropological Societies in existence, lands us only at the very threshold of such knowledge. And that collective information, be it remembered, as year by year it gradually increases, only brings us the more surely to a settled conviction of *existing* diversity, which is, moreover, so marked and found to consist in such very important anatomical |127| and physiological differences, that the growing conviction among most anthropological students is, that this so strongly marked diversity, is aboriginal, and consequently ineradicable. But whatever may be the value of these convictions, those who hold them have at least been guided in their search after truth by the laws of induction. They have examined the facts, they have investigated the data, and have deduced their conclusions from the elements so obtained.   While Mr. Mill, disdaining such laborious processes, leaps at once, according to the old high *à priori* method, to the magnificent assumption of racial equality, and then proceeds in undoubting confidence to all its far-stretching conclusions and momentous consequences.

But postponing for the present any further consideration of his processes, let us glance at Mr. Mill's assumption, that the capacity for liberty is simply a question of educational preparation, and with which, race has nothing whatever to do.   What says history on the aptitude of the various divisions of mankind for political liberty? And here we must carefully distinguish between the wild license of the savage and the legalised liberty of the civilised citizen of a constitutional state.   There is, no doubt, plenty of the former in the Indian wigwams of America, or the Hottentot kraals of South Africa, but such license is only a prelude to the direst despotism, at the first dawn of civilisation, as we see in the case of the Indian monarchies of Peru and Mexico.   It is the same with the rude freedom of the Mongolic nomads, which at once degenerates into the paternal despotism of China, as soon as they have exchanged their migratory habits as shepherds, for the settled occupations which accompany agriculture and its necessary concomitants in the mechanical arts.   Leaving savagism then behind, where, in truth, we do not so much see the presence of liberty as the absence of government, what Negroid or Mongolic people have ever developed constitutional freedom such as that once existing at Athens and Rome, and now enjoyed in Britain and the United States.   Nay, what people far removed from the Ethnic area of Europe have ever accomplished this?   For the Ionian Greeks, the Jews and the Phoenicians, together with the Carthaginian descendants of the latter, were at least Mediterranean races; and as we have already observed, with many European characteristics.   And of the people of Europe, do all show an equal aptitude for liberty?   Leaving out the classic type, as being in a sense historically past, do the existing Teutons, Celts and Sclavons manifest the same capacity for achieving and retaining liberty?   We would not however dwell too forcibly on the diversities in this respect, at present attaching to the various members of the great and nobly-endowed European family, as we are quite willing to admit, that many of these specialities are |128|

largely, if not wholly due to educational accidents. And indeed we
are prepared to acknowledge, that all Caucasian types on the
European area, may, with due preparation, be found fit for working
the complex machinery of a constitutional monarchy. History,
however, informs us that the Classic and Teutonic divisions alone
have yet shown any decided and inherent qualification for political
liberty, and that where there is not at least a large admixture of one
or both, liberty is either wholly absent or enjoyed by a very fitful
and uncertain tenure.

But distinct from, if not above and beyond political liberty, is
that which attaches to the individual. Men may be politically free,
yet socially enslaved. They may not dare to say or do what the
law allows, being overawed by the despotism of fashion or the
prescription of precedent. This is the state of the great majority
of respectable persons throughout Europe. But history narrates
instances where this authority of custom has been fossilised into
law. Egypt and India are notable examples. Here again Mr. Mill
treats this subject in the abstract, quite independently of all considerations of race, and yet, as in the case of political liberty, it
obviously has some connection with type. Some races submit far
more slavishly to the tyranny of custom than others. In the lower
types, indeed, individuality, in the nobler sense of that very expres-
sive and much-embracing term, is strictly speaking, unknown. This
is a subject deserving of far more investigation than it has yet
received. There is obviously more individuality in the Teutonic
than the Celtic type. There was, perhaps, more of it in the Roman
than the Greek, and there is decidedly more of it in the European
than the Asiatic. Speaking nationally, there is more of it in
England than in France, and more of it in lowland Scotland than
in England.

In the treatment of this subject we must carefully distinguish
between those moral monstrosities who are only marked by oddity,
by crotchets in thought, and eccentricities in action, from those
truly individualised personalities, really characterised by originality
and by its accompanying independence in thought and conduct.
The latter are doubtless rare in all races, and when carefully studied
are generally found to present *physical* as well as moral attributes
indicative of peculiarly effective development, at least in certain
directions. The head and face of Caesar, were, no doubt, especially

Roman.   He did not depart from his racial type by anything at all abnormal.   Yet he was a unique individuality.   He was so because he was the most strongly pronounced, shall we say it, the most distinctly specialised, mentally and physically, of all his racially vigorous countrymen.

This matter goes down to great depths.   We would not willingly fatigue even the general reader by a set treatise, aiming to be |129| exhaustive; but without a few more remarks and illustrations, it is impossible that our meaning should be fully understood.   Specialisation is the test of development.   From the zoophyte to man the march is steadily in this direction.   In the vegetable kingdom it is the blossom and the fruit that constitute the invididual—never fully born out of the maternal matrix, the plant proper, being strictly speaking, a congeries of imperfectly developed individualities, that never advance beyond the foetal stage.   We have the analogues of this in the corals, the polypi, and the mollusca, and growing fainter, in the spawn of fish.   This, however, is simply the stage of physical aggregation, above and beyond which is that of the moral sphere.   The ant and the bee have no distinct individuality of will and character.   They are the blind and unresisting instrumentalities of a common purpose.   They are the integral parts of a larger whole—the hill or the hive.   Now, among men, the community is the plant, the hive, the moral matrix, whereto all its human blossoms still inhere.

We begin now then to understand how it is that the higher races manifest more individuality than the lower; they are less foetal in their character, both morally and physically.   It has been long observed that the Negroid and Mongolic races are far less distinctly marked physiognomically than the Caucasian.   They keep much closer to the common type; we may add, in mind as well as body.   And among Caucasian peoples, the same remark applies to the Sclavons, who are, it may be observed parenthetically, to Europe, what the Mongols proper are to Asia, the imperfectly-developed children of the North-eastern wilderness.

Again in this inquiry, as in that connected with the aptitude of various races for political liberty, we must carefully distinguish between the uncultured rudeness of the savage, and the true individuality of the vigorously constituted citizen of some free, yet civilised community.   The first is only raw material waiting for the stamp of social despotism.   It is simply wax, wanting nothing but the seal.   Neither must we wholly ignore the influence of institutions, on the spirit of successive ages.   Thus, for example, we quite agree with Mr. Mill that our more immediate present, is less favourable to individuality, at least in the outward life, than some ages which have preceded it.   We are less under the tyranny of power, but we are more under the despotism of fashion, than the men of the eighteenth century.   These oscillations are unavoidable, even in the highest races, whose strongly individualised members constituting but a small minority, are ever liable to suffer by "the pressure from without," on the part of the numerically preponderant mediocrity, by whom they |130| are surrounded.   But this is something very distinct from the inherent tendency to fossilisation manifested by Asiatics, more especially those of the farther Orient.   Yet, from his neglect of all racial considerations, Mr. Mill confounds these two things. . . .   Towards the conclusion of the third chapter of his otherwise admirable work on liberty, where he is speaking of "individuality, as one of the elements of wellbeing," Mr. Mill warns us that "the modern *régime* of public opinion is, in an unorganised form, what the Chinese educational and political systems are in an organised; and unless individuality shall be able successfully to assert itself against this yoke, Europe, notwithstanding its noble antecedents, and its professed Christianity, will tend to become another China."   Here it is very obvious that the acute logician is in blissful ignorance of any ethnic distinctions as attaching to Mongolic China, or Caucasian Europe.   In other words, he proceeds in his argument on the utterly fallacious assumption, that the racial element in the problem is identical in both instances, whereas, the merest tyro in Anthropology could inform him that the diversity is not only great, but greater than it is yet possible to define in all its elements of corporeal structure and mental constitution, and in the far-reaching consequences resulting from them.

But, lest we should labour under any misapprehension in this matter, Mr. Mill thus proceeds in his next paragraph.   "What is it that has preserved Europe from this lot?   What has made the European family of nations an improving, instead of a stationary portion of mankind?   *Not any superior excellence in them*, which, when it exists, exists as the effect, and not as the cause; but *their remarkable diversity of character* and culture.   Individuals, classes, nations, have been extremely unlike one another: they have struck out a great variety of paths, each leading to something valuable."   And farther on, "Europe is, in my judgment, wholly indebted to this plurality of paths, for its progressive and many-sided development."   Oh, Anthropological reader, how shall we proceed to define such science and such *logic* as the foregoing? How speak with due severity, yet with proper respect, of such *self-contradictory* utterances, more especially from the mouth of the master?   Shall we leave the matter, duly emphasised with italics, which, of course, are our own, to speak for itself, or shall we endeavour to make such palpable absurdities still more palpable? For the Anthropologist, most assuredly, nothing more is needed than the quotation, its own all-sufficient answer.   Not, |131| however, to be too severe on Mr. Mill, we may observe that the direct contradiction involved in the italicised divisions of his sentence, arises from the fact, that in accordance with the principles of his school, he regards character as being *wholly* the product of circumstances, and not of circumstances acting on organisation.   We must remember that he does not believe in ethnic areas, nor in zones of population.   That the earth, in virtue of its telluric, climatic, and other influences, can and does produce different kinds of plants and animals, he would readily admit.   But his political idola utterly forbid his applying the same principles to, or seeing correspondent facts in man.   If a Chinaman differs from an Englishman, this, according to his philosophy, is altogether due to an accident of education, and not in any measure to inherent proclivities, dependant upon hereditarily transmitted specialities of structure and function, these very specialities being in large part due to racial type, itself the distinctive product of a given Ethnic area.   In short, Mr. Mill does not believe in race; and hence the grave errors of his otherwise-admirable works.

And yet there are sentiments, even in some of his earlier writings, which might well have guarded him from these mistakes of his later years.   Here, for instance, is an extract from his article on Bentham, in *the London and Westminster Review* for August, 1838, and reprinted in his Dissertations.   "For the philosphy of matter, the materials are the properties of matter; for moral and political philosophy, *the properties of man, and of man's position in the*

world."   And farther on in the same paragraph, "If in his survey
of human nature and life he has left any element out, then,
wheresoever that element exerts any influence, his conclusions will
fail, more or less, in their application."   Precisely so.   Mr. Mill
in his otherwise masterly "surveys of human nature and life," has
left out the very important element of race, and as a necessary
result, "wheresoever that element exerts any influence, his conclusions fail in their application," that is, however, truthful to his own
race, the Teutonised Celts of Britain, they are, more or less, inappl-
icable to all other races, more especially those separated from us by
such broad lines of demarcation as the Negroid and Mongolic
populations of Central Africa and Eastern Asia.   Of course, Mr.
Mill and his friends will reply, that in the passage in question, and
in others of similar import, which might be readily found scattered
through his writings, he was not speaking of man in his *physical*
relationships at all.   And we readily grant this.   It is not a part
of his philosophic vocation to contemplate man under a material,
or, to speak somewhat more definitively, a corporeal aspect.   It
rather suits his purpose, or shall we say, it better comports with
|132| his frame of mind to speak in "vague generalities" about
"human nature" and other "abstractions," which "he has not
translated into realities," or subjected to "an exhaustive method of
classification," to use some of the pet phrases of the great master
of codification, whose life and labours constitute the subject-matter
of the article from which we have just been quoting.

    Mr. Mill very justly accords great praise to Bentham for never
"reasoning about abstractions till they have been translated into
realities."   Will he pardon us for hinting to him that the abstractions, "man," and "human nature," need such a translation?   When
we, as Anthropologists, hear of man, we want to know what kind
of man.   That he is of the GENUS *homo* is not enough for us, we
want to know his *species*, and, if possible, the very variety to which
he belongs.   And any naturalist will inform Mr. Mill that he
requires precisely the same kind of information about an animal,
before he can pronounce in any detail upon its qualities and
attributes, upon its structure and its habits.   We can, however,
quite understand, that all these things are infinitely beneath the
notice of Mr. Mill and his school, who, from the lofty empyrean of
their closet philosophy, can afford to look down with unutterable

pity upon people who concern themselves about such trifles as the development of the Negro brain, and the possible correlationship of mind to so insignificant an organ!   What, forsooth, has the proportion of the viscera in different races, to do with "Political Economy," saving and except that some stomachs are more prone to a carnivorous diet than others, and so, perhaps, cost rather more for their sustenance to the body politic?   And what have strong or weak impulses, dominant passions, or predominant principles to do with law making, more especially that which is done in the closet?   Having your chart of "human nature," can't you codify at your ease, for all times and countries, all climes and races?   What is to hinder you?   Nothing, my esteemed friend and most profound philosopher, absolutely nothing, we reply, except that most inconvenient of all possible obstructions, FACT; the world-old and world-wide fact of racial diversity, which has hitherto bid defiance to prophets and priests, to princes and legislators, in their benevolent endeavours to convert all mankind to one religion, and subject them to the beneficent restraint of one form of law and government.

The perversity of Mr. Mill in rejecting anthropology as an instrument for investigating the diversities of national character is something marvellous, as an instance of what may almost be called judicial blindness of intellect.   Listen to his oracular utterances in the same article from which we have just been quoting: "That which alone causes any material interests to exist, which alone enables any body of human |133| beings to exist as a society, is national character."   And in the next page, "A philosophy of laws and institutions, not founded on a philosophy of national character, is an absurdity."   Amen, and again amen, say we, from the anthropological standpoint.   Why this is the very pith and marrow of the whole matter.   It is what we have been preaching from the very first.   It is the burthen of our discourse.   It is the very truth which we wish to impress upon statesmen and legislators, and we may add upon political economists, if it be right to name them apart from the foregoing.   Oh, Mr. Mill, how nearly transparent is the veil, which nevertheless hides us from each other!   It is very obvious that the great logician sees everything, but the fact in nature of organic speciality.   To that, from his bookish education, he is blind, perhaps hopelessly so now.   Shall we then blame him?   Certainly not, but with all his greatness, we must yet, from

the very depths of our soul, pity him.   To be so near the truth, and
yet from a prejudgment to miss it!   To be forced to accept a
conclusion, and yet from inveterate prejudice, to ignore the very
data on which it is based!   What will a more enlightened posterity
say to the melancholy humiliation of so sad a position!

But, to use the words of Mr. Mill when speaking of Bentham,
"it is an ungracious task to call a great benefactor of mankind to
account for not being a greater."   Mr. Mill is so enlightened and
so liberal, with such a breadth of culture and such a true catholicity
of sentiment on almost every other subject, that we are almost
ashamed to take him thus severely to account for his deficiencies
and prejudices on the subject of race.   But as anthropologists we
cannot but regard it as very important, and indeed we may say
without exaggeration, all important, in reference to the very topics
treated of, in all other respects, so ably by the great master of logic
and political economics, and while we have not the smallest hope
of converting him from the error of his ways, we would fain preserve
some of his pupils and followers from falling into similar mistakes.
We are not lacking in respect for Mr. Mill, nor we trust, wanting
in the power to appreciate his great and commanding abilities, and
the truly noble purposes to which, with life-long assiduity, he has
applied them.   But we cannot blind ourselves to his egregious
fallacies, not can we persuade ourselves that these fallacies, bearing
as they do directly on practical questions, are wholly innocuous.
They have led him, and they have led inferior men, to make demands
for the ruder races, such as science, the science of man, cannot
sanction,—demands founded on ignorance of the great facts of race,
and in opposition to the laws of nature.   Demands all the more
dangerous, because coinciding with that pseudo-philanthrophy of
our age, which starting from groundless assumptions, enthroned as
first |134| principles, proceeds to their stupendous conclusions, in
defiance alike of the revelations of science and the teachings of
experience.   A philanthropy that aims at uniformity where there
is diversity; and which, disregarding alike anthropology and history,
endeavours to set up the creed and code of Caucasian Christendom
as the sole standard to which humanity in all its varieties must
hasten to conform.   A philanthropy based on the absurdity of a
dogma, and which, therefore, can only end in the mortification of
defeat, while productive of incalculable mischief in the process of

experimentally demonstrating the fallacy of its principles and the groundlessness of its expectations.

We have, in the earlier part of the present article, spoken rather severely of the school to which Mr. Mill belongs.   Let it not, however, be for one moment supposed that we would apply these remarks, in all their severity, to him individually, even in his speciality as a writer on legislation and political economy.   He has too much good sense, and we may add, too much good feeling, to allow the errors of his school to wholly dominate his better nature. He is in the noblest sense the master of this school, for he is conducting it *through* many of its old errors into higher truths. He sees as clearly as any anthropologist the utter absurdity of attempting to impose European institutions on Asiatic slaves or African savages—in their own country.   But because he persistently regards their disqualification for the immediate possession of polit- ical liberty, with its equal rights and representative government, as simply a matter of defective education, he does not hesitate to claim the franchise for the recently liberated Negro of the Southern States of America.   To him in this connection, the term Negro simply implies a person who has, till within the last few months, unfor- tunately held an inferior *social* position.   But it does not imply, as it does to the anthropologist, a being of inferior *organic* consti- tution, in whom corporeal function and animal impulse too readily dominate moral sentiment and intellectual aptitude, a being who is not merely a barbarian in his *habits*, but a savage in his *hereditary* proclivities.   To this phase of the question, Mr. Mill is both blind and deaf.   He will not or he cannot *see* the facts of racial diversity for himself, and he refuses to listen to the statements and conclusions of those who have made this subject the study of a life.   To their scientific investigations and the results so far obtained by most carefully conducted observation, results steadily cumulative, he responds, on the old *à priori* method, that is from the seemingly impregnable stronghold of a preconception, in the very foolish words which we have prefixed to this paper.   Now these words may perhaps be quite worthy of the school which Mr. Mill so ably represents, and we can conceive of his followers and admirers applauding them to the echo, but they |135| are not worthy of him.   The ablest logician of the nineteenth century should not be so childishly facile in the assumption of his premises.   Reasoning, to be of any value, demands something more than unassailable *concatenation*. It must have a tenable *basis*. It must have unassailable data. Now the data in reference to race are the concrete *facts* of race, not *abstract* political principles; they are facts obtained by the process of induction, not first principles evolved by a process of thought. Mr. Mill, in short, has overstepped his province. He has intruded into the domain of science, and hence the unpleasant necessity laid upon us, of warning him off, we trust with respectful civility, but we also hope in words "of no uncertain sound".

SIX

FREDERIC WILLIAM FARRAR (1831–1903)

Aptitudes of Races

Transactions of the Ethnological Society
Volume 5, 1867, pp. 115–26

Farrar was a clergyman whose appointments included the Head-mastership of Marlborough (1871–6) and the Deanery of Canter-bury (1895–1903). In 1866 Darwin, an admirer of his Essay on the Origin of Language *(1860), successfully nominated him for Fellowship of the Royal Society. Though most of his writing was on theological subjects, Farrar is remembered best for such pain-fully sentimental school novels as* Eric, or Little by Little *(1858), which proclaim the virtues of 'muscular Christianity' and reflect the influence of Thomas Arnold. Like the latter, Farrar had strong views on the importance of race in social explanation. In 1874 some 550 of his Marlborough boys underwent anthropological measurement because of their Headmaster's desire to assist Galton's efforts to collect such data. In this paper, read to the Ethnologists on 27 March 1866 when he was still Classical Master at Harrow, Farrar presents his recommendations about racial classification on a basis of three broad categories. He discusses first 'the irreclaimably savage' who comprise, in the main, black stocks; then, 'the semi-civilized' brown and yellow peoples whose limited capabilities are exemplified best in the 'utilitarian mediocrity' of Chinamen; finally, the Semitic and Aryan breeds who share between them the credit for all the great achievements of human civilization. Farrar's clerical status adds particular poignancy to the piece. For he not only embraces an unashamedly polygenetic approach but also suggests how the very inferiority of non-white races makes the application to them of Christian*

141

charity more rather than less necessary. The latter point would have appealed much more readily to most members of the Ethnological Society than the former.

The great Linnaeus, in his *Systema Naturae*, discriminates, with his usual acuteness, the intellectual and moral characteristics of four great human families. The Homo Americanus he describes as obstinate, contented, free; the Homo Europaeus as fickle, keen, inventive; the Homo Asiaticus as grave, dignified, avaricious; the Homo Afer as cunning, lazy, careless. The American, he said, was governed by habit; the European by institutions (?); the Asiatic by opinions; the African by caprice. Undoubtedly some of these remarks show an insight into national character not unworthy of a mind as keen in its intuitions as it was laborious and patient in research; but the part of it which seems most liable to exception is the sweeping geographic generalisation involved in the term Homo Asiaticus. It is true that America from north to south appears to be inhabited mainly by one race of aborigines, who, with but single exception, speak a variety of languages all characterised by a cumbrous and peculiar polysynthetic structure. It is also true that the whole of Europe, with the comparatively insignificant exception of Finns, Lapps, Turks, and probably a few scattered remnants of other races, is occupied by the descendants of one great family of mankind. But it is certain that in Africa we find several deeply, and, to all appearance, primordially distinct varieties of man; and it is certain that we find in Asia the representatives of human species, who are now, and have been for immemorial years, as distinct from each other as every physical, intellectual, and moral difference can possibly make them.

A modern writer has expressed a wish that a map should be constructed sufficiently pictorial to pourtray at a glance the many-coloured interchanges of the earth's surface, and to give "such a view as the stork and the swallow might see far off as they lean upon the Sirocco wind." Such a map, representing the pale circles of Arctic and Antarctic snow, the green sunlit expanse of the temperature region, and the gorgeous colourings of fauna and flora in the torrid zone, would indeed be beautiful. Yet how valueless it would be in comparison with one so drawn up as to represent the habits and peculiarities of the human tribes who inhabit these widely-sundered regions; which should enable us to catch a glimpse of the stunted Esquimaux cowering in his igloo |116| of snow,—of which he seems to have borrowed the conception from the seals on which he feeds,—or tossed on the spray in his coracle of skin; of the hideous Bosjesman chasing the ostrich on foot over the burning desert, or, like the ostrich, scraping his miserable lair out of the sands of the parched karoo; of the quivered Indian hunting the buffalo over his immeasurable pampas, and requiring many square miles for the sustenance of every individual of his race; of the squalid Fuegian, "a poor wretch, stunted in growth, his hideous face bedaubed with white paint, his body filthy and greasy; his hair tangled, his voice discordant, his gestures violent;" of the depraved, mud-daubed, lark-heeled inhabitant of the greater Andaman; of the placid, sensual, conservative Chinese; and side by side with these, of the handsome, highly-civilised, richly-endowed, divinely-ennobled races, who, emerging from their mountain cradle in Asia, have occupied, as the natural lords and masters, the fairest portions in every quarter of the globe.

Yet we believe that these and all other races may be reduced to *Three* great classes or divisions; and it is to establish, or rather, I should say, to recall the antique and deep-lying distinctions between these three classes that the present paper is written.   I do not for a moment say how the members of these classes may be supposed to be mutually related; I do not for a moment wish to infer that each great class sprang from an original pair; indeed it must be admitted that Ethnology has not yet obtained sufficient evidence to give a final decision on any such questions.   All that I want to establish is that they seem to belong to three distinct and different *strata or stages of humanity*; and that they appeared (to use the vaguest possible word which can conceal our necessary ignorance as to the beginning of every creative act) that they appeared at different chronological epochs upon the surface of the earth.   Those three classes are the Savage races, the Semi-civilised races; and finally the two Civilised races.   The facts on which I shall dwell, tend to show that these races have always been as distinct as they now are, and that it is impossible for their limits to be confused either by degeneracy on the one hand, or progress on the other. Of course if an unlimited series of years be postulated, the difficulties are lessened, though they are even then by no means removed.   But at any rate *the only scientific choice* appears to be between the doctrine of development on the one hand, or a polygenism on the other, which admits the existence not of Cuvier's three races, or Blumenbach's five, or St. Vincent's fifteen, but of a much larger number of primitive species falling under three well-marked groups.

First, then, by the Savage races, I mean those that are *irreclaimably* savage; and I hope that, from what I say of them |117| the word "irreclaimably" will not be found to involve any *petitio principii*. I do not apply it to *all* savages; but I think it must be admitted as being applicable to by far the largest number of savage races who have hitherto had the chance of rising from their abject condition.

With the exception of Madeira, the Azores, and a few other islands, there is hardly a single country which, when first discovered, was found destitute of inhabitants; and it is a very remarkable fact that every race, including even some of the semi-barbarous, tell us, in their far-reaching traditions, of other races who preceded them, and whom they found inhabiting the countries to which they came. The Greeks and the Romans never attempted to conceal that their lands were won by victorious immigration. The Egyptians spoke of the gigantic and shadowy races, the Νέκυεσ, or dead ones, as they called them, who preceded that line of demigods which reigned before the first Pharaoh. The Arabians regarded themselves as successors of the genii. The Canaanites, as we know from Scripture, ousted and almost exterminated the Nephilim, Rephaim, Anakim, and other antediluvian races. The Aryans confessedly won Hindostan by expelling from it those previous tribes whom they contemptuously represent as monkeys, demons, or savages, with whom however they probably intermarried, and of whom traces are still to be found. According to Fa Hian, the Chinese traveller, the first people in Ceylon were demons and dragons, who are probably intended for the original Yakkahs. The North American Indians do not claim to have made the vast mound-temples and tumuli which occur on many of their plains and river valleys, but attribute them to an antecedent race. The natives of New Zealand say that, on arriving, they found there an inferior people, whom they hunted down like wild beasts. Britain was once occupied by cannibal savages who were ousted by the Kelt, and who appear in various early traditions as ghosts or giants. Even the all-but-immemorial Chinese, the least likely of all nations to make any such admission, freely acknowledge that they were not the first possessors of the vast plains which they have held from unknown centuries, but that when their mysterious king Fo-hi appeared, circled with a rainbow, from the north-west, they drove out an aboriginal race who still survive in Formosa, in Hainan, and in the mountainous regions, under the significant name of Miautszee, or children of the soil.   Who, then, were these races, who appear in the traditions of all but the most barbarous nations? I believe the answer to be that they were the squalid, primeval allophylian races, whose ghastly relics, consisting of half-gnawed bones and coarse implements of flint, have been found so abundantly of late years in fluviatile deposits, and stalactite flooring of deep caves, but |118| respecting whose origin nothing is known, except that they lived on the earth with the mammoth and the elk, the cave-hyaena and the cave-bear, for long ages before the first civilised races had appeared upon the globe.

If it be asked whether any *representatives* of such tribes still survive, we may point to many.   Such are the tallow-coloured Bosjesmen who, when not living on worms and pismires, are glad to squabble for the putrid carcase of the hyaena and the antelope; the leather-skinned Hottentot, whose hair grows in short tufts like a worn out shoe-brush, with spaces of scalp between; the degraded, gibbering Yamparico, whose food consists of vermin; the aborigines of Victoria, among whom new-born babes are, when convenient, killed and eaten by their parents and brothers; the Alforese of Ceram, who live in families in the trees; the Banaks, who wear lumps of fat meat ornamentally in the cartilage of the nose; the forest tribes of Malacca; the wild people of Borneo, whom the Dayaks hunt as though they were monkeys; the hairy Ainos of Yesso, who annually pay their tribute of fish and skin to the Japanese; the pigmy Dokos, south of Abyssynia, whose nails are grown long, like vultures' talons, that they may dig up ants, and tear the skins of serpents, which they devour raw; the Veddahs of Ceylon, who have gutturals and grimaces instead of languages, who have no God, no notions of time or distance, no name for hours, days, and years, and who cannot count beyond five upon their fingers.   Many tribes like these, in the lowest mud of barbarism, so far from having traditions or traces of preceding tribes, attribute their origin directly to lions (like the Sahos), to goats (like the Dagalis), or with contented unanimity to the ape, on whose deformed resemblance to themselves they look without any particle of horror and repugnance, as on a type to which they are assimilated by their own abject degradation, fierce squalor, and protuberant jaws.

A picture of some such race of primeval troglodytes may be found in a very ancient document, the 30th chapter of the Book of Job. Famine, darkness, solitude—a life in the desolate wilderness—a squalid subsistence upon roots and mallows, expulsion as criminals and outcasts from human society and human sympathy, idiotic and semi-bestial noises as they crouched among bushes and under the nettles,—these are the lineaments of that repulsive portraiture. And how does Job speak of them? as "children of nothing;" as "viler than the earth"; as wretches "whose father he would have disdained to set with the dogs of his flock." The description reads like that of a Bosjesman or an Australian, and it is hard to believe that the writer of Job, or the Jews generally, could have regarded people, of whom they could thus speak, as members with themselves of the same original stock. Indeed it |119| would be easy to adduce direct proofs that, in spite of the apparent teaching of Genesis, they did not so regard them. Yet the picture is not half so revolting as that photograph of modern savages, with which several modern travellers have presented us. Take Sir George Grey's picture of an Australian,—"altogether a disgusting spectacle, stepping out of the carcase of a putrid whale, ill-tempered, violent, rubbed from head to feet with stinking oil, gorged to repletion with putrid meat, and suffering from cutaneous disorders, brought on by high feeding." Or take Dr. Mouatt's picture of dead Andamaners. "Their expression as it had been settled by the hand of death was truly repulsive and frightful. Their features distorted by the most violent passions were too horrible for anything of human mould, and I could regard them only as the types of the most ferocious and relentless fiends. Their aspect was really that of demons. I doubt whether Fuseli in depicting the worst and most violent passions of humanity ever imagined anything so horrible as the visages upon which we now looked." Gross ignorance, total nudity, and promiscuous intercourse, will give a notion of their moral condition; and to complete the picture of other savages would demand the introduction of features darker and deadlier still. To read one such description of savage life is to read all; in short, the savage is not a stately, free, noble creature, presenting the happy spectacle of unsophisticated innocence and primeval liberty, but too generally a wretch, depraved, hideous, and sanguinary; his body equally disgustful to the eye and to the nose, and his grotesque existence divided between "a mistrust of life, and a still greater mistrust of death, which he dreads like fire." They are, says Mr. Darwin, who, unlike the whole company of those who have romanced about them, has had the opportunity of personally inspecting them, "they are men whose very signs and expressions are less intelligible to us than those of the domesticated animals; men who do not possess the instinct of those animals, but yet appear to boast of human reason, or at least of acts consequent on that reason. *I do not believe it possible to describe or paint the difference between savage and civilised man.* It is the difference between a wild and tame animal."

If it be asked what is the history of these races, the answer is extremely simple. They have no history. They have not originated a single discovery; they have not promulgated a single thought; they have not established a single institution; they have not hit upon a single invention. Of the seven or eight civilisations which the world has seen, not one, if we except the Egyptian,—which has been grossly exaggerated, which was probably due, such as it was, to Semitic and Aryan influences, and which was deeply marked by the Negritian stains of cruelty and |120| Fetichism,—not one has been achieved by a black race. The features of these tribes are invariable and expressionless, and their minds characterised by a dead and blank uniformity. Among them generation hands on no torch to generation, but each century sees them in the same condition as the last, learning nothing, inventing nothing, improving nothing, living on in the same squalid misery and brutal ignorance; neither wiser nor better than their forefathers of immemorial epochs back, mechanically carrying on only a few rude mechanical operations as the bee continues to build her waxen hexagon, and the spider to spin his concentric web; but in all other respects as little progressive, and apparently as little perfectible, as the dogs which they domesticate, or the monkeys which chatter in their woods. They are without a past and without a future, doomed, as races infinitely nobler have been before them, to a rapid, an entire, and, perhaps for the highest destinies of mankind, an inevitable extinction. They have not added one iota to the knowledge, the arts, the sciences, the manufactures, the morals of the world, nor out of all their teeming myriads have they produced one single man whose name is of the

slightest importance in the history of our race.   Were they all to be
merged to-morrow in some great deluge, they would leave behind them
no other trace of their existence than their actual organic remains.

And I call them *irreclaimable* savages for two reasons: *the one*
is, that I find this to be the practical verdict of all who have been
thrown most closely into contact with them; *the other*, that, so far
from being influenced by civilisation, they disappear from before
the face of it as surely and as perceptibly as the snow retreats before
the advancing line of sunbeams.

If no attempt had ever been made to reclaim them, no one could
call them irreclaimable.   There is indeed a very favourite method
of disproving this.   A few isolated instances are adduced of individual savages trained up to a certain point by civilised races.
"I shall not wait," says De Gobineau, "for the partisans of the
equality of races to come and show me such and such a passage
from such and such a missionary or traveller, from which it appears
that a Yolof showed himself a vigorous carpenter, that a Hottentot
became a good servant, that a Kaffir dances and plays the violin,
or that a Bambarra is acquainted with arithmetic."   Even, however,
if we take such individual cases, the single savages who have been,
after complete isolation from their fellows, with all appliances and
aids to boot, in any way reclaimed or instructed, offer very few and
not very hopeful instances.   Jemmy Button, Admiral Fitzroy's
Fuegian, who was petted in England even by royalty, "as a passably
finished man," was found twenty years after by Captain Parker
Snow, "rude, shaggy, half-repulsive," in |121| every respect like his
fellow-savages, to whom literally the *only* civilisation which he had
communicated was a knowledge of some of our most degraded
English words.   Miago, the Australian, who was so kindly trained
by the officers of the *Beagle*, soon after voluntarily returned as a
savage to the bush, and was soon seen almost naked, painted all
over, after having been concerned in several murders.   Benilong,
another Australian, after living for some time in London, resumed
with full choice the savage life.   A Hottentot boy, long and carefully
instructed by Governor Van der Stel, after years of kindness and
education, stripped off his European dress before the Governor,
clothed himself in sheepskins, and emphatically renounced both
civilisation and Christianity.   Hundreds of such instances might
be quoted, and every one will recollect how hopelessly this incapacity

for improvement frustrated in Australia the generous and benevolent efforts of Mr. Threlkeld and of Governor Maquairie.

In fact the real, wild, pagan, savage not only has a *horror* for civilisation, but deliberately *despises* it. An old Indian chief spoke to Dr. Daniel Wilson, "with the unimpressible indifference of the true Indian, of the civilisation of the European intruders as a thing good enough for the white man, but in which neither he nor his people had any interest." Neither as individuals nor as races have they ever adopted it. Barely 300 years ago the Red race were the sole and undisputed lords of the rivers, the prairies, and the forests of America. Now, as a people, they barely exist, and in the late terrible civil war though they saw the encroaching strangers decimating each other by sea and land, and one half of them standing in terror of a third, or black race, introduced still more recently than themselves, they looked on with a strange and terrible apathy, which does not even borrow energy from despair. They deliberately refuse every opportunity of improvement, from which their conscience, their whole nature, their very blood revolts, and as though they were the indisputable "proletarians of humanity", they accept with a mysterious horror and depression of mind, their inevitable lot. Their very spirits are broken, and they watch with frigid indifference the approaching extinction of their type and race.

Or, again, let us take one specimen of the 100,000,000 of Africa, and that not the most degraded types, Hottentots, or Bosjesmen, or even Amakoso Kaffirs, but a much higher race, the pure-blooded negro. With keen senses, and singularly powerful physique, yet, mainly owing to his salient animality, and the crimes of cruelty laziness, and superstition which, if we may accept the accounts of hosts of successive travellers, mark his native condition, he is not untameable like the Indian, but so mentally apathetic as to bow his shoulder to the yoke of race after race of Asiatics and Euro-|122| peans. Ever since civilisation has existed, he has been conterminous to, and even in contact with it from an unknown period. Yet this natural imitativeness has given him no proficiency even in the mechanical arts. He did not learn architecture, writing, or organisation from the Egyptians; the brilliant Phoenician could not teach him so simple a lesson as the taming of his native elephant; neither Dutch, nor French, nor Spaniards, nor Americans, nor Anglo-Saxons have weaned him, on his native continent from his cannibalism, his rain-doctors, his medicine-men, his mumbo-jumbo, his gris-gris and ju-jus. St. Domingo, "the only episode" in the history of all the dark races put together, only proves their incapability as a race under the most favourable circumstances, of maintaining, without constant and rapid retrogression even a poor imitation of civilised life. The grand qualities which secure the continuous advance of mankind, the generalising power of pure reason, the love of perfectibility, the desire to know the unknown, and, last and greatest, the ability to observe new phenomena and new relations,—these mental faculties seem to be deficient in all the dark races. But, if so, how are they to be civilised? What hope is there for their progress? As they were probably the earliest to appear on the earth's surface, "covering the soil since an epoch which must be determined by Geology rather than by history," so will the vast majority of them in all probability be the first to disappear by a decay, from which not even the sweet influences of Christianity, at least as *we* have taught it, have hitherto been able to rescue more than a small and insignificant number.

For many of them *have* disappeared already. The Tasmanian has perished; the Australian is dying out; the Carib has disappeared from the West Indies; the Maori race is diminishing; the Esquimaux is decreasing in numbers; the North American Indian dwindling away by a process of extinction which has already obliterated innumerable tribes. Savage and civilised life *cannot* co-exist side by side, and even when savages adopt the externalities of civilisation, they seem to wither away with a kind of weary nostalgia, a pining sickness, a deeply-seated despair, and an inevitable decay. They learn with terrible and fatal facility the worst vices of civilisation, without acquiring one of its nobler lessons. To our disgrace it must be admitted, that the steps of the Caucasian man over the earth's surface have too often been dipped in tears and blood; and that his worst vices have spread like a leprosy among these rude and ignorant children of nature. But if he has imparted to them his diseases, his fire-water, and his implements of war, he has at least put down cannibalism, suttee, infanticide, and human sacrifices with the strong arm of power, nor has his conduct been solely an *exemplar vitiis imitabile*. The savage *might* have learnt many great and glorious lessons; |123| he *has* learnt only what is vicious and degrading. Hence it is that these races—the lowest types of humanity, and presenting its most hideous features of moral and intellectual degradation—are doomed to perish;—not, let us hope, by the criminality of superior races, *to whom the very weakness and inferiority of these races ought to constitute their most powerful claim to protection, justice, and pity*, but because darkness, sloth, and brutal ignorance cannot co-exist with the advance of knowledge, industry, and light.   "It is written in the Book of Destiny," says a recent traveller, "that man must either advance or perish."

These low and perishing races then, the congeners, if not the representatives, of those early sporadic allophylians, whose deformed skulls and cannibal relics are turned up here and there, appear to me, on these, and on other grounds, some of which I have already laid before the Society, to have no genetic connection with the other races to which I shall now allude, but as they were the first to appear in the annals of humanity they seem likely to be the earliest to vanish, and in many regions at any rate to leave no traces of their ignoble type.   A great philosopher has called this "a desolating belief."   I do not see why it should be more desolating that the certain fact that even in the same family man is divided from man by immeasurable and ineffaceable distinctions; but whether desolating or not, is it not the conclusion to which we are led by a vast mass of unmistakeable evidence?   If so, is it a sound reverence "to model Providence after our fashion"?

And, now, if we mount to a second stage or stratum of humanity, we *again* find that difference of aptitude, which appears to prove a radical, permanent, and an original difference of race.   Let us take the most advanced and eminent family of the Mongolian race—the Chinese.   They will furnish the best possible example of that *arrested development*, that "mummified intelligence," as Bunsen happily calls it, that stopping short at a certain stage, which seems to characterise the earliest civilisations, no less certainly than absolute *immobility* has ever characterised the Black and Red types of mankind.

China represents a spectacle all the more astounding from the fact that it survives as the sole representative of those primitive materialistic utilitarian civilisations which mark in human history the time when races, hitherto unknown and in all respect superior to the dark races, began to appear.   Every product of these civilisations seems to be ingenious but imperfect, to betray, as I said before, an *arrested development.* They invented writing, but it stopped at ideography and hieroglyphics; their art had no perspective and no ideality; their science no progressiveness; their religion no enthusiasm; their literature no warmth; their |124| administration no vigour. Everything in them is marked with the plague-spot of utilitarian mediocrity; they reduce everything to the dead level of vulgar practical advantage, and hence the inventions, which they possessed centuries before the Europeans, stop short at the lowest point. Their compass is but a plaything; their ships painted tubs; their sculpture only grotesque; their architecture a repetition of children's toys; their painting found its consummation in a "grimacing activity;" their gunpowder mere pyrotechny; their printing only by wooden blocks; their very language a petrified fragment of primeval periods—flexionless, monosyllabic, and infinitely awkward. The unmarked features, the serene, blandly-smiling face, the tendency to physical obesity and mental apathy, the feeble, tranquil, childish, gluttonous sensuality, mark the race. And when a handful of barbarian French and English made these 300,000,000 repeal some of their immemorial laws, what spectacle did this fossil nation display? "They mistook," says Dr. Knox, "the big drum of the 18th Irish Foot for an unknown and dangerous machine, and kept firing at it during the greater part of the action, so that they killed nobody." They lighted a fire inside an iron tube to frighten us with the smoke, and put on huge and hideous masks that we might mistake them for monsters; and finally, with almost asinine ignorance, they put great lights beside their guns to see to fire by at night, thus gratuitously making an excellent mark for our gunners without benefiting themselves in the slightest degree. The age of Pericles alone, short as it was, with its eternal ideals of art and science, was worth a hundred centuries of that frightful torpor, that slumber of death, that immemorial congealment which characterises the so-called wisdom of the Chinese, and proves that—

"Better twenty [*sic*] years of Europe, than a cycle of Cathay."

How vast the contrast presented by the two races whose history begins latest, and who belong to the highest stratum, the Tertiary deposits of humanity, the Semitic and Aryan stocks. To the Semite belong pre-eminently a pure religion, iconoclasm, monotheism, and

probably writing.   It is but a few days' journey among a Semitic
population from Mecca to Sinai, and from Sinai to Jerusalem—the
three mother-haunts of Christianity, Judaism and Islam, the three
greatest and noblest religions of mankind.   On the other hand to
the Aryan belong science, philosophy, and art; to his race belong
the Greeks, the Romans, the English, the French, |125| the Germans,
the Italians, the Spaniards; to his race Homer, Aristotle, Cicero,
Charlemagne, Da Vinci, Columbus, Shakespeare, Newton, Göthe,
Kant.   To him and to the Semite belong every single discovery
that has adorned, every single thought that has ennobled, every
single influence that has elevated and purified our race.   To them
we owe writing, coinage, commerce, navigation.   To them belong
the steam-engine, the printing-press, the ship, the light-house, the
electric telegraph.   To them belong all that is ideal and exquisite
in painting, poetry, and sculpture.   To them are due discovery and
colonisation.   Vast islands and continents, like New Zealand and
America, where before their arrival for untold ages, unalterable and
degraded savages, black and red, had been miserably living on the
pupae of the wood-ant, or on each other, they have in a few years
transformed into richly cultivated, prosperous, and densely inhabited
countries, the seats of new civilisation and the homes of gigantic
empire.   Can one single step, can one single discovery be named in
the mental and religious progress of mankind which was not due to
them?   Has there ever been one single tribe of their brotherhood
which was marked by the stolid unprogressiveness of the Mongol,
or which for thousands of years have ever been known to have
existed in that abysmal degradation which seems to have been the
normal condition of many races, Black and Red?

Here, then, we have *marked*, and so far as any evidence can show,
primordial differences of aptitude in salient representatives of the
great stages of mankind.   We believe that the *lowest* of them are
the *eldest* brothers of our race, and that they, or savages like them,
have existed for 30,000 years on the surface of the earth.   But
they are vanishing fast, and signs are not wanting to show that
even the Brown and Yellow races, so far above them, may in turn
give way.   To the Aryan, *i.e.*, to the youngest and latest race which
has appeared in human history, apparently belong the destinies of
the future.   The races whose institutions and inventions are despotism, fetichism, and cannibalism,—the races who rest content in

administrative formalism, placid sensuality, and unprogressive decrepitude, can hardly hope to contend permanently in the great struggle for existence with that noblest division of the human species whose intelligent energy and indomitable perseverance have won for it, from Peru to China, from Spitzbergen to the Falkland Isles, so wide an empire and so unapproachable a rank.

Perhaps it will be asked in conclusion, do you then disbelieve in the future of mankind? do you not believe in "a common humanity transcending all divisions of tribe and race?"   Both questions admit of a brief answer.   I *do* believe in the future of humanity; but all testimony leads me to the certainty that it will |126| not be achieved, or even in any way promoted, by Yamparicos or Fuegians.   And I *do* believe in a common humanity, although I do not believe that all races are equally gifted, or all descended from a common pair. Here, as in other cases, the endowments of men are unequal; but *for that very reason we must rear a strong barrier of Religion and Right against the encroachments of the stronger upon their less privileged brethren.*   Driven by the evidence of centuries to doubt the perfectibility of the negro, I yet abhor slavery from my heart. Believing that all men are children of a common Father, and partakers of a common Redemption, I do not require the notion of a physical or genetic unity as a motive to philanthropy.   Though but a single race should ultimately be proved to have descended from that great Protoplast of Eden, such a conviction will not shake the sense of universal charity in any mind which has only thereby been deepened in the belief that there is a *far higher unity* in the fact that for every child of humanity there is "one God and Father of us all."

SEVEN

THOMAS HUXLEY (1825–95)

The Forefathers and Forerunners of the English People

Pall Mall Gazette
10 January 1870, pp. 8–9

Huxley is rightly renowned as 'Darwin's bulldog'. None did more than he to promote amongst the public at large an acceptance of his friend's evolutionary theory. The election of Huxley to preside over the 1870 gathering of the British Association for the Advancement of Science was a significant landmark in Darwinism's progress towards general respectability. This Liverpool meeting was also vital in the process of rapprochement between the Ethnological and Anthropological Societies. In 1863 Huxley had declined a diploma from the latter, describing the organization as 'that nest of imposters'; and when in 1868 he became President of the Ethnological Society the Anthropologists' journal mocked the rival concern for having become 'little more than a sort of Darwinian club'. Relations between the two societies were easing when on 9 January 1870 Huxley delivered the following lecture in a popular series arranged by the National Sunday League. It was published next day in the Pall Mall Gazette *and reprinted some months later, together with critical correspondence, in Volume 8 of the* Anthropological Review, *pp. 197–216.*

Here Huxley does not deny in principle the great importance of race; he accepts, for instance, that 'physical, mental, and moral peculiarities go with blood'. On the other hand, he is aiming to combat ideas (like those of Jackson and Hunt) which favour 'the determination of political by natural relationships'. His overriding contention is that in Europe stocks are now mixed to a degree where policies based on racial differentiation are simply unwork-

157

able. This thesis is expounded with reference to the British mainland, and to Ireland where the rhetoric of struggle between Celt and Anglo-Saxon, or Teuton, has flourished most notably. Regarding both territories, Huxley's stress is on the similarity and mixture between the Celtic and Teutonic portions of the great Aryan family. He regards racial explanation as no more helpful in Irish politics than in those of the English West Country. Huxley concedes that in the distant past the Celts and Teutons probably did have to confront an Iberian race foreign to them. But he can find no evidence to indicate that this darker stock was any less well endowed with an aptitude for civilization. In any case, Huxley deems it now impossible to distinguish Aryan from Iberian elements, and suggests that anyone who continues to claim insight into some appropriate political discrimination between them 'makes a statement . . . as baseless in natural science as it is mischievous in politics'.

Of late years ethnology, the science which is concerned with the natural history of man, has had a good deal to do with practical politics.   A vague though powerful sentiment has become developed in favour of the determination of political by natural relation-ships.   There seems to be a tacit assumption that men ought to associate themselves according to their natural kinships; and that all barriers, natural or artificial, should be broken down which either separate men of one blood from coalescing into a political entity or, on the other hand, bind together into one nation those who are of different blood.

Panslavism, the aspirations after German unity and Italian unity, the talk about the Latin as contradistinguished from the Germanic or Slavonic nations, are so many practical shapes of this belief; and the advocates of these several views, so far as they are consistent and logical (which, perhaps, is not very far), appeal to ethnology to bear them out.   Among our own people the nationality doctrine takes a shape which is painfully familiar to every one who attends to the course of political events.   I mean the antagonism of the Celt and the Teuton, or Anglo-Saxon, most conspicuously represented by the Irish and the English constituents of the population of our islands.

A leading article on the affairs of Ireland in any popular English paper is pretty certain to contain some allusion to the Celt and his assumed peculiarities.   If the writer means to be civil, the Celt is taken to be a charming person, full of wit and vivacity and kindliness, but, unfortunately, thoughtless, impetuous, and unstable, and hav-ing standards of right and wrong so different from those of the Anglo-Saxon that it would be absurd, not to say cruel, to treat him in the same way; or if the instructor of the public is angry, he talks of the Celt as if he were a kind of savage, out of whom no good ever has come or ever will come, and whose proper fate is to be kept as a hewer of wood and a drawer of water for his Anglo-Saxon master.   This is the picture of the lion by the man.   Any Irish national paper will supply you with the picture of the man by the lion.   Here, again, according to the temper of the moment, the portrait of the Anglo-Saxon varies—from a stolid, good-natured kind of fellow, whose main fault is that he is incapable of compre-hending the Celtic nature and aspirations, down to the well-known "base, brutal, and bloody, Saxon," with whose features that great limner, the late Daniel O'Connell, made us all so familiar. Nor are the ethnological assumptions involved in these views of the antagonism of the Celt and the Teuton confined to mere popular scribblers or demagogues. Grave and able disputants dealing with such a problem as the Irish land question have much to say about the necessity of respecting Celtic peculiarities, and take their countrymen seriously to task for their narrowness in supposing that what is good for Teutonic is good for Celtic races of mankind.

Now this is neither the time nor the place for political discussion. I do not propose to express an opinion, one way or another, about Irish affairs or Celtic nationality. The subject which I purpose to deal with lies much more within my own province. I propose to inquire what foundation there is for these ethnological assumptions of the politician. Who are the Celts? Who are the Teutons? What sort of grounds are afforded by scientific investig-|9|ation for the belief that these two stocks of mankind are so different as to require different political institutions? And supposing such grounds to exist, are the Celtic and the Teutonic stocks among us so distinctly separable that it is practicable to make such distinctions between them? Let us try to deal with these questions in succession.

At the present moment, the languages which are spoken by the natives of these islands belong to two very different groups. There is, on the one hand, the English group, represented by a great variety of dialects—the lowland Scotch, the Suffolk, and the Dorset dialects, for example, being so different that the speakers of each might have a good deal of difficulty in understanding one another. On the other hand, there is the Celtic group—comprising the Cymric spoken in Wales, and formerly in Cornwall, and the Gaelic spoken in the highlands of Scotland, the Isle of Man, and Ireland. The speakers of Cymric and Gaelic are not intelligible to one another. They are like French and Italian, totally distinct, though allied, languages. We call the people who speak Cymric and Gaelic Celts, while the English-speaking population is roughly called Anglo-Saxon, except, so far as we have reason to believe, that it comprises people who formerly spoke Celtic tongues.

But here, to begin with, is a plain source of confusion. Physical, mental, and moral peculiarities go with blood, and not with language. In the United States, the negroes have spoken English for generations, but no one on that ground would call them Englishmen, or expect them to differ physically, mentally, or morally from other negroes.   And hence, assuming in the first place that we are justified in calling all speakers of Celtic dialects Celts; and assuming, in the second place, that these Celts are a different stock from the Anglo-Saxons; our first business, before these assumptions can bear any practical fruit, is to ascertain what part of the present population of these islands is Celtic by blood in addition to that part which still speaks Cymric or Gaelic.   This is a very difficult inquiry, and has resulted, as yet, in more uncertainties than certainties.   I will put before you those results which, to the best of my knowledge and belief, may be depended upon.

At the time of Caesar's invasion, now nearly 2,000 years ago, there is every reason to believe that the population of Britain, from Land's End to John o'Groat's House, spoke Cymric dialects, while the inhabitants of Ireland all spoke Gaelic.   The whole population of these islands, therefore, so far as their language is concerned, was Celtic, but the Britons belonged to the Cymric division, and the Hibernians to the Gaelic division.   The English language did not exist, and there is no evidence that any Teutonic dialect was spoken within our coasts.   The Romans, as you know, never entered Ireland, but they held Britain for four centuries.   England is full of the remains of their wonderful works, and has much more to show as the result of the Roman occupation than India would exhibit of ours if we left that country.   Nevertheless, the Roman blood and Roman language seem to have made no more impression on the ancient British people than the English blood and language have on the Hindoos.   For my present purpose, therefore, their influence may be neglected. When the Romans evacuated Britain the Cymric Celts were attacked on two sides—on the north by the Scots and the Picts, on the east and south by the Angles and Saxons.   The Scots were Gaelic-speaking Irish, who speedily won a foothold in the highlands, and have remained there ever since. But though they subjugated, and probably in a great measure destroyed, the Cymri, who were their predecessors, they only sub- stituted one Celtic population for another.   Who the Picts were, and whence they came, no one knows with certainty; but the balance of evidence to my mind is in favour of their being a Teutonic population, derived either from Scandinavia or North Germany.

If they were a Teutonic population, they harried and ravaged all

Scotland north of the Firths of Forth and Clyde so effectually, in conjunction with their allies, the Scots, that the Celtic element in Caithness, Sutherland, and the east coast of Scotland, must have been practically abolished.

Leaving the Picts aside, however, it is certain that for something like five hundred years these islands were encircled by a sort of fiery girdle of Teutonic invaders, Angles, Saxons, Jutes, Danes, and Norsemen—who sometimes entered into alliances with the Celts; but more frequently made war upon them with indescribable ferocity, and eventually gained fixed possessions in all parts of Britain and Ireland.

Upon the eastern and south-eastern coast of Britain, which was most exposed to the invaders, the Celts seem to have been absolutely exterminated over vast districts—a Celtic name of a river or a hill being all that is left to show that they once existed. But as, in the slow progress of centuries, the Teutonic conquests were pushed farther and farther westward, the antagonism of savagery and civilisation, of paganism and Christianity, ceased to exist. The Teuton was content to dominate instead of exterminating, and in the western parts of England and Lowland Scotland, as well as in Wales and the Highlands, the change of blood effected by the Saxon and Danish conquests has been, on the whole, insignificant. One is apt to forget that a couple of centuries ago there was as little English spoken in Cornwall as there now is in Wales, and that not only Cornish men but Devonshire men are as little Anglo-Saxons as Northumbrians are Welsh. The Norman Conquest is hardly worth mentioning from an ethnological point of view. What new blood the Normans introduced was Celtic as well as Teutonic. They and their language have alike been smothered in the English nationality, which, from the facts which have been stated, it is simply absurd to call Anglo-Saxon.

Let us now to turn to Ireland. The study of the so-called history of that country before the Norman invasion in the twelfth century is not a hopeful undertaking for the searcher after fact, but some points are clear. It is certain, for example, that the Norsemen and the Danes had an immense deal of intercourse—sometimes friendly, sometimes very much the reverse—with Ireland. Burnt Njal, the hero of the wonderful Icelandic Saga, which Dr. Dasent has made accessible to all of us, bears, like many of his compatriots, an Irish

name.   It is, in fact, the Norse representative of the Irish O'Neil.
And Dr. Dasent tells me that a lively slave trade was carried on for
centuries between Scandinavia and Ireland.   Burnt Njal's Saga tells
of Icelanders who took an active share in Irish wars.   We know
that Norse chiefs long ruled one part of the country, and that Danes
occupied all the chief maritime towns.   It is inconceivable that all
these conquests should have taken place without a large infusion
of Teutonic blood among the Irish people.

Then came the Norman conquest, and the spread of Normans and
Englishmen among the landholders of the country, by intermarriage,
force, or fraud.   The English policy of those days was to set up an
England in Ireland which should be strong enough to keep the
native Irish in check, but weak enough to depend on the support
and execute the will of the English Government.   The practical
result was, firstly, a constant condition of civil war and anarchy;
and, secondly, the forcing of all the Norman and English who had
intermarried with the Irish into identifying themselves with the
Celts in name and language, and becoming the leaders of every so-
called national movement.   From these causes, the state of Ireland
was bad enough under the Plantagenets; but when the Reformation
came the Irish as a body, and without distinction of Teutonic or
Celtic elements, declined to have anything to do with it, and the
antagonism of religion was added to other antagonisms.   From the
time of Elizabeth to that of Cromwell, the country was devastated
by the most ferocious and savage warfare, until, in the middle of
the seventeenth century, it is probable that the population of Ireland
was reduced to less than a million.

Ireland was a terrible thorn in the sides of the statesmen of the
Commonwealth.   They sent Cromwell over, and he dealt with the
Irish at Drogheda and elsewhere in such fashion that to this day
his name remains the symbol of ruthless cruelty in the mind of the
Irish peasant.   If you see an old ruin, it is Cromwell who destroyed
it; and his heaviest malediction is the curse of Cromwell.   I believe
this is rather hard upon the Lord Protector, who was a merciful
man enough when he had his own way; but whosesoever the
responsibility may be, it is certain that Ireland was dealt with by
the Puritans as no country has been dealt with in civilised times.
If you look into the records of that period, you will find that they
"sought the Lord" a good deal about it, and the result of their

seekings was this.   They formed what we should now call a joint-stock company, with limited liability, for the conquest of Ireland—who were called the "Adventurers."   Every adventurer was to receive land, proportioned to the stock invested, when Ireland was conquered.   Well, Cromwell and Ireton between them not only conquered but crushed Ireland, so far as she was Catholic.   Then the Government divided the land—all Ireland except Connaught—into parcels, which were allotted partly to the adventurers and partly to the army, and offered the pre-existing Catholic population, no matter whether it was Teutonic or Celtic in blood, the choice of two alternatives—emigration into Connaught or beyond the seas.   It is computed that some forty thousand able-bodied men were drafted off into the armies of foreign sovereigns, who rejoiced to have their services, and inflicted many a blow on England by their help.   Those who remained—old, young, rich, and poor—were ordered in the late autumn to leave their homes and their crops, and betake themselves to the wilds and wastes of Connaught.   Suppose the first Napoleon had successfully invaded England, and that about August he had ordered all the Protestants in England east of the Severn and north of the Dee to give up their land to French Catholics, and take themselves off to Cornwall and Wales, he would have performed a feat exactly comparable to the so-called Cromwellian settlement of Ireland.   It is true that the laws of nature, more merciful than those of man, prevented the complete carrying out of the orders of the Parliament.   The English superseders of the old proprietors found that land without labourers was almost as valueless a present as a steam-engine without coal. Hence many of the peasantry were allowed to remain, and many were brought back from Connaught.   But the invaders remained as the dominant caste, and in the north as the bulk of the population.   And a large part of Ireland has thus been as completely Teutonised by the Lowland Scotch and the eastern English as these people were themselves Teutonised by the Saxon and Norse invasions.

If one wishes to think of a representative Irishman, the image of the "Tipperary Boy," with all his merits and all his faults, involuntarily presents itself to those who have known Irishmen. But I believe that I am affirming no more than there is warranty for, if I declare that a native of Tipperary is just as much or as little an Anglo-Saxon as a native of Devonshire.   And, if you want to know why a Tipperary man occasionally "tumbles" his landlord, and a Devonshire man does not, you must seek the cause of the difference in something else than in the presence of Celtic blood in the one and not in the other.

To sum up, there is full evidence to prove that in Ireland as well as in Britain the present population is made up of two parties—the one primitive, so far as history goes, and speaking a Celtic tongue; the other, secondary and intrusive, and speaking a Teutonic tongue. We have absolutely no knowledge of the relative proportions of these two parties in England and in Ireland; but it is quite possible, and I thank probable, that Ireland, as a whole, contains less Teutonic blood than the eastern half of England, and more than the western half.   Thus, assuming that Celtic speech and Teutonic speech are making two separate groups of races of mankind, I absolutely deny that the past affords any reason for dealing with the people of Ireland differently from that which may be found to answer with the people of Devonshire, or *vice versa.*   And, if this is true, I think that the sooner we leave off drawing political distinctions between Celts and Saxons the better.   But, as an ethnologist, I go further than this.   I deny that there is sufficient proof of the existence of any difference whatever, except that of language, between Celt and Teuton.   And my reason for this seeming paradox is the following.   All the accounts which have been handed down to us by the Romans and the Greeks of the physical character of the Celtic speaking peoples known to them, and whom they called Gauls or Kelts, agree in ascribing to these terrible enemies of theirs a tall stature, fair hair of a reddish or yellow tinge, blue eyes, and fair skins.   Such were the Gauls whom Caesar conquered.   Such were the Gauls who settled in Asia Minor, to whom the Epistle to the Galatians was written; such again were the Britons with whom Caesar fought in North-eastern Britain.   But all the ancient authors give exactly the same account of the physical character of the ancient Germans.   There is not a doubt that they also were tall, blue-eyed, fair-haired, and fair-skinned; so, without doubt, were all the other Teutonic speaking people—whether Angles, Saxons, Danes, or Norsemen.   So close was the physical resemblance of the Celts and the Teutons who, in the early days of the Roman Empire, inhabited the right and the left banks of the Rhine, that it was, and is, a matter of discussion whether particular rights belonged to the one division or the other—and we hear of Celtic tribes who tried to pass themselves off as of German origin—an imposture which could not have been attempted had any clear physical difference existed between the two stocks.   I am unaware of any evidence of the existence of a dark-complexioned people speaking a Celtic dialect outside of Britannia (Ireland).   But it is quite certain that, in the time of Tacitus, the Silures, who inhabited South Wales and Shropshire, were a dark-complexioned people; and, if Irish tradition is to be trusted for anything, we must credit its invariable assertion that only the chief Irish tribes—that of the Milesians—consisted of dark-haired, black-eyed people.   And the commonest observation will convince you of the existence of a dark and a light stock, and of all the shades produced by their intermixture in Ireland and Britain at the present day.   In Ireland, as in Britain, the dark stock predominates in the west and south, the fair in the east and north.

The same fact was observed in France long ago by William Milne-Edwards.   The population of Eastern and Northern France is, on the whole, fair—that of Western and Southern France is, on the whole, dark.   Turn to Caesar, and you will find the reason of this singular distribution of complexion.   To the south of the Garonne, he tells us, the population consisted of the Aquitani, who spoke a language which was not Celtic.   This language is that which is now spoken by the people who inhabit the shores of the Bay of Biscay, and who are called Basques by foreigners.   Hence the language is termed Basque, but they themselves call it Euskaldunac.   It is a language which is the despair of philologers, inasmuch as it presents not a trace of affinity with any other European or Asiatic tongue.   People speaking this language were the primitive inhabitants, not only of the south of France, but of Spain, whence they are called Iberians, and they have been traced as far west as Sicily.   But in all directions they have been broken up by Celtic and other invasion; and wherever the Celts have penetrated, they have substituted their own language for the Euskaldunac, the mixed population—a Celtiberian—everywhere, so far as I know, speaking Celtic, and not Euskarian dialects.   But, just as the Celtic language has been lost in Cornwall, while the proportion of Celtic blood remains unchanged, so the Iberian blood has remained, although all traces of the language may have been

obliterated.   I believe it is this Iberian blood which is the source
of the so-called black Celts in Ireland and in Britain; and I may
mention three circumstances, upon which I do not wish to lay too
much weight, but which, so far as they go, are in favour of my
hypothesis.   The first is, that all Irish tradition derives the Milesians from Spain; the second is, that the termination *uri*, in the
name of the Siluri, is characteristically Euskarian; the third is, that
Tacitus expressly compares the Silures with the Aquitani.   When
the genealogy of the English people is thoroughly worked out, we
find that our forefathers are reduced to two stocks—the one, a
lightly made, short, dark-complexioned people, the Iberians who,
as far as they can be traced back, talked Euskaldunac, a language
which has not the least resemblance to any other spoken in Europe;
the other, a tall, big limbed, fair people, who, as far as we can trace
them, have always talked some form or other of the languages of
that great Aryan family to which German, Latin, Greek, Persian,
and the Sanskrit belong, and of which the Celtic tongues are outlying
members.   In everything which constitutes a race, these Aryan or
Celtic and Teutonic nations are of one race.   In every particular
by which races of mankind differ, the Iberians and the Aryans are
of different races.

Thus English political ethnology offers two problems:—1.   Is
there any evidence to show that the Iberians and the Aryans differ
in their capacity for civilisation, or in their intellectual and moral
powers?   All I can say is, that I know of none. Whether in Greece
or Rome, in modern Italy, France, Germany, or England, the dark
stock and the light have run neck and neck together. 2.   Is there
any evidence to show that there is what may be called a political
difference between the Celtic Aryan and the Germanic Aryan?   I
must say again that I can find none.   And one of the keenest
observers who ever lived, and who had the opportunity of comparing
the Celt and the German side by side—I mean Julius Caesar—tells
us especially that the Gauls in former days were better men than
the Germans—that they had been corrupted by contact with civilisation, and that even in his day the races who held the Black
Forest in possession were the equals of the Germans in frugality,
hardiness, and every virtue of man or warrior.   Put side by side
with this the picture of the Saxon when, England fairly won, he
sank into the slothful enjoyment of his possessions; and after the

Conquest fell so low that the invective of Giraldus Cambrensis
against the Saxons of his day, as idle worthless fellows, cowards,
and liars, fit only to be drudges and menials, reads just like an
extract from an English or American leading article against the low
Irish.   Do not let what I have said mislead you into the notion
that I disbelieve in the importance of race.   I am a firm believer
in blood, as every naturalist must be, and I entertain no doubt that
our Iberic forefathers have contributed a something to the making
of the modern Englishman totally distinct from the elements
which he has inherited from his Aryan forefathers.   But which is
the Aryan element and which the Iberian I believe no man can tell,
and he who affirms that any quality needful for this, that, or the
other form of political organisation is present in the one and absent
in the other, makes a statement which I believe to be as baseless
in natural science as it is mischievous in politics.   I say again that
I believe in the immense influence of that fixed hereditary transmission which constitutes a race.   I believe it just as I believe in
the influence of ancestors upon children.   But the character of a
man depends in part upon the tendencies he brought with him into
the world, and in part upon the circumstances to which he is
subjected—sometimes one group of influence predominates, sometimes the other.   And there is this further truth which lies within
every one's observation—that by diligent and careful education you
may help a child to be good and wise and keep it out of evil and
folly. But the wisest education cannot ensure its being either good
or wise; while, on the other hand, a few years of perverted ingenuity
would suffice to convert the best child that ever lived into a monster
of vice and wickedness.   The like applies to those great children,
nations and their rulers, who are their educators.   The most a good
government can do is to help its people to be wise and noble, and
that mainly by clearing obstacles out of their way.   But a thoroughly bad government can debauch and demoralise a people for
generations, discouraging all that is good, cherishing all that is evil,
until it is as impossible to discover the original nobleness of the
stock, as it is to find truthfulness and self-restraint in a spoiled and
demoralised child.   Let Englishmen ponder these things.   If what
I have to say in a matter of science weighs with any man who has
political power, I ask him to believe that the arguments about the
difference between Anglo-Saxons and Celts are a mere sham and

delusion. And the next time the Irish difficulty rises before him I ask him, in the first place to read Mr. Prendergast's book on the Cromwellian Settlement, and then to put before himself these plain questions:—Firstly, Are the essentially Celtic people of Devonshire and Cornwall orderly, contented, industrious Englishmen, or are they not? And, secondly, is there the smallest probability that the folk who sang, "And shall Trelawney die?" would have been what they are if they had been dealt with as the people of Tipperary were by our pious Puritan ancestors? And if he answers the first question in the affirmative, and the second in the negative, as he certainly will, he will have fulfilled Dr. Johnson's condition for dealing with all great questions—"Sir, first clear your mind of cant."

EIGHT

KELBURNE KING (1823–86)

An Inquiry into the Causes which have led
to the Rise and Fall of Nations

*Anthropologia: containing the Final Proceedings
of the London Anthropological Society*
Only Volume, 1876, pp. lvi–lxvi

*King was far from being an eminent Victorian, but he can be
valued as an example of the provincial professional man with an
active interest in promoting general debate on current social and
scientific affairs. He spent most of his working life as Surgeon to
the Royal Infirmary at Hull, in which city he was particularly
prominent as an advocate of sanitary reform. He served three
terms as Mayor and was President of the Hull Literary and
Philosophical Society from 1864 to 1869 and 1872 to 1875. He
was also a member of the Anthropological Institute, and of the
short-lived London Anthropological Society to which this paper
was read on 12 March 1875. It reveals his enthusiasm for racial
determinism – something which may well have been acquired, or
at least strengthened, by his association with Robert Knox whom
he assisted as an anatomical demonstrator in the later 1840s. In
the first section of his paper, omitted here, King reviews and
dismisses arguments supporting the opinion that it is such factors
as geography, climate, forms of government, or religion which
bring about the predominance of certain nations. Thereafter he
proceeds to assert, as an alternative explanation, the significance
of blending between certain relatively allied stocks. He contends
that such mixture can sometimes produce 'a race superior to
either of the parent stocks', which for a time multiplies and excels
but which is also condemned to lapse eventually into decay.
King's argument is developed with reference to a wide range of
historical examples. It concludes by touching upon the relevance*

171

*of race to the contemporary condition of the United States, where
a waning of vigour in the English stock may at last be discernible,
and the recently established German Reich where a new mixed
and conquering breed appears to be emerging.*

Although history, in the usual sense of the term, is not considered to be a subject for anthropological investigations, there is one view of historical events which brings them within our scope, and to this I would call your attention.   In so far as history details the acts of kings, statesmen, or generals, it is outside our pale; but when we take broad views of the great events in the written records of our race, and trace them to the results of racial differences, we bring the broad stream of history within the cognizance of the science which concerns itself with the natural history of man; and the subject to which, in this meeting, I wish to call your attention is the effect of intermixture of highly developed and allied races in producing what we may call new races, who occasionally excel in mental and physical qualities any of their ancestors, assume great predominance during a longer or shorter period of time, but seem, as far as we can judge from the records of the past, to have a shorter, if more brilliant, existence than the purer races from which they are derived.   During the period of their greatness these mixed peoples exhibit a wonderful physical development and fecundity, not only becoming greatly more numerous in their own country, but overflowing their borders, occupying other seats either as colonists or conquerors, or both; and this material development is accompanied by a corresponding intellectual progress—the great epochs of literary brightness usually marking the maturity of one or other of these mixed races.

First of all I would divide the races of man as we know them at present, or have studied them in history, into two great classes, the pure and the mixed; and I would limit the consideration of races to those which are nearly allied.   The boundaries occupied by the white, the yellow, the black, and the red races are pretty well defined, and have remained so, except when disturbed by conquest or colonization, during the whole period of history.   But when I speak of mixed races, I would limit myself to the blendings of allied races, excluding altogether such compound races as are formed by the |lvii| mixture of black and white, white and red, red and black, and other hybrid races.   The distinction between the parents is too great to permit of any beneficial admixture, and such hybrid races are usually of little account, as they ordinarily die out or return to one or other of their primitive forms.   I would also confine myself to the consideration of the white race, and more especially to what

is commonly called the Aryan division, though I believe the laws
I am about to lay down would apply equally to the Semitic peoples,
and probably also to the other great subdivisions of the human
family.

Limiting ourselves then, to the European races, I would divide
them into the pure and the mixed.   The pure races, the Pelasgians,
the Iberians, the Celts, the Germans, the Scandinavians, the Sclaves,
are all members of the great Aryan family.   The first occupied
Greece and Italy; the second the Peninsulas of Spain and Portugal;
the third France, Britain, and Ireland; the fourth Germany from
the Rhine to the Oder, from the Baltic to the Alps and the
Carpathians; the fifth, the Peninsulas of Denmark, Norway, and
Sweden; and the sixth the whole countries beyond these limits, the
greater part of Old Prussia, of Russia, of Poland, of what is now
Turkey in Europe, and Bohemia.

What I would lay down as the law of ascendancy in Europe is,
that an admixture of two or more of these races has occasionally
produced a race superior to either of the parent stocks, which for
a time multiplies with extraordinary rapidity, during which it
becomes the predominant race for the time being, but eventually
either dies out altogether, or returns to one or other of its primitive
forms.   The pure races, on the other hand, hold their old boundaries
with wonderful pertinacity, and as in the case of the Basque
Provinces of Spain, sometimes show a capacity of outliving many
separate races who have at different times held the reins of government but have successively died out or been absorbed in the
general ranks of the population.   We have, then, pure races, fixed
comparatively in geographical distribution, in numbers, in habits,
and generally in languages, distinguished by permanence; and the
mixed races, rapidly increasing in numbers, throwing out colonies
in all directions, obtaining great, sometimes universal, dominion,
but finally receding to their original boundaries, losing their peculiarities, and suffering a decay as marked as their former rise and
progress.

A conquering race, then, I take it, arises from the admixture of
several nearly allied races, bound together usually be resistance to
a superior force, or welded together by foreign conquest.   The race
so formed has a period of maturity, during which it increases greatly
in numbers, excels in literature, science, and the arts, then ceases

to extend in number, loses its pre-eminence in intellectual development, and finally either ceases to exist altogether, or takes on a
lower form of life, corresponding probably to some one or other of
the races from which it was originally derived.

Let us look shortly at the history of some of the most remarkable
|lviii| dominant races of the ancient and modern world, and see
whether their history is accordant with this theory.   First, with
respect to the Greeks.   Grote considers that the Greek was a special
creation.   Like his own Pallas, he started full grown and full armed
from the head of Zeus.   But Bishop Thirlwall considers that the
islands of the Egean were from a very remote antiquity, "steps by
which Asia and Europe exchanged a part of their wretched population," while in the north flying or conquering tribes would continually pass southwards; thus a mixed race would be formed, loosely
connected, but most probably acting together in some coherent way,
as proved by the legends of the Trojan war.   Then came the
wonderful events of the Persian invasion; the extraordinary outburst
of literature and art which followed, and is unequalled to this day
in the world's history; then the welding together of the whole race
by the conquests of Philip and Alexander, the final predominance,
established by Alexander, of the Greek nation all over the East;
which lasted, little affected by the subsequent Roman conquest,
until a new history was begun for these countries by the conquests
of Mahomet and his successors.   But long before the final overthrow
of Greek ideas and influence, the nation had lost its peculiar
character.   The population declined.   It sent out no more colonies,
gave no new impulse to thought, and ceased even to be original in
art.   Though the Greek language and nation still survive, the
characters of a dominant race have long been gone, and "Greece is
living Greece no more."

Let us now turn to the Romans, the successors and conquerors
of the Greeks.   Like them they originated from a mixture of many
races, out of which ultimately sprang the great Roman race, which
multiplied exceedingly, stamped on all southern, western, and central
Europe an impression which lasts to this day, swallowed up in its
empire all the known world worth the trouble of conquering, then
gradually dissolved and disappeared, dying out both as to the
numbers and the distinctive qualities of the race.

The Romans never claimed to be children of the soil.   They were

composed of Latin and Oscan tribes, added to an original Pelasgic
stock common to them with the Greeks.   They showed in their
early history signs of a great, new, and energetic race having
appeared on the scene of history.   So late as 380 B.C. the city was
taken by the Gauls, but a hundred years after it was the mistress
of Central Italy, and pressed hard on the Grecianized southern
portion of the peninsula.   Pyrrhus, king of Epirus, the last representative soldier of Greece, came to the assistance of his fellow-
countrymen, and Rome for the first time measured swords with a
non-Italian power.   The result was prophetic of the future.   Pyrrhus, the greatest warrior of his time, went home discomfited, and
no Italian power for the future could cope with Rome.   Then came
the Carthaginian struggle, which lasted more than a hundred years
(264 to 146 B.C.), and left Rome the most powerful state in the
world.   The Romans were then clearly the |lix| dominant race.
After Hannibal had failed, no accidental genius could hope to turn
the scale against

"The master mould of nature's heavenly hand,
Wherein were cast the heroic and the free,
The beautiful, the brave, the lords of earth and sea,
The commonwealth of kings—the men of Rome."

The conquests of Africa, of Greece, of the East, of Spain, and of
Gaul followed in rapid succession, and such was the pride of race,
that a Roman citizen claimed and was allowed peculiar privileges
all over the civilized world.   Then appeared that remarkable fecundity which distinguishes the mixed and conquering race.   "Wherever
the Roman conquers he inhabits, is a very just observation of
Seneca, confirmed by history and experience" (Gibbon).   "The
native of Italy," says Gibbon, "allured by pleasure or interest,
hastened to enjoy the advantages of victory, and we may remark
as a proof of the vast system of colonization which prevailed, and
which yet could not prevent the continual increase of population
in both city and country, that forty years after the conquest of Asia
80,000 Roman citizens were massacred in one day by the cruel
orders of Mithridates."   "These voluntary exiles were engaged for
the most part in the occupations of commerce, agriculture, and
farming the revenue.   But after the legions were rendered permanent by the emperors, the provinces were peopled by a race of

soldiers, and the veterans, whether they received the reward of their services in money or land, usually settled with their families in the country where they had honourably spent their youth." Pliny tells us that no less than twenty-five colonies were settled in Spain, nine in Britain, of which London, Colchester, Lincoln, Chester, Glouces-ter, York, and Bath still remain considerable cities.

As in spite of this prodigious emigration the population at home continually increased, it is evident that the reproductive powers of the race were at this time prodigious. Literature, science, and art shared in the general progress. The eloquence of the Roman forum was as celebrated as the genius of the soldier or the administrative talent of the governor of the provinces. Rome reached its acme and then came the inevitable decline. Symptoms of this decay began to show themselves even before the culmination of the Roman power under Trajan. Tacitus notes as one of the signs of his times that the Roman citizens in Gaul, who shortly after the death of Augustus numbered nearly 3,000,000, had diminished to little more than 500,000. The race of independent freemen had disappeared. The bone and sinew of the country were gone, and nothing was left except a few overgrown patricians on the one hand, and a multitude of serfs on the other. But no wasting war, no dire pestilence nor consuming famine, no external calamity had occurred to decimate the descendants of the hardy veterans of Rome. Nor can the imperial government be blamed justly for this decay, for during the hundred years that followed the death of Julius Caesar the population increased more rapidly, the external power and material prosperity |lx| advanced higher than they had ever done before. When Rome reached the zenith of her power and her population, the indispensable condition on which all mixed races acquire their dominion began to be exacted; her population ceased to increase, then began to diminish, till for the purposes of extensive dominion it may be said to have altogether disappeared. Yet for a long time the remnant of the Roman race struggled manfully against their fate. Whenever 30,000 legionaries could be collected, the most overpowering odds of the German barbarians or Arabian zealots contended in vain. There is something grand in the vigour displayed up to the very last. Stilicho, with but a comparative handful of legionaires, baffled the warlike genius of Alaric and his hordes of Goths; and Belisarius under even more hopeless circumstances made for himself,

as Gibbon says, "a name that can never die." But valour and genius
were alike unavailing.   Destiny could not long be averted, and the
Roman empire fell because the Roman race had disappeared.

Mark what happened then.   The governors were gone, the
governed were left.   I shall speak to-night only of the western
portion of the empire, though the lesson to be derived from the
conquests of the Arabs and of the Turks in the East is precisely the
same.   Spain, Gaul, Britain, and Italy itself were deprived of their
defenders, who were recalled to protect the heart of the empire, now
removed to Byzantium.   The vacuum was soon felt in that vast
ocean of barbarism which extended from the Rhine and the Danube
to the Wall of China.   Its surges had been often felt by the Romans
when at the height of their power.   The Provincials who had
imbibed Roman art, civilization, and law, had totally lost the use
of arms and martial exercises, which a conquering race, few comparatively in numbers, can never be expected to foster or even to
permit on the part of the conquered.   They now fell an easy prey
to the hosts of barbarians who flocked from their forests to enter
upon the possession and enjoy the spoils of what had been the
Roman provinces.   This process of occupation went on during the
whole of the fifth century.   When Alaric was leading his Goths to
the sack of Rome (A.D. 410), he passed through the plains of Aquae
Sextiae (Verona), and saw there whitening in the sun the huge bones
of the Teutones who had fallen five hundred years before under the
disciplined valour of Marius and the Roman legions.   The men of
Alaric were neither stronger nor braver than their kinsfolk; but
there was now no Marius to withstand them, and had there been,
there were no Roman legions for him to command.   Thus Franks,
Burgundians, Goths and Visigoths, Angles and Saxons, Longobardi,
and many other barbarous tribes, were installed as masters in the
once opulent and prosperous Roman provinces.   Spain (410), Gaul
(Clovis at Soissons, 480), Britain (455 to 586), and Italy (476), after
longer or shorter periods of resistance, all fell ultimately under the
power of one or other of the German tribes who were hastening to
divide the plunder of the western world.   But these new rulers |lxi|
were not a conquering race in the same sense as the Greeks and
Romans had been.   They emigrated in whole tribes from poorer
and less genial to richer and more fertile territories.   They found
decaying populations accustomed to servitude, and they accepted

the situation, and sat in the seats of the former masters. They left their native country, not because the race was multiplying with the rapidity which characterizes the early maturity of a mixed race, but because the conditions of life were easier in the lands to which they emigrated than in those which they left. They brought with them neither a higher culture nor a purer religion, for in these respects they were inferior to the conquered. Neither were they guided by any great idea or policy, nor did they add anything to the power or prestige of the country from which they came. What they did bring was new blood, bone and muscle, so to speak, to the populations among whom they settled, among whom they ruled, and by whom they were in most instances gradually absorbed. In this way there sprang up the mixed races of modern Europe, and we find once more that new races superior to any of the parent stocks began to appear upon the scene. But what a dreary period intervened! What an interminable series of violence and bloodshed, fraud and treachery, distinguished, or rather darkened, the long period during which the German tribes held undisputed sway over the fairest countries in Europe! Once, indeed, under Charles the Great, there seemed a probability of a really great empire being built up (768 to 814). But the genius of one or even of several men produces no lasting effect, except it works in harmony with physical law. The empire of Charles broke in pieces after his death, and it was not until the new, mixed, and conquering races reappeared on the scene that anything like settled government and continuous good order prevailed in Europe.

From the tenth to the fifteenth century these new races showed themselves in Italy, Spain, France, and England. Time forbids my entering on the long and difficult subject of the Italian and French races; but I shall endeavour very shortly to show that in Spain and in Britain new races arose out of an admixture of several, and that they displayed all the characters of the old dominant classical nations.

The Spaniards, then, are, first of all, a mixed race. This is easily shown. The Pyrenees were forced by barbarians in the year 411. Suevi, Alans, and Vandals entered the devoted province. Their ravages were dreadful. "Towns pillaged and burnt, the country laid waste, the inhabitants massacred without distinction of age or sex, were but the beginning of evils. Famine and pestilence made awful havoc. The wild beasts made war on the human species, and the latter consumed the very corpses of the dead; nay, mothers are said to have killed their children to feed on their flesh." The Vandals ultimately crossed the Straits of Gibralter to subdue northern Africa, and the other barbarians were gradually brought into subjection by the Visigoths. One of their kings finally |lxii| succeeded in forming a kind of government about the year 522, and the Goths remained masters of Spain for two hundred years. Everyone knows how their power was broken, and their last king, Roderick, killed in battle, in the year 711, by the Saracens, who extended their dominion over the whole peninsula with remarkable rapidity, burst through the barrier of the Pyrenees, and in 833 received on the field of Tours, at the hands of Pepin, the first signal and, as it turned out, decisive and permanent defeat which had yet occurred to the followers of the Arabian Prophet. A kind of sentimental regret is often expressed for the royal Goth slain in battle by infidel invaders, fighting in defence of his country and kingdom. But we cannot feel much sympathy for the ruin which overtook the Goths. Their cruel despotism over their slaves; their horrible persecution of such as differed from them in religion, must brand the memory of these tyrants and bigots with everlasting infamy. The Visigothic monarchy was founded in usurpation and blood, and its end corresponds to its beginning. "It deserved to fall and it fell." Under the Saracens Spain enjoyed great prosperity. "Their empire reached its culminating point in the latter half of the tenth century." Commerce flourished and riches were accumulated in an unexampled degree; a powerful navy was formed and maintained in full activity; arts and sciences were cultivated with ardour; many splendid public works were undertaken; the king was the friend of industry, of merit, and of poverty, and generally the government may be described as enlightened, beneficent, and powerful, when compared with that which had preceded it. The Christians were driven into Asturias, where Pelagius and his successors maintained an independent sovereignty. As Arabian power declined, these last emerged from their fastnesses and gradually pressed southwards, till, in 1211, Alfonzo of Castile gained a crowning victory over the Mohammedans at Tolosa; and afterwards all Spain, except the powerful and brilliant kingdom of Granada, was under the government of Christian princes. After a long and glorious existence Granada finally surrendered to Ferdinand the Catholic, in 1491.   All Spain was governed by Ferdinand and Isabella, and the Spanish race may be said to have reached its maturity—the product of the admixture of Iberian, Roman, Germanic, and Saracenic blood—bound together by the bond of recent conquest of the mixed Christian and Saracenic races.   It was a wonderful race, worthy of the best of its ancestors, and during the sixteenth century was the most powerful nationality in Europe.   Italy, Spain, France, and the Low Countries were overshadowed by its might, and our own England regarded it as little less than a manifestation of divine favour that its existence was spared and its honour preserved in its contest with the gigantic Spanish power.   Cervantes, Calderon, Lope de Vega, and many other writers formed a dramatic literature hardly inferior to that of our own Elizabethan era.   "Don Quixote" has been thought by many great thinkers, eminently by Coleridge, the greatest book that has ever been written.   Murillo, and Velasquez and others, rendered the Spanish school of painters |lxiii| only less illustrious than the Italian.   Don Juan, the Prince of Parma, and other famous warriors raised her military reputation to the highest pitch, and the Spanish infantry continued to be esteemed the first in Europe till defeated and almost destroyed at Rocroi in 1643 by the great Condé, then only twenty-two years of age.   Nor was its influence confined to Europe.   Like other similar races, its population found its boundaries too narrow for its expansive force, and the whole of South America and that great and rich region now called Central America were peopled by Spanish colonists.   Spain was truly unfortunate in its government; its blood was spilt and its treasures squandered in projects which could not add to the national power and prosperity, and after a period of extraordinary greatness came an almost equally sudden collapse.   But long after the government had sunk into a state of almost bewildering weakness and apathy, the Spanish power remained great, and the character of the Spaniard was universally respected.   A familiar instance of this is the representation of the Spaniards by Defoe, in his immortal tale of "Robinson Crusoe." My hearers will remember that Will Atkins and the other Englishmen are represented as strong, but mischievous, self-willed, and often wrong-headed men; but the Spaniards are grave, prudent, self-controlled, and sagacious.   Though generally opposed to England in religion and policy, we must admit that, after reaching her climax,

Spain has often shown great recuperative power.   Under the first
three Bourbon kings she made (1700 to 1783) rapid strides in
national prosperity, and by nearly doubling her population proved
that the elements of greatness had not yet died out.   But the events
of the French revolution and those which have succeeded have had
generally a depressing influence on the Spanish Peninsula; and
though a firm hand is still capable of uniting her scattered powers
and restoring her to a respectable place among the nations of
Europe, as we have seen in the case of the governments of O'Donnel
and Prim, the conquering element has disappeared from the Spanish
blood; and I fear we may have to say of Spain as was said of another
decayed nationality by the British poet, whose eye was the most
piercing and his pinion the strongest of all who have sung in our
language since Milton—"Her glorious day is o'er, but not her years
of shame."

That the English are a conquering race cannot be denied—an
empire on which the sun never sets; a population of subject states
and colonies exceeding that of any other empire in the world; a
population at home which has doubled within the last fifty years,
yet has borne an emigration sometimes numbering one thousand a
day; a military history in some respects unrivalled; and a position
in literature, science, and the arts, at least equal to that of any
other nationality for the last three hundred years—these are all
unmistakable signs of a dominant race, and of one which has not
yet passed its climax.   Then, as to our origin.   I know that Mr.
Freeman always speaks of the Angles and Saxons as our fathers;
and no doubt the Teutonic is a very strong element in the English
people and character.   But when Mr. Freeman asks, rather |lxiv|
indignantly "Are you a Welshman??"I answer, No; but neither am
I a German.   The Teutonic invaders of England did their work
more thoroughly than their kinsfolk in France and Spain; but even
by Mr. Freeman's own showing it was only in the south-east of
England that the Britons were exterminated.   The cruelties practised by the Visigoths and other German tribes in Spain were
equalled or exceeded by Jutes, Angles, and Saxons in England; and
the general history of the conquerors here is not unlike that of the
Visigoths in Spain.   There was a heptarchy constantly engaged in
cruel and meaningless wars.   Then followed an attempt at firm and
stable government by able leaders, as Egbert, Alfred, Edward the

Elder, and other kings of the race of Cerdic. But the same incapacity to mould subject races and to form a powerful united kingdom was evident in England, as in the conquered continental provinces. Hardly had Egbert united the different states of the heptarchy, when the Scandinavians, Danes, and Norse began to plunder the country, as the Angles and Saxons had done before; and though often defeated they settled in large numbers along the northern and eastern coasts. Lincolnshire was a Danish colony; and we find the Danes not only invading the southern coasts, but penetrating as far inland as Oxford and Northampton. Eventually the Danish dynasty displaced the Saxon, and from 1013 to 1042 Danish sovereigns sat on the English throne. This could not have happened unless at least a third of the country was in the hands of the Danes, not merely in the way of military occupation, but inhabited by Danes, or people of Danish descent. Now when it is remembered that the Celtic language is to this day spoken in Wales, and that it has died out in Cornwall only within a recent period, and that large districts in the west of England, Cumberland, Lancashire, Somerset, Devon, and all the country between the Severn and the present boundaries of Wales, are admitted by Mr. Freeman to have been only conquered, and that there the Britons were not exterminated, we have clearly—putting the Roman element aside—three races: the Briton, the Teuton, and the Scandinavian, all entering into the composition of the English people. But to complete their amalgamation there was an external force required, and that was supplied by the Norman conquest. That terrible event trod down all distinction of the subject races; a bridge was thrown across the Channel, by which Normans and Angevins flowed over in a continuous stream for a hundred and fifty years; and then in the reign of our first Edward began to appear the first traces of the new race, which is neither German, nor Dane, nor Welsh, but has its own individuality, is inferior to none of its predecessors, and when it has passed away will be always known as the great English race.

There are two subjects on which I should wish to say a very few words, and without which this lecture will hardly bring down my own ideas quite to the present time: one relates to America; the other to the new empire of Germany.

We hear a great deal of a new England on the other side of the

|lxv| Atlantic, and of the connection in blood between us and the people of the United States. "Blood," we are told, "is thicker than water," and we fondly hope that our cousins, as we think them, must on the whole be actuated mainly by friendly feelings towards ourselves. The friendship of England and America is necessary to the world's progress; but that friendship must be based on feelings of mutual respect and mutual interests, not on any sentimental idea of blood relationship.   Observe, as one of the signs of the times, the answer given to Mr. Froude by the American press: "We do not care for the England of the past."   They say in effect: "We have but little English blood in our veins."   This is no doubt an exaggeration, but it is founded on truth.   It would seem as if the English race loses muscle and fat, and gains length in America. The statistics of their army prove that the American-born recruits exceed in stature, but are inferior in weight, strength, and girth, to Irish, German, and English-born recruits.   What is almost more serious is that the birth-rate is continually diminishing, the race is losing its *fecundity*, and the population is maintained and increased only by European immigration.   The birth-rate of the foreign Americans in the United States is about 1 to 30 of the population; of the native Americans about 1 to 40; while the birth-rate for England in the first half of 1872 was 1 to 28.   But English blood is not that which flows most freely into America; and if the English already settled there cannot (for 230 years) maintain their numbers and their strength, one of two things must happen—the American race will not survive the cessation of European immigration, or, if so, it will be by the formation of a new race formed of German, Irish-Celt, and Scandinavian, speaking probably the English language, but not really allied to England in blood or in sentiment. The failure of the English-descended American stock is put down to various causes: intemperance in eating, in drinking, smoking, the enormous consumption of patent medicines, the hasty manner of eating, the practice of eating an excess of fine-flour bread, the abuse of tea and coffee, the increased use of a rich, highly-seasoned and stimulating diet, and the constant employment of iced water.   These it will be at once apparent may accompany but cannot cause a general degeneracy in physical development and national reproduction.   The cause has to be sought deeper, and may arise from the incapacity of the English race to keep up its physique and its

numbers on American soil—a very serious subject for contemplation, and one which may exercise no little influence on the fortunes and fates of the future.

One other point, and I have done.   I have spoken of the Germans as a pure race, inhabiting fixed boundaries, which they overflowed only when a vacuum was caused, so to speak, by the decay of the Romans.   Their emigrations were guided by no fixed policy; they settled down in their new seats and lost all connection with the country from which they came; plundering the subject races, and giving them in return very little except the benefit to be derived centuries |lxvi| after by the admixture of a strong, vigorous, and muscular race.   But it will be asked, is this description compatible with the history of the last ten years during which Germany has certainly displayed all the characteristics of a conquering nation; has engaged in great and eminently successful wars; has conquered large territories which it has incorporated in its empire, careless of the approval or disapproval of the inhabitants?   This is all true, but it does not affect my theory.   In past times the Germans extended their influence over many of the Sclavonic tribes lying to their east.   These acquired the German language; some are now incorporated with the great Russian empire, others form part of the old Prussian monarchy.   There a new mixed race has been forming for some time.   It has at length taken the crown, as it has for long wielded the sword of Germany.   Turning to our physical test of reproduction, we find that the birth-rate of the purely German states, as Hanover, is 1 to 32; of Bavaria, 1 to 29; but the birth-rate of Prussia is 1 to 26.   As in the case of the Hellenes, the Romans, the Spanish Asturians, and the Normans, a little leaven leaveneth the whole mass.   So we have in Prussia a new race with all the attributes of the old conquering races using the great German nationality for a lever, and entering on the career for the future, be it for good or for evil, of a conquering race.

It is only when I have brought this subject to a conclusion that I see how feebly and imperfectly I have been able to bring before you one of the most momentous questions of history.   It is a subject on which I have thought much and long, and I fear, to the great annoyance of my friends, have also talked too much and too long.   But if everything that concerns our race is interesting and worthy of thought, it cannot be denied that a surpassing interest

must attacn to all that belongs to those races which in the history
of Europe have done the most to impress civilization, knowledge,
laws, and arts on the rest of mankind.

NINE

HERBERT SPENCER (1820–1903)

The Comparative Psychology of Man

Popular Science Monthly
Volume 8, 1876, pp. 257–69

Even before Darwin became a household name Spencer had established himself as a most influential proponent of the view that every aspect of reality should be studied in terms of development from lower to higher stages. This conviction eventually provided the basis for his 'Synthetic Philosophy', articulated between 1862 and 1893 in a whole series of volumes covering such topics as sociology, psychology, biology, epistemology, and ethics. Spencer's politics centred on a laissez-faire aspiration to maximize personal liberty, for the fit at least, by demonstrating that the laws of social evolution operate best with minimal interference from the state. But the related idea of progress – a movement towards ever more coherent heterogeneity – also includes images of racial hierarchy. Here commentators have noted Spencer's tendency to waver between hereditarian and environmentalist modes of social explanation. He certainly did believe in the possibility of men inheriting modifications that had been stimulated originally by environmental factors. Yet there were tight practical limits to Spencer's support for such Lamarckianism. According to him, a major feature of those stocks which had not advanced much beyond primitiveness was their simple and uncreative reflex response to external conditions. Races which had not already derived much benefit from the inheritance of acquired characteristics were unlikely to improve significantly in the future. On these terms the gulf in attainment could only widen.

The paper reprinted here was read to the Anthropological

Institute on 22 June 1875. The Popular Science Monthly *published it during the following January, and later in 1876 it appeared again as the very first article in the inaugural issue of* Mind. *Spencer pleads that anthropologists should give the same attention to categorizing 'psychical' differences between races as they have hitherto devoted to classifying physical distinctions. He schedules the questions that must be tackled if such a comparative human and racial psychology is to be properly established. The answers at which he hints suggest very clearly his willingness to talk in terms of inferior and superior breeds. On his own premises, it is difficult to see how his concluding remarks about education have much relevance to the former, who stand condemned by their 'great rigidity of general character'. Spencer's address also warns against any mixture between markedly different races, while proposing that adaptive advantages may yet stem from alliance between types that are only mildly divergent.*

While discussing with two members of the Anthropological Institute the work to be undertaken by its psychological section, I made certain suggestions which they requested me to put in writing. When reminded, some months after, of the promise I had made to do this, I failed to recall the particular suggestions referred to; but, in the endeavour to remember them, I was led to glance over the whole subject of comparative human psychology.   Hence resulted the following paper:

That making a general survey is useful as a preliminary to deliberate study, either of a whole or of any part, scarcely needs showing.   Vagueness of thought accompanies the wandering about in a region without known bounds or landmarks.   Attention devoted to some portion of a subject, in ignorance of its connection with the rest, leads to untrue conceptions.   The whole cannot be rightly conceived without some knowledge of the parts; and no part can be rightly conceived out of relation to the whole.

To map out the comparative psychology of man must also conduce to the more methodic carrying on of inquiries.   In this, as in other things, division of labor will facilitate progress; and, that there may be division of labor, the work itself must be systematically divided.

We may conveniently separate the entire subject into three main divisions, arranged in the order of increasing speciality.

The first division will treat of the degrees of mental evolution of different human types, generally considered: taking account of both the mass of mental manifestation and the complexity of mental manifestation.   This division will include the relations of these characters to physical characters—the bodily mass and structure, and the cere-|258|bral mass and structure.   It will also include inquiries concerning the time taken in completing mental evolution, and the time during which adult mental power lasts; as well as certain most general traits of mental action, such as the greater or less persistence of emotions and of intellectual processes.   The connection between the general mental type and the general social type should also be here dealt with.

In the second division may be conveniently placed apart, inquiries concerning the relative mental natures of the sexes in each race. Under it will come such questions as these: What differences of mental mass and mental complexity, if any, existing between males

and females, are common to all races?   Do such differences vary
in degree, or in kind, or in both?   Are there reasons for thinking
that they are liable to change by increase or decrease?   What
relations do they bear in each case to the habits of life, the domestic
arrangements, and the social arrangements?   This division should
also include in its scope the sentiments of the sexes toward one
another, considered as varying quantitatively and qualitatively; as
well as their respective sentiments toward offspring, similarly
varying.

For the third division of inquiries may be reserved the more
special mental traits distinguishing different types of men.   One
class of such specialities results from differences of proportion
among faculties possessed in common; and another class results
from the presence in some races of faculties that are almost or quite
absent from others.   Each difference in each of these groups, when
established by comparison, has to be studied in connection with the
stage of mental evolution reached, and has to be studied in connection with the habits of life and the social development, regarding
it as related to these both as cause and consequence.

Such being the outlines of these several divisions, let us now
consider in detail the subdivisions contained within each.

I—Under the head of general mental evolution we may begin
with the trait of—

1. *Mental Mass.*—Daily experiences show us that human beings
differ in volume of mental manifestation.   Some there are whose
intelligence, high though it may be, produces little impression on
those around; while there are some who, when uttering even com-
monplaces, do it so as to affect listeners in a disproportionate
degree.   Comparison of two such makes it manifest that, generally,
the difference is due to the natural language of the emotions.
Behind the intellectual quickness of the one there is not felt any
power of character; while the other betrays a momentum capable
of bearing down opposition—a potentiality of emotion that has
something formidable about it.   Obviously the varieties of mankind
differ much in respect of this trait.   Apart from kind of feeling,
they are unlike in amount of feeling.   The dominant races overrun
the inferior races mainly in virtue of the |259| greater quantity of
energy in which this greater mental mass shows itself.   Hence a

series of inquiries, of which these are some: (*a*) What is the relation between mental mass and bodily mass?   Manifestly, the small races are deficient in it.   But it also appears that races much upon a par in size—as, for instance, an Englishman and a Damara—differ considerably in mental mass.   (*b*.) What is its relation to mass of brain? and, bearing in mind the general law that, in the same species, size of brain increases with size of body (though not in the same proportion), how far can we connect the extra mental mass of the higher races with an extra mass of brain beyond that which is proper to their greater bodily mass?   (*c*.) What relation, if any, is there between mental mass and the physiological state expressed in vigor of circulation and richness of blood, as severally determined by mode of life and general nutrition?   (*d*.) What are the relations of this trait to the social state, as predatory or industrial, nomadic or agricultural?

2. *Mental Complexity.*—How races differ in respect of the more of less involved structures of their minds will best be understood, on recalling that unlikeness between the juvenile mind and the adult mind among ourselves which so well typifies the unlikeness between the minds of savage and civilized.   In the child we see absorption in special facts.   Generalities even of a low order are scarcely recognized; and there is no recognition of high generalities.   We see interest in individuals, in personal adventures, in domestic affairs; but no interest in political or social matters.   We see vanity about clothes and small achievements; but little sense of justice: witness the forcible appropriation of one another's toys.   While there have come into play many of the simpler mental powers, there has not yet been reached that complication of mind which results from the addition of powers evolved out of these simpler ones. Kindred differences of complexity exist between the minds of lower and higher races; and comparisons should be made to ascertain their kinds and amounts.   Here, too, there may be a subdivision of the inquiries: (*a*.) What is the relation between mental complexity and mental mass?   Do not the two habitually vary together?   (*b*.) What is the relation to the social state, as more or less complex?—that is to say, Do not mental complexity and social complexity act and react on each other?

3. *Rate of Mental Development.*—In conformity with the biological law, that the higher the organisms the longer they take to

evolve, members of the inferior human races may be expected to complete their mental evolution sooner than members of the superior races; and we have evidence that they do this.   Travellers from all regions comment, now on the great precocity of children among savage and semi-civilized peoples, and now on the early arrest of their mental progress.   Though we scarcely need more proofs that this general contrast exists, there remains to be asked the question, whether it is |260| consistently maintained throughout all orders of races, from the lowest to the highest—whether, say, the Australian differs in this respect from the Hindoo, as much as the Hindoo does from the European.   Of secondary inquiries coming under this sub-head may be named several: (*a*.) Is this more rapid evolution and earlier arrest always unequally shown by the two sexes; or, in other words, are there in lower types proportional differences in rate and degree of development, such as higher types show us?   (*b*.) Is there in many cases, as there appears to be in some cases, a traceable relation between the period of arrest and the period of puberty? (*c*.) Is mental decay earlier in proportion as mental evolution is rapid?   (*d*.) Can we in other respects assert that, where the type is low, the entire cycle of mental changes between birth and death—ascending, uniform, descending—comes within a shorter interval?

4. *Relative Plasticity.*—Is there any relation between the degree of mental modifiability which remains in adult life, and the character of the mental evolution in respect of mass, complexity, and rapidity?   The animal kingdom at large yields us reasons for associating an inferior and more rapidly-completed mental type with a relatively automatic nature.   Lowly-organized creatures, guided almost entirely by reflex actions, are in but small degrees changeable by individual experiences.   As the nervous structure complicates, its actions become less rigorously confined within preëstablished limits; and, as we approach the highest creatures, individual experiences take larger and larger shares in moulding the conduct: there is an increasing ability to take in new impressions and to profit by the acquisitions.   Inferior and superior human races are contrasted in this respect.   Many travellers comment on the unchangeable habits of savages.   The semi-civilized nations of the East, past and present, were, or are, characterized by a greater rigidity of custom than characterizes the more civilized nations of the West.   The histories

of the most civilized nations show us that in their earlier times the modifiability of ideas and habits was less than it is at present. And, if we contrast classes or individuals around us, we see that the most developed in mind are the most plastic. To inquiries respecting this trait of comparative plasticity, in its relations to precocity and early completion of mental development, may be fitly added inquiries respecting its relations to the social state, which it helps to determine, and which reacts upon it.

5. *Variability.*—To say of a mental nature that its actions are extremely inconstant, and at the same time to say that it is a relatively unchangeable nature, apparently implies a contradiction. When, however, the inconstancy is understood as referring to the manifestations which follow one another from minute to minute, and the unchangeableness to the average manifestations, extending over long periods, the apparent contradiction disappears; and it becomes com-|261|prehensible that the two traits may, and ordinarily do, coexist. An infant, quickly weary with each kind of perception, wanting ever a new object, which it soon abandons for something else, and alternating a score times a day between smiles and tears, shows us a very small persistence in each kind of mental action: all its states, intellectual and emotional, are transient. Yet, at the same time, its mind cannot be easily changed in character. True, it changes spontaneously in due course; but it long remains incapable of receiving ideas or emotions beyond those of simple orders. The child exhibits less rapid variations, intellectual and emotional, while its educability is greater. Inferior human races show us this combination, great rigidity of general character, with great irregularity in its passing manifestations. Speaking broadly, while they resist permanent modification they lack intellectual persistence, and they lack emotional persistence. Of various low types we read that they cannot keep the attention fixed beyond a few minutes on any thing requiring thought even of a simple kind. Similarly with their feelings: these are less enduring than those of civilized men. There are, however, qualifications to be made in this statement; and comparisons are needed to ascertain how far these qualifications go. The savage shows great persistence in the action of the lower intellectual faculties. He is untiring in minute observation. He is untiring, also, in that kind of perceptive activity which accompanies the making of his weapons and orna-

ments: often persevering for immense periods in carving stones, etc. Emotionally, too, he shows persistence not only in the motives prompting these small industries, but also in certain of his passions—especially in that of revenge. Hence, in studying the degrees of mental variability shown us in the daily lives of the different races, we must ask how far variability characterizes the whole mind, and how far it holds only of parts of the mind.

6. *Impulsiveness.*—This trait is closely allied with the last: unenduring emotions are emotions which sway the conduct now this way and now that, without any consistency. The trait of impulsiveness may, however, be fitly dealt with separately, because it has other implications than mere lack of persistence. Comparisons of the lower human races with the higher appear generally to show that, along with brevity of the passions, there goes violence. The sudden gusts of feeling which men of inferior types display are excessive in degree as they are short in duration; and there is probably a connection between these two traits: intensity sooner producing exhaustion. Observing that the passions of childhood illustrate this connection, let us turn to certain interesting questions concerning the decrease of impulsiveness which accompanies advance in evolution. The nervous processes of an impulsive being are less remote from reflex actions than are those of an unimpulsive being. In reflex actions we see a simple stimulus passing suddenly into movement: little or no control |262| being exercised by other parts of the nervous system. As we ascend to higher actions, guided by more and more complicated combinations of stimuli, there is not the same instantaneous discharge in simple motions; but there is a comparatively deliberate and more variable adjustment of compound motions, duly restrained and proportioned. It is thus with the passions and sentiments in the less developed natures and in the more developed natures. Where there is but little emotional complexity, an emotion, when excited by some occurrence, explodes in action before the other emotions, have been called into play; and each of these, from time to time, does the like. But the more complex emotional structure is one in which these simpler emotions are so coördinated that they do not act independently. Before excitement of any one has had time to cause action, some excitement has been communicated to others—often antagonistic ones—and the conduct becomes modified in adjustment to the combined dic-

tates.   Hence results a decreased impulsiveness, and also a greater persistence.   The conduct pursued, being prompted by several emotions coöperating in degrees which do not exhaust them, acquires a greater continuity; and while spasmodic force becomes less conspicuous, there is an increase in the total energy.

Examining the facts from this point of view, there are sundry questions of interest to be put respecting the different races of men: (*a*.) To what other traits than degree of mental evolution is impulsiveness related: Apart from difference in elevation of type: the New-World races seem to be less impulsive than the Old-World races.   Is this due to constitutional apathy?   Can there be traced (other things equal) a relation between physical vivacity and mental impulsiveness?   (*b*.) What connection is there between this trait and the social state?   Clearly a very explosive nature—such as that of the Bushman—is unfit for social union; and, commonly, social union, when by any means established, checks impulsiveness.   (*c*.) What respective shares in checking impulsiveness are taken by the feelings which the social state fosters—such as the fear of surrounding individuals, the instinct of sociality, the desire to accumulate property, the sympathetic feelings, the sentiment of justice?   These, which require a social environment for their development, all of them involve imaginations of consequences more or less distant; and thus imply checks upon the promptings of the simpler passions. Hence arise the questions—In what order, in what degrees, and in what combinations do they come into play?

7. One further general inquiry of a different kind may be added: What effect is produced on mental nature by mixture of races? There is reason for believing that, throughout the animal kingdom, the union of varieties that have become widely divergent is physically injurious; while the union of slightly-divergent varieties is physically beneficial.   Does the like hold with the mental nature?   Some facts seem |263| to show that mixture of human races extremely unlike produces a worthless type of mind—a mind fitted neither for the kind of life led by the higher of the two races, nor for that led by the lower—a mind out of adjustment to all conditions of life. Contrariwise, we find that peoples of the same stock, slightly differentiated by lives carried on in unlike circumstances for many generations, produce by mixture a mental type having certain superiorities.   In his work on "The Huguenots," Mr. Smiles points

out how large a number of distinguished men among us have
descended from Flemish and French refugees; and M. Alphonse de
Candolle, in his "Histoire des Sciences et des Savants depuis deux
Siècles," shows that the descendants of French refugees in Switz-
erland have produced an unusually great proportion of scientific
men.   Though, in part, this result may be ascribed to the original
natures of such refugees, who must have had that independence
which is a chief factor in originality, yet it is probably in part due
to mixture of races.   For thinking this, we have evidence which
is not open to two interpretations.   Prof. Morley draws attention
to the fact that, during seven hundred years of our early history,
"the best genius of England sprang up on the line of country in
which Celts and Anglo-Saxons came together."   In like manner,
Mr. Galton, in his "English Men of Science," shows that in recent
days these have mostly come from an inland region, running
generally from north to south; which we may reasonably presume
contains more mixed blood than do the regions east and west of
it.   Such a result seems probable *a priori*.   Two natures respectively adapted to slightly unlike sets of social conditions may be
expected by their union to produce a nature somewhat more plastic
than either—a nature more impressible by the new circumstances
of advancing social life, and therefore more likely to originate new
ideas and display modified sentiments.   The comparative psychology of man may, then, fitly include the mental effects of mixture;
and among derivative inquiries we may ask, How far the conquest
of race by race has been instrumental in advancing civilization by
aiding mixture, as well as in other ways?

II.—The second of the three leading divisions named at the outset
is less extensive.   Still, concerning the relative mental natures of
the sexes in each race, questions of much interest and importance
may be raised:

1. *Degree of Difference between the Sexes.*—It is an established
fact that, physically considered, the contrast between males and
females is not equally great in all types of mankind.   The bearded
races, for instance, show us a greater unlikeness between the two
than do the beardless races.   Among South American tribes, men
and women have a greater general resemblance in form, etc., than
is usual elsewhere.   The question, then, suggests itself, Do the

mental natures of the sexes differ in a constant or in a variable degree?   The differ- |264| ence is unlikely to be a constant one; and, looking for variation, we may ask what is its amount, and under what conditions does it occur?

2. *Difference in Mass and in Complexity.*—The comparisons between the sexes, of course, admit of subdivisions parallel to those made in comparisons between the races.   Relative mental mass and relative mental complexity have chiefly to be observed.   Assuming that the great inequality in the cost of reproduction to the two sexes is the cause of unlikeness in mental mass, as in physical mass, this difference may be studied in connection with reproductive differences presented by the various races, in respect of the ages at which reproduction commences, and the period over which it lasts. An allied inquiry may be joined with this; namely, how far the mental developments of the two sexes are affected by their relative habits in respect to food and physical exertion?   In many of the lower races, the women, treated with great brutality, are physically very inferior to the men; excess of labor and defect of nutrition being apparently the combined causes.   Is any arrest of mental development simultaneously caused?

3. *Variation of the Differences.*—If the unlikeness, physical and mental, of the sexes is not constant, then, supposing all races have diverged from one original stock, it follows that there must have been transmission of accumulated differences to those of the same sex in posterity.   If, for instance, the prehistoric type of man was beardless, then the production of a bearded variety implies that within that variety the males continued to transmit an increasing amount of beard to descendants of the same sex.   This limitation of heredity by sex, shown us in multitudinous ways throughout the animal kingdom, probably applies to the cerebral structures as much as to other structures.   Hence the question, Do not the mental natures of the sexes in alien types of man diverge in unlike ways and degrees?

4. *Causes of the Differences.*—Is any relation to be traced between this variable difference and the variable parts the sexes play in the business of life?   Assuming the cumulative effects of habit on function and structure, as well as the limitation of heredity by sex, it is to be expected that, if in any society the activities of one sex, generation after generation, differ from those of the other, there

will arise sexual adaptations of mind.   Some instances in illustration
may be named.   Among the Africans of Loango and other districts,
as also among some of the Indian Hill-tribes, the men and women
are strongly contrasted as respectively inert and energetic: the
industry of the women having apparently become so natural to
them that no coercion is needed.   Of course, such facts suggest an
extensive series of questions.   Limitation of heredity by sex may
account both for those sexual differences of mind which distinguish
men and women in all races and for those which distinguish them
in each race, or each so-|265|ciety.   An interesting subordinate
inquiry may be, how far such mental differences are inverted in
cases where there is inversion of social and domestic relations; as
among those Khasi Hill-tribes whose women have so far the upper
hand that they turn off their husbands in a summary way if they
displease them.

5. *Mental Modifiability in the Two Sexes.*—Along with comparisons of races in respect to mental plasticity may go parallel
comparisons of the sexes in each race.   Is it true always, as it
appears to be generally true, that women are less modifiable than
men?   The relative conservatism of women—their greater adhesion
to established ideas and practices—is manifest in many civilized and
semi-civilized societies.   Is it so among the uncivilized?   A curious
instance of greater adhesion to custom by women than by men is
given by Dalton, as occurring among the Juangs, one of the lowest
wild tribes of Bengal.   Until recently the only dress of both sexes
was something less than that which the Hebrew legend gives to
Adam and Eve.   Years ago the men were led to adopt a cloth
bandage round the loins, in place of the bunch of leaves; but the
women adhere to the aboriginal habit: a conservatism shown where
it might have been least expected.

6. *The Sexual Sentiment.*—Results of value may be looked for
from comparisons of races made to determine the amounts and
characters of the higher feelings to which the relation of the sexes
gives rise.   The lowest varieties of mankind have but small endow-
ments of these feelings.   Among varieties of higher types, such as
the Malayo-Polynesians, these feelings seem considerably developed:
the Dyaks, for instance, sometimes display them in great
strength.   Speaking generally, they appear to become stronger with
the advance of civilization.   Several subordinate inquiries may be

named: (*a.*) How far is development of the sexual sentiment dependent upon intellectual advance—upon growth of imaginative power?   (*b.*) How far is it related to emotional advance; and especially to evolution of those emotions which originate from sympathy: What are its relations to polyandry and polygyny? (*c.*) Does it not tend toward, and is it not fostered by, monogamy? (*d.*) What connection has it with maintenance of the family bond, and the consequent better rearing of children?

III.—Under the third head, to which we may now pass, come the more special traits of the different races:

1. *Imitativeness.*—One of the characteristics in which the lower types of men show us a smaller departure from reflex action than do the higher types is, their strong tendency to mimic the motions and sounds made by others—an almost involuntary habit which travellers find it difficult to check.   This meaningless repetition, which seems to imply that the idea of an observed action cannot be framed in the mind of the observer without tending forthwith to discharge itself in the action conceived (and every ideal action is a nascent form of the |266| consciousness accompanying performance of such action), evidently diverges but little from the automatic; and decrease of it is to be expected along with increase of self-regulating power.   This trait of automatic mimicry is evidently allied with that less automatic mimicry which shows itself in greater persistence of customs.   For customs adopted by each generation from the last, without thought or inquiry, imply a tendency to imitate which overmasters critical and skeptical tendencies: so maintaining habits for which no reason can be given.   The decrease of this irrational mimicry, strongest in the lowest savage and feeblest in the highest of the civilized, should be studied along with the successively higher stages of social life, as being at once an aid and a hindrance to civilization; an aid in so far as it gives that fixity to the social organization without which a society cannot survive; a hindrance in so far as it offers resistance to changes of social organization that have become desirable.

2. *Incuriosity.*—Projecting our own natures into the circumstances of the savage, we imagine ourselves as marvelling greatly on first seeing the products and appliances of civilized life.   But we err in supposing that the savage has feelings such as we should

have in his place.   Want of rational curiosity respecting these incomprehensible novelties is a trait remarked of the lowest races wherever found; and the partially-civilized races are distinguished from them as exhibiting rational curiosity.   The relation of this trait to the intellectual nature, to the emotional nature, and to the social state, should be studied.

3. *Quality of Thought.*—Under this vague head may be placed many sets of inquiries, each of them extensive: (*a.*) The degree of generality of ideas; (*b.*) The degree of abstractness of the ideas; (*c.*) The degree of definiteness of the ideas; (*d.*) The degree of coherence of the ideas; (*e.*) The extent to which there have been developed such notions as those of *class*, of *cause*, of *uniformity*, of *law*, of *truth*.   Many conceptions, which have become so familiar to us that we assume them to be the common property of all minds, are no more possessed by the lowest savages than they are by our own children; and comparisons of types should be so made as to elucidate the processes by which such conceptions are reached.   The development under each head has to be observed: (*a.*) Independently in its successive stages; (*b.*) In connection with the coöperative intellectual conceptions; (*c.*) In connection with the progress of language, of the arts, and of social organization.   Already linguistic phenomena have been used in aid of such inquiries; and more systematic use of them should be made.   Not only the number of general words, and the number of abstract words, in a people's vocabulary should be taken as evidence, but also their *degrees* of generality and abstractness; for there are generalities of the first, second, third, etc., orders and abstractions similarly ascending in degree.   *Blue* is an abstraction referring to one class of |267| impressions derived from visible objects; *color* is a higher abstraction, referring to many such classes of visual impressions; *property* is a still higher abstraction, referring to classes of impressions received not through the eyes alone, but through other sense-organs.   If generalities and abstractions were arranged in the order of their extensiveness and in their grades, tests would be obtained which, applied to the vocabularies of the uncivilized, would yield definite evidence of the intellectual stages reached.

4. *Peculiar Aptitudes.*—To such specialities of intelligence as marked different degrees of evolution have to be added the minor ones related to modes of life: the kinds and degrees of faculty which

have become organized in adaptation to daily habits—skill in the
use of weapons, powers of tracking, quick discrimination of individual objects.   And under this head may fitly come inquiries
concerning some race-peculiarities of the aesthetic class, not at
present explicable.   While the remains from the Dordogne caves
show us that their inhabitants, low as we must suppose them to
have been, could represent animals, both by drawing and carving,
with some degree of fidelity, there are existing races, probably
higher in other respects, who seem scarcely capable of recognizing
pictorial representations.   Similarly with the musical faculty.
Almost or quite wanting in some inferior races, we find it in other
races, not of high grade, developed to an unexpected degree, instance
the negroes, some of whom are so innately musical that, as I have
been told by a missionary among them, the children in native
schools, when taught European psalm-tunes, spontaneously sing
seconds to them.   Whether any causes can be discovered for race-
peculiarities of this kind is a question of interest.

    5. *Specialities of Emotional Nature.*—These are worthy of
careful study, as being intimately related to social phenomena—to
the possibility of social progress, and to the nature of the social
structure.   Of those to be chiefly noted there are—(*a.*) Gregariousness or sociality—a trait in the strength of which races differ
widely: some, as the Mantras, being almost indifferent to social
intercourse; others being unable to dispense with it.   Obviously the
degree of the desire for the presence of fellow-men affects greatly
the formation of social groups, and consequently underlies social
progress.   (*b.*) Intolerance of restraint.   Men of some inferior
types, as the Mapuché, are ungovernable; while those of other types,
no higher in grade,. not only submit to restraint, but admire the
persons exercising it.   These contrasted traits have to be observed
in connection with social evolution; to the early stages of which
they are respectively antagonistic and favorable.   (*c.*) The desire
for praise is a trait which, common to all races, high and low, varies
considerably in degree.   There are quite inferior races, as some of
those in the Pacific States, whose members sacrifice without stint
to gain the applause which lavish generosity brings; while, elsewhere,
applause is sought with less eagerness.   Notice should be |268| taken
of the connection between this love of approbation and the social
restraints, since it plays an important part in the maintenance of

them.   (*d*.) The acquisitive propensity.   This, too, is a trait the
various degrees of which, and the relations of which to the social
state, have to be especially noted.   The desire for property grows
along with the possibility of gratifying it; and this, extremely small
among the lowest men, increases as social development goes on.
With the advance from tribal property to family property and
individual property, the notion of private right of possession gains
definiteness, and the love of acquisition strengthens.   Each step
toward an orderly social state makes larger accumulations possible,
and the pleasures achievable by them more sure; while the resulting
encouragement to accumulate leads to increase of capital and further
progress.   This action and reaction of the sentiment and the social
state, should be in every case observed.

6. *The Altruistic Sentiments.*—Coming last, these are also highest.   The evolution of them in the course of civilization shows us
very clearly the reciprocal influences of the social unit and the social
organism.   On the one hand, there can be no sympathy, nor any
of the sentiments which sympathy generates, unless there are fellow-
beings around.   On the other hand, maintenance of union with
fellow-beings depends in part on the presence of sympathy, and the
resulting restraints on conduct.   Gregariousness or sociality favors
the growth of sympathy; increased sympathy conduces to closer
sociality and a more stable social state; and so, continuously, each
increment of the one makes possible a further increment of the
other.   Comparisons of the altruistic sentiments resulting from
sympathy, as exhibited in different types of men and different social
states, may be conveniently arranged under three heads: (*a*.) Pity,
which should be observed as displayed toward offspring, toward the
sick and aged, and toward enemies.   (*b*.) Generosity (duly discrim-
inated from the love of display) as shown in giving; as shown in the
relinquishment of pleasures for the sake of others; as shown by
active efforts on others' behalf.   The manifestations of this sentiment, too, are to be noted in respect of their range—whether they
are limited to relatives; whether they extend only to those of the
same society; whether they extend to those of other societies; and
they are also to be noted in connection with the degree of providence—whether they result from sudden impulses obeyed without
counting the cost, or go along with a clear foresight of the future
sacrifices entailed.   (*c*.) Justice.   This most abstract of the altruistic

sentiments is to be considered under aspects like those just named, as well as under many other aspects—how far it is shown in regard to the lives of others; how far in regard to their property, and how far in regard to their various minor claims.   And the comparisons of men in respect of this highest sentiment should, beyond all others, be carried on along with observations on the accompanying |269| social state, which it largely determines—the form and actions of government; the character of the laws; the relations of classes.

   Such, stated as briefly as consists with clearness, are the leading divisions and subdivisions under which the Comparative Psychology of Man may be arranged.   In going rapidly over so wide a field, I have doubtless overlooked much that should be included.   Doubtless, too, various of the inquiries named will branch out into subordinate inquiries well worth pursuing.   Even as it is, however, the programme is extensive enough to occupy numerous investigators who may with advantage take separate divisions.

   Though, after occupying themselves with primitive arts and products, anthropologists have devoted their attention mainly to the physical characters of the human races, it must, I think, be admitted that the study of these yields in importance to the study of their psychical characters.   The general conclusions to which the first set of inquiries may lead cannot so much affect our views respecting the highest classes of phenomena as can the general conclusions to which the second set may lead.   A true theory of the human mind vitally concerns us; and systematic comparisons of human minds, differing in their kinds and grades, will help us in forming a true theory.   Knowledge of the reciprocal relations between the characters of men and the characters of the societies they form must influence profoundly our ideas of political arrangements.   When the interdependence of individual nature and social structure is understood, our conceptions of the changes now taking place, and hereafter to take place, will be rectified.   A comprehension of mental development as a process of adaptation to social conditions, which are continually remoulding the mind, and are again remoulded by it, will conduce to a salutary consciousness of the remoter effects produced by institutions upon character, and will check the grave mischiefs which ignorant legislation now causes.   Lastly, a right theory of mental evolution as exhibited by humanity at large, giving a key, as it does, to the evolution of the individual mind, must help to rationalize our perverse methods of education, and so to raise intellectual power and moral nature.

TEN

EDWARD AUGUSTUS FREEMAN (1823–92)

Race and Language

Contemporary Review
Volume 29, 1877, pp. 711–41

Freeman must be ranked amongst the most vigorous promoters of Anglo-Saxonism in his age. As a historian, whose career culminated in the Regius Professorship at Oxford, he associated all that was best about the English past with the free Teutonic origins of the nation. It has been remarked that he never really recovered from having so fortunate a surname. In this essay, however, we find that the racial determinism which he employed far too easily elsewhere is carefully qualified. The piece takes up a major issue in nineteenth-century debate about race everywhere in Europe – the connections between breed and speech. Freeman considers the manner in which the recent intensification of nationalism, especially in Central Europe, has been affected by belief in such linkage. He counters the tendency, still common in the 1870s, to stress unduly the correlation between linguistic and racial kinship. None the less he is also keen to indicate that there are senses in which language does constitute at least 'a presumption of race'. Freeman shows that this is all the more important precisely because questions of racial 'belonging' have a subjective as well as objective element. Indeed, his essay shows an especially acute awareness of the ability of the race-concept to serve as the basis for political myths. The text concludes by suggesting that one prerequisite for true statemanship in the contemporary world is a grasp of the power of such racial identifications to transcend the boundaries of mere nationhood.

Those who have read their newspapers during the last few months
with becoming care must have been, perhaps a little startled, perhaps
a little amused, at the story of a deputation of Hungarian students
going to Constantinople to present a sword of honour to an Ottoman
general.   The address and the answer dwelled on the ancient kindred
of Turks and Magyars, on the long alienation of the dissevered
kinsfolk, on the return of both in these later times to a remembrance
of the ancient kindred and to the friendly feelings to which such
kindred gave birth... |712| The Magyar students seem to have
meant their address quite seriously.   And the Turkish general, if
he did not take it seriously, at least thought it wise to shape his
answer as if he did.   As a piece of practical politics, it sounds like
Frederick Barbarossa threatening to avenge the defeat of Crassus
upon Saladin, or like the French of the Revolutionary wars making
the Pope Pius of those days, answerable for the wrongs of Vercin-
getorix.   The thing sounds like comedy, almost like conscious
comedy.   But it is a kind of comedy which may become tragedy,
if the idea from which it springs gets so deeply rooted in men's
minds as to lead to any practical consequences.   As long as talk of
this kind does not get beyond the world of hot-headed students, it
may pass for a craze.   It would be more than a craze, if it should
be so widely taken up on either side that the statesmen on either
side find it expedient to profess to take it up also.

   To allege the real or supposed primaeval kindred between Magyars
and Ottomans as a ground for political action, or at least for political
sympathy, in the affairs of the present moment, is an extreme
case—some may be inclined to call it a *reductio ad absurdum*—of
a whole range of doctrines and sentiments which have in modern
days gained a great power over men's minds. |713| They have gained
so great a power that those who may regret their influence cannot
afford to despise it.   To make any practical inference from the
primaeval kindred of Magyar and Turk is indeed pushing the doctrine
of race, and of sympathies arising from race, as far as it well can
be pushed.   Without plunging into any very deep mysteries, without
committing ourselves to any dangerous theories in the darker regions
of ethnological inquiry, we may perhaps be allowed at starting to
doubt whether there is any real primaeval kindred between Turk
and Magyar.   It is for those who have gone specially deep into the
antiquities of the non-Aryan races to say whether there is or is

not. At all events, as far as the great facts of history go, the kindred is of the vaguest and most shadowy kind. It comes to little more than the fact that Magyars and Ottomans are alike non-Aryan invaders, who have made their way into Europe within recorded times, and that both have, rightly or wrongly, been called by the name of Turks. These do seem rather slender grounds on which to build up a fabric of national sympathy between two nations, when several centuries of living practical history all pull the other way. It is hard to believe that the kindred of Turk and Magyar was thought of when a Turkish Pasha ruled at Buda. Doubtless Hungarian Protestants often deemed, and not unreasonably deemed, that the contemptuous toleration of the Moslem Sultan was a lighter yoke than the persecution of the Catholic Emperor. But it was hardly on grounds of primaeval kindred that they made the choice. The ethnological dialogue held at Constantinople does indeed sound like ethnological theory run mad. But it is the very wildness of the thing which gives it its importance. The doctrine of race, and of sympathies springing from race, must have taken very firm hold indeed of men's minds before it could be carried out in a shape which we are tempted to call so grotesque as this.

The plain fact is that the new lines of scientific and historical inquiry which have been opened in modern times have had a distinct and deep effect upon the politics of the age. The fact may be estimated in many ways, but its existence as a fact cannot be denied. Not in a merely scientific or literary point of view, but in one strictly practical, the world is not the same world as it was when men had not yet dreamed of the kindred between Sanscrit, Greek, and English, when it was looked on as something of a paradox to hint that there was a distinction between Celtic and Teutonic tongues and nations. Ethnological and philological researches—I do not forget the distinction between the two, but for the present I must group them together—have opened the way for new national sympathies, new national antipathies, such as would have been unintelligible a hundred years ago. A hundred years ago a man's political likes and |714| dislikes seldom went beyond the range which was suggested by the place of his birth or immediate descent. Such birth or descent made him a member of this or that political community, a subject of this or that prince, a citizen—perhaps a subject—of this or that commonwealth. The political community

of which he was a member had its traditional alliances and traditional emnities, and by those alliances and enmities the likes and
dislikes of the members of that community were guided.   But those
traditional alliances and enmities were seldom determined by theories about language or race. Men might in this or that place be
discontented under a foreign government; but, as a rule, they were
discontented only if subjection to that foreign government brought
with it personal oppression, or at least political degradation.
Regard or disregard of some purely local privilege or local feeling
went for more than the fact of a government being native or
foreign.   What we now call the sentiment of nationality did not go
for much; what we call the sentiment of race went for nothing at
all.   Only a few men here and there would have understood the
feelings which have led to those two great events of our own time,
the political reunion of the German and Italian nations after their
long political dissolution.   Not a soul would have understood the
feelings which have allowed Panslavism to be a great practical
agent in the affairs of Europe, and which have made talk about
"the Latin race," if not practical, at least possible.   Least of all,
would it have been possible to give any touch of political importance
to what would have then seemed so wild a dream as a primaeval
kindred between Magyar and Ottoman.

   That feelings such as these, and the practical consequences which
have flowed from them, are distinctly due to scientific and historical
teaching there can, I think, be no doubt.   Religious sympathy and
purely national sympathy are both feelings of much simpler growth,
which need no deep knowledge nor any special teaching.   The cry
which resounded through Christendom when the Holy City was
taken by the Mussulmans, the cry which resounded through Islam
when the same city was taken by the Christians, the spirit which
armed England to support French Huguenots and which armed
Spain to support French Leaguers, all spring from motives which
lie on the surface.   Nor need we seek for any explanation but such
as lies on the surface for the natural wish for closer union between
Germans or Italians parted off by purely dynastic arrangements
from men who are their countrymen in everything else.   Such a
feeling has to strive with the counter feeling which springs from
local jealousies and local dislikes; but it is a perfectly simple feeling,
which needs no subtle research either to arouse or to understand

it.   So, if we |715| draw our illustrations from events which are
going on at the present moment, there is nothing but what is
perfectly simple in the feeling which calls Russia, as the most
powerful of Orthodox states, to the help of her Orthodox brethren
everywhere, and which calls the members of the Orthodox Church
everywhere to look to Russia as their protector.   The feeling may
have to strive against a crowd of purely political considerations,
and by those purely political considerations it may be outweighed.
But the feeling is in itself altogether simple and natural.   So again,
the people of Montenegro and of the neighbouring lands in Herze-
govina and by the *Bocche* of Cattaro feel themselves countrymen
in every sense but the political accident which places one section
of them under a rule purely national, another section under a rule
civilized but foreign, a third under a rule at once foreign and
barbarous.   They are drawn together by a tie which every one can
understand, by the same tie which would draw together the people
of three adjoining English counties, if any strange political accident
should part them asunder in like manner.   The feeling here is that
of nationality in the strictest sense, nationality in a purely local or
geographical sense.   It would exist all the same if Panslavism had
never been heard of; it might exist though those who feel it had
never heard of the Slavonic race at all.   It is altogether another
thing when we come to the doctrine of race, and of sympathies
founded on race, in the wider sense.   Here we have a feeling which
professes to bind together, and which as a matter of fact has had
a real effect in binding together, men whose kindred to one another
is not so obvious at first sight as the kindred of Germans, Italians,
or Slaves who are kept asunder by nothing but a purely artificial
political boundary.   It is a feeling at whose bidding the call to
union goes forth to men whose dwellings are geographically far
apart, men who may have had no direct dealings with one another
for years or for ages, men whose languages, though the scholar may
at once see that they are closely akin, may not be so closely akin
as to be mutually intelligible for common purposes.   A hundred
years back the Servian might have cried for help to the Russian on
the ground of common Orthodox faith; he would hardly have called
for help on the ground of common Slavonic speech and origin.   If
he had done so, it would have been rather by way of grasping at
any chance, however desperate or far-fetched, than as putting

forward a serious and well understood claim which he might expect
to find accepted and acted on by large masses of men.   He might
have received help, either out of genuine sympathy springing from
community of faith or from the baser motive that he could be made
use of as a convenient political tool.   He would have got but little
help purely on the ground of a community of blood and |716| speech
which had had no practical result for ages. When Russia in earlier
days interfered between the Turk and his Christian subjects, there
is no sign of any sympathy felt or possessed for Slaves as Slaves.
Russia dealt with Montenegro, not, as far as one can see, out of any
Slavonic brotherhood, but because an independent Orthodox state
at enmity with the Turk could not fail to be a useful ally.   The
earlier dealings of Russia with the subject nations were far more
busy among the Greeks than among the Slaves.   In fact, till quite
lately, all the Orthodox subjects of the Turk were in most European
eyes looked on as alike Greeks.   The Orthodox Church has been
commonly known as the Greek Church; and it has often been very
hard to make people understand that the vast mass of the members
of that so-called Greek Church are not Greek in any other sense.
In truth we may doubt whether, till comparatively lately, the subject
nations themselves were fully alive to the differences of race and
speech among them.   A man must in all times and places know
whether he speaks the same language as another man; but he does
not always go on to put his consciousness of difference into the
shape of a sharply drawn formula.   Still less does he always make
the difference the ground of any practical course of action.   The
Englishman in the first days of the Norman Conquest felt the
hardships of foreign rule, and he knew that those hardships were
owing to foreign rule.   But he had not learned to put his sense of
hardship into any formula about an oppressed nationality.   So,
when the policy of the Turk found that the subtle intellect of the
Greek could be made use of as an instrument of dominion over the
other subject nations, the Bulgarian felt the hardship of the state
of things in which, as it was proverbially said, his body was in
bondage to the Turk and his soul in bondage to the Greek.   But
we may suspect that that neatly turned proverb dates only from the
awakening of a distinctly national Bulgarian feeling in modern
times.   The Turk was felt to be an intruder and an enemy, because
his rule was that of an open oppressor belonging to another creed.

The Greek, on the other hand, though his spiritual dominion brought undoubted practical evils with it, was not felt to be an intruder and an enemy in the same sense. His quicker intellect and superior refinement made him a model. The Bulgarian imitated the Greek tongue and Greek manners; he was willing in other lands to be himself looked on as a Greek. It is only in quite modern times, under the direct influence of the preaching of the doctrine of race, that a hard and fast line has been drawn between Greeks and Bulgarians. That doctrine has cut two ways. It has given both nations, Greek and Bulgarian alike, a renewed national life, national strength, national hopes, such as neither of them had felt for ages. In so doing, it has done one of the best and most hopeful works |717| of the age. But in so doing, it has created one of the most dangerous of immediate political difficulties. In calling two nations into a renewed being, it has arrayed them in enmity against each other, and that in the face of a common enemy in whose presence all lesser differences and jealousies ought to be hushed into silence.

There is then a distinct doctrine of race, and of sympathies founded on race, distinct from the feeling of community of religion, and distinct from the feeling of nationality in the narrower sense. It is not so simple or easy a feeling as either of those two. It does not in the same way lie on the surface; it is not in the same way grounded on obvious facts which are plain to every man's understanding. The doctrine of race is essentially an artificial doctrine, a learned doctrine. It is an inference from facts which the mass of mankind could never have found out for themselves, facts which, without a distinctly learned teaching, could never be brought home to them in any intelligible shape. Now what is the value of such a doctrine? Does it follow that, because it is confessedly artificial, because it springs, not from a spontaneous impulse, but from a learned teaching, it is therefore necessarily foolish, mischievous, perhaps unnatural? It may perhaps be safer to hold that, like many other doctrines, many other sentiments, it is neither universally good nor universally bad, neither inherently wise nor inherently foolish. It may be safer to hold that it may, like other doctrines and sentiments, have a range within which it may work for good, while in some other range it may work for evil. It may in short be a doctrine which is neither to be rashly accepted nor rashly cast aside, but one which may need to be guided, regulated, modified, according

to time, place, and circumstance. I am not now called on so much
to estimate the practical good and evil of the doctrine as to work
out what the doctrine itself is, and to try to explain some difficulties
about it.   But I must emphatically say that nothing can be more
shallow, nothing more foolish, nothing more purely sentimental,
than the way of speaking of those who think that they can simply
laugh down or shriek down any doctrine or sentiment which they
themselves do not understand.   A belief or a feeling which has a
practical effect on the conduct of great masses of men, sometimes
on the conduct of whole nations, may be very false and very
mischievous; but it is in every case a great and serious fact, to be
looked gravely in the face.   Men who sit at their ease and think
that all wisdom is confined to themselves and their own clique may
think themselves vastly superior to the great emotions which stir
our times, as they would doubtless have thought themselves vastly
superior to the emotions which stirred the first Saracens or the first
Crusaders.   But the emotions are there all the same, and |718| they
do their work all the same.   The most highly educted man in the
most highly educated society cannot sneer them out of being with
a "but" or a "probably."

But it is time to pass to the more strictly scientific aspect of the
subject.   The doctrine of race, in its popular form, is the direct
offspring of the study of scientific philology; and yet it is just now,
in its popular form at least, somewhat under the ban of scientific
philologers.   There is nothing very wonderful in this.   It is in fact
the natural course of things, which might almost have been reckoned
on beforehand.   When the popular mind gets hold of a truth, it
seldom gets hold of it with strict scientific precision.   It commonly
gets hold of one side of the truth; it puts forth that side of the truth
only.   It puts that side forth in a form which may not be in itself
distorted or exaggerated, but which practically becomes distorted
and exaggerated, because other sides of the same truth are not
brought into their due relation with it.   The popular idea thus
takes a shape which is naturally offensive to men of strict precision,
and which men of strict scientific precision have naturally, and from
their own point of view quite rightly, risen up to rebuke.   Yet it
may often happen that, while the scientific statement is the only
true one for scientific purposes, the popular version may also have
a kind of practical truth for the somewhat rough and ready purposes

of a popular version.   In our present case scientific philologers are
beginning to complain, with perfect truth and perfect justice from
their own point of view, that the popular doctrine of race confounds
race and language.   They tell us, and they do right to tell us, that
language is no certain test of race, that men who speak the same
tongue are not therefore necessarily men of the same blood.   And
they tell us further that, from whatever quarter the alleged popular
confusion came, it certainly did not come from any teachings of
scientific philologers.   The truth of all this cannot be called in
question.   We have too many instances in recorded history of
nations laying aside the use of one language and taking to the use
of another, for any one who cares for accuracy to set down language
as any sure test of race.

***

|720| The study of men's skulls is a study which is strictly physical,
a study of facts over which the will of man has no direct control.
The study of men's languages is strictly an historical study, a study
of facts over which the will of man has a direct control.   It follows
therefore at once from the very nature of the two studies that
language cannot be an absolutely certain test of physical descent.
A man cannot, under any circumstances, choose his own skull; he
may, under some circumstances, choose his own language.   He
must keep the skull which has been given him by his parents; he
cannot, by any process of taking thought, determine what kind of
skull he will hand on to his own children.   But he may give up the
use of the language which he has learned from his parents, and he
may determine what language he will teach to his children.   The
physical characteristics of a race are unchangeable, or are changed
only by influences over which the race itself has no direct control.
The language which the race speaks may be changed, either by a
conscious act of the will or by that power of fashion which is in
truth the aggregate of countless unconscious acts of the will.   And,
as the very nature of the case thus shows that language is no sure
test of race, so the facts of recorded history equally prove the same
doctrine.   Both individuals and whole nations do in |721| fact often
exchange the language of their forefathers for some other language.
A man settles in a foreign country.   He learns the language of that
country; sometimes he forgets the use of his own language.   His

children may perhaps speak both tongues; if they speak one tongue only, it will be the tongue of the country where they live. In a generation or two all trace of foreign origin will have passed away. Here then language is no test of race. If the great-grandchildren speak the language of their great-grandfathers, it will simply be as they may speak any other foreign language. Here are men who by speech belong to one nation, by actual descent to another. If they lose the physical characteristics of the race to which the original settler belonged, it will be due to intermarriage, to climate, to some cause altogether independent of language. Every nation will have some adopted children of this kind, more or fewer, men who belong to it by speech, but who do not belong to it by race. And what happens in the case of individuals happens in the case of whole nations. The pages of history are crowded with cases in which nations have cast aside the tongue of their forefathers, and have taken instead the tongue of some other people. Greek in the East, Latin in the West, became the familiar speech of millions who had not a drop of Greek or Italian blood in their veins. The same has been the case in later times with Arabic, Persian, Spanish, German, English. Each of those tongues has become the familiar speech of vast regions where the mass of the people are not Arabian, Spanish, or English, otherwise than by adoption. The Briton of Cornwall has, slowly but in the end thoroughly, adopted the speech of England. In Ireland itself the crimes of the Saxon are for the most part denounced in the Saxon tongue. In the American continent full-blooded Indians preside over commonwealths which speak the tongue of Cortes and Pizarro. In the lands to which all eyes are now turned, the Greek, who has been busily assimilating strangers ever since he first planted his colonies in Asia and Sicily, goes on busily assimilating his Albanian neighbours. So between renegades, Janissaries, and mothers of all nations, the blood of many a Turk must be physically anything rather than Turkish. The inherent nature of the case, and the witness of recorded history, join together to prove that language is no certain test of race, and that the scientific philologers are doing good service to accuracy of expression and accuracy of thought by emphatically calling attention to the fact that language is no such test.

But, on the other hand, it is quite possible that the truth to which our attention is just now most fittingly called may, if put forth too broadly and without certain qualifications, lead to error quite as great as the error at which it is aimed.   I do not suppose |722| that any one ever thought that language was, necessarily and in all cases, an absolute and certain test.   If anybody has thought so, he has put himself altogether out of court by shutting his eyes to the most manifest facts of the case.   But there can be no doubt that many people have given too much importance to language as a test of race.   Though they have not wholly forgotten the facts which tell the other way, they have not brought them out with enough prominence.   And I can further believe that many people have written on the subject in a way which cannot be justified from a strictly scientific point of view, but which may have been fully justified from the point of view of the writers and speakers them-selves.   It may often happen that a way of speaking may not be scientifically accurate, but may yet be quite near enough to the truth for the purposes of the matter in hand.   It may, for some practical, or even historical purpose, be really more true than the statement which is scientifically more exact.   Language is no certain test of race; but if a man, struck by this wholesome warning, should run off into the belief that language and race have absolutely nothing to do with one another, he had better have gone without the warning.   For in such a case the last error would be worse than the first.   The natural instinct of mankind connects race and language.   It does not assume language as an infallible test of race; but it does assume that language and race have something to do with one another.   It assumes that, though language is not an accurately scientific test of race, yet it is a rough and ready test which does for many practical purposes.   To make something more of an exact definition, one might say that, though language is not a test of race, it is, in the absence of evidence to the contrary, a presumption of race—that, though it is not a test of race, yet it is a test of something which, for many practical purposes, is the same as race.

Professor Max Müller warned us long ago that we must not speak of a Celtic skull.   Mr. Sayce has more lately warned us that we must not infer from community of Aryan speech that there is any kindred in blood between this or that Englishman and this or that Hindoo.   And the warning is scientifically true.   Yet any one who begins his studies on these matters with Professor Müller's famous Oxford Essay will practically come to another way of looking at things. He will fill his mind with a vivid picture of the great Aryan family, as yet one, dwelling in one place, speaking one tongue, having already taken the first steps towards settled society, recognizing the domestic relations, possessing the first rudiments of government and religion, and calling all these first elements of culture by names of which traces still abide here and there among the many nations of the common stock. He will go on to draw pictures equally vivid of the several |723| branches of the family parting off from the primaeval home. One great branch he will see going to the south-east, to become the forefathers of the vast, yet isolated, colony in the Asiatic lands of Persia and India. He watches the remaining mass sending off wave after wave, to become the forefathers of the nations of historical Europe. He traces out how each branch starts with its own share of the common stock; how the language, the creed, the institutions, once common to all, grow up into different, yet kindred, shapes, among the many parted branches which grew up, each with an independent life and strength of its own. This is what our instructors teach us as being the true origin of nations and their languages. And, in drawing out the picture, we cannot avoid, our teachers themselves do not avoid, the use of language which implies that the strictly family relation, the relation of community of blood, is at the root of the whole matter. We cannot help talking about the family and its branches, about parents, children, brothers, sisters, cousins. The nomenclature of natural kindred exactly fits the case; it fits it so exactly that no other nomenclature could enable us to set forth the case with any clearness. Yet we cannot be absolutely certain that there was any real community of blood in the whole story. We really know nothing of the origin of language or the origin of society. We may make a thousand ingenious guesses; but we cannot prove any of them. It may be that the group which came together, and which formed the primaeval society which spoke the primaeval Aryan tongue, were not brought together by community of blood, but by some other cause which threw them in one another's way. If we accept the Hebrew genealogies, they need not have had any community of blood nearer than common descent from Adam and Noah. That is, they need not have been all children of Shem, of

Ham, or of Japheth; some children of Shem, some of Ham, and some of Japheth may have been led by some cause to settle together. Or if we believe in independent creations of men, or in the development of men out of mollusks, the whole of the original society need not have been descendants of the same man or the same mollusk.   In short, there is no theory of the origin of man which requires us to believe that the primaeval Aryans were a natural family; they may have been more like a club or an accidental party of fellow-travellers.   And if we accept them as a natural family, it does not follow that the various branches which grew into separate races and nations, speaking separate, though kindred, languages were necessarily marked off by more immediate kindred.   It may be that there is no nearer kindred among Persians or Greeks or Teutons than the general kindred of all Aryans.   For, when this or that party marched off from the common home, it does not follow that those who marched off together were neces-|724|sarily immediate brothers and cousins.   The party which grew into Hindoos or into Teutons may not have been made up exclusively of one set of near kinsfolk.   Some of the children of the same parents or forefathers may have marched one way, while others marched another way, or stayed behind.   We may, if we please, indulge our fancy by conceiving that there actually may be family distinctions older than distinctions of nation and race.   It may be that the Gothic Amali and the Roman Aemilii—I throw out the idea as a mere illustration—were branches of a family which had taken a name before the division of Teuton and Italian.   Some of the members of that family may have joined the band of which came the Goths, while other members joined the band of which came the Romans.   There is no difference but the length of time to distinguish such a supposed case from the case of an English family, one branch of which settled in the seventeenth century at Boston in Massachusetts, while another branch stayed behind at Boston in Holland.   Mr. Sayce says truly that the use of a kindred language does not prove that the Englishman and the Hindoo are really akin in race; for, as he adds, many Hindoos are men of non-Aryan race who have simply learned to speak tongues of Sanscrit origin.   He might have gone on to say, with equal truth, that there is no positive certainty that there was any community in blood among the original Aryan group itself, and that, if we admit such community of blood in the original Aryan group, it does not follow that there is any further special kindred between Hindoo and Hindoo or between Teuton and Teuton.   The original group may not have been a family, but an artificial union.   And, if it was a family, those of its members who marched together east or west or north or south may have had no tie of kindred beyond the common cousinhood of all.

Now the tendency of this kind of argument is to lead to something a good deal more startling than the doctrine that language is no certain test of race.   Its tendency is to go on further, and to show that race is no certain test of community of blood.   And this comes pretty nearly to saying that there is no such thing as race at all. For our whole conception of race starts from the idea of community of blood.   If the word "race" does not mean community of blood, it is hard to see what it does mean.   Yet it is certain that there can be no positive proof of real community of blood, even among those groups of mankind which we instinctively speak of as families and races.   It is not merely that the blood has been mingled in after times; there is no positive proof that there was any community of blood in the beginning.   No living Englishman can prove with absolute certainty that he comes in the male line of any of the Teutonic settlers in Britain in the fifth or sixth centuries.   I say in the male line, because any one |725| who is descended from any English king can prove such descent, though he can prove it only through a long and complicated web of female successions.   But we may be sure that in no other case can such a pedigree be proved by the kind of proof which lawyers would require to make out the title to an estate or a peerage.   The actual forefathers of the modern Englishman may chance to have been, not true-born Angles or Saxons, but Britons, Scots, in later days Frenchmen, Flemings, men of any other nation who learned to speak English and took to themselves English names.   But supposing that a man could make out such a pedigree, supposing that he could prove that he came in the male line of some follower of Hengest or Cerdic, he would be no nearer to proving original community of blood either in the particular Teutonic race or in the general Aryan family.   If direct evidence is demanded, we must give up the whole doctrine of families and races, as far as we take language, manners, institutions, anything but physical conformation, as the distinguishing marks of races and families.   That is to say, if we wish never to use any word of whose accuracy we cannot be perfectly certain, we must leave off speaking of races and families at all from any but the purely physical side. We must content ourselves with saying that certain groups of mankind have a common history, that they have languages, creeds, and institutions in common, but that we have no evidence whatever to show how they came to have languages, creeds, and institutions in common.   We cannot say for certain what was the tie which brought the members of the original group together, any more than we can name the exact time and the exact place when and where they came together.

We may thus seem to be landed in a howling wilderness of scientific uncertainty.   The result of pushing our inquiries so far may seem to be to show that we really know nothing at all.   But in truth the uncertainty is no greater than the uncertainty which attends all inquiries in the historical sciences.   Though a historical fact may be recorded in the most trustworthy documents, though it may have happened in our own times, though we may have seen it happen with our own eyes, yet we cannot have the same certainty about it as the mathematician has about the proposition which he proves to absolute demonstration.   We cannot have even that lower degree of certainty which the geologist has with regard to the bare order of succession between this and that stratum.   For in all historical inquiries we are dealing with facts which themselves come within the control of human will and human caprice, and the evidence for which depends on the trustworthiness of human informants, who may either purposely deceive or unwittingly mislead. A man may lie; he may err. |726| The triangles and the rocks can neither lie nor err.   I may with my own eyes see a certain man do a certain act; he may tell me himself, or some one else may tell me, that he is the same man who did some other act; but as to his statement I cannot have absolute certainty, and no one but myself can have absolutely certainty as to the statement which I make as to the facts I saw with my own eyes.   Historical evidence may range through every degree from the barest likelihood to that undoubted moral certainty on which every man acts without hesitation in practical affairs.   But it cannot get beyond this last standard.   If then we are ever to use words like race, family, or even nation, to denote groups of mankind marked off by any kind of historical, as distinguished from physical, characteristics, we must be content to use those words, as we use many other words, without being able to prove that our use of them is accurate, as mathematicians judge of accuracy.   I cannot be quite sure that William the Conqueror landed at Pevensey, though I have strong reasons for believing that he did so.   And I have strong reasons for believing many facts about race and language about which I am much further from being quite sure than I am about William's landing at Pevensey.   In short, in all these matters, we must be satisfied to let presumption very largely take the place of actual proof; and, if we only let presumption in, most of our difficulties at once fly away.   Language is no certain test of race; but it is a presumption of race.   Community of race, as we commonly understand race, is no certain proof of original community of blood; but it is a presumption of original community of blood.   The presumption amounts to moral proof, if only we do not insist on proving such natural community of blood as would satisfy a genealogist. It amounts to moral proof, if all that we seek is to establish a relation in which the community of blood is the leading idea, and in which, where natural community of blood does not exist, its place is supplied by something which by a legal fiction is looked upon as its equivalent.

If then we do not ask for scientific, for what we may call physical, accuracy, but if we are satisfied with the kind of proof which is all that we can ever get in the historical sciences—if we are satisfied to speak in a way which is true for popular and practical purposes—then we may say that language has a great deal to do with race, as race is commonly understood, and that race has a great deal to do with community of blood.   If we once admit the Roman doctrine of adoption, our whole course is clear.   The natural family is the starting point of everything; but we must give the natural family the power of artificially enlarging itself by admitting adoptive members.   A group of mankind is thus formed, in which it does not follow that all the members have |727| any natural community of blood, but in which community of blood is the starting point, in which those who are connected by natural community of blood form the original body within whose circle the artificial members are admitted.   A group of mankind thus formed is something quite different from a fortuitous concurrence of atoms.   Three or four

brothers by blood, with a fourth or fifth man whom they agreed to
look on as filling in everything the same place as a brother by blood,
form a group which is quite unlike an union of four or five men,
none of whom is bound by any tie of blood to any of the others.
In the latter kind of union the notion of kindred does not come in
at all.   In the former kind the notion of kindred is the groundwork
of everything; it determines the character of every relation and
every action, even though the kindred between some members of
the society and others may be owing to a legal fiction and not to
natural descent.   All that we know of the growth of tribes, races,
nations, leads us to believe that they grew in this way.   Natural
kindred was the groundwork, the leading and determining idea; but,
by one of those legal fictions which have had such an influence on
all institutions, adoption was allowed to count as natural
kindred.*. . .

|728| Now it is plain that, as soon as we admit the doctrine of
artificial kindred, that is as soon as we allow the exercise of the law
of adoption, physical purity of race is at an end.   Adoption treats
a man as if he were really the son of a certain father; it cannot
really make him the son of that father.   If a brachykephalic father
adopts a dolichokephalic son, the legal act cannot change the shape
of the adopted son's skull.   I will not undertake to say whether,
not indeed the rite of adoption, but the influences and circumstances
which would spring from it, might not, in the course of generations,
affect even the skull of the man who entered a certain *gens*, tribe,
or nation by artificial adoption only.   If by any chance the adopted
son spoke a different language from the adopted father, the rite of
adoption itself would not of itself change its language.   But it
would bring him under influences which would make himself adopt
the language of his new *gens* by a conscious act of the will, and
which would make his children adopt it by the same unconscious
act of the will by which each child adopts the language of his
parents.   The adopted son, still more the son of the adopted son,
became, in everything but physical descent, in speech, in feelings,

* I am here applying to this particular purpose a line of thought which both
myself and others have often applied to other purposes.   See above all Sir Henry
Maine's Lecture "on Kinship as the Basis of Society" in the "Lectures on the Early
History of Institutions;" and I would refer also to my own lecture on "the State"
in "Comparative Politics."

in worship, one with the *gens* into which he was adopted. He became one of that *gens* for all practical, political, historical purposes. It is only the physiologist who could deny his right to his new position. The nature of the process is well expressed by a phrase of our own law. When the nation—the word itself keeps about it the remembrance of birth as the groundwork of everything—adopts a new citizen, that is a new child of the state, he is said to be naturalized. That is, a legal process puts him in the same position, and gives him the same rights, as a man who is a citizen and a son by birth. It is assumed that the rights of citizenship come by nature, that is by birth. The stranger is admitted to them only by a kind of artificial birth; he is naturalized by law; his children are in a generation or two naturalized in fact. There is now no practical distinction between the Englishman whose forefathers landed with William, or even between the Englishman whose forefathers sought shelter from Alva or from Lewis the Fourteenth, and the Englishman whose forefathers landed with Hengest. It is for the physiologist to say whether any difference· can be traced in their several skulls; for all practical purposes, historical or political, all distinction between these several classes has passed away.

We may in short say that the law of adoption runs through everything, and that it may be practised on every scale. What adoption is at the hands of the family, naturalization is at the hands |729| of the state. And the same process extends itself from adopted or naturalized individuals to large classes of men, indeed to whole nations. When the process takes place on this scale, we may best call it assimilation. Thus Rome assimilated the continental nations of Western Europe to that degree that, allowing for a few scraps and survivals here and there, not only Italy, but Gaul and Spain, became Roman. The people of those lands, admitted step by step to the Roman franchise, adopted the name and tongue of Romans. It must soon have been hard to distinguish the Roman colonist in Gaul or Spain from the native Gaul or Spaniard who had, as far as in him lay, put on the guise of a Roman. This process of assimilation has gone on everywhere and at all times. Which of the nations that come into close contact shall assimilate the other, or whether neither shall assimilate the other, depends on a crowd of circumstances. Sometimes the conquerors assimilate their subjects; some-

times they are assimilated by their subjects.   Which form the
process takes in each particular case will depend, partly on their
respective numbers, partly on their degrees of civilization.   A small
number of less civilized conquerors will easily be lost among a
greater number of more civilized subjects, and that even though
they give their name to the land and people which they conquer.
The modern Frenchman represents, not the conquering Frank, but
the conquered Gaul, or as he called himself, the conquered
Roman.   The modern Bulgarian represents, not the Finnish conqueror, but the conquered Slave.   And so we might go on with
endless other cases.   The point is that the process of adoption,
naturalization, assimilation, has gone on everywhere.   No nation
can boast of absolute purity of blood, though no doubt some nations
come much nearer to it than others.   When I speak of purity of
blood, I leave out of sight the darker questions which I have already
raised with regard to the groups of mankind in days before recorded
history.   I assume great groups like Celtic, Teutonic, Slavonic, as
having what we may call a real corporate existence, however we
may hold that that corporate existence began.   My present point
is that no existing nation is, in the physiologist's sense of purity,
purely Celtic, Teutonic, Slavonic, or anything else.   All races have
assimilated a greater or less amount of foreign elements.   Taking
this standard, one which comes more nearly within the range of our
actual knowledge than the possibilities of unrecorded times, we may
again say that, from the purely scientific or physiological point of
view, not only is language no test of race, but that, at all events
among the great nations of the world, there is no such thing as
purity of race at all.

But, while we admit this truth, while we even insist upon it from
the strictly scientific point of view, we must be allowed to look at
it |730| with different eyes from a more practical standing point.
This is the standing point, whether of history which is the politics
of the past, or of politics which are the history of the present.
From this point of view, we may say unhesitatingly that there are
such things as races and nations, and that to the grouping of those
races and nations language is the best guide.   We cannot undertake
to define with any philosophical precision the exact distinction
between race and race, between nation and nation.   Nor can we
undertake to define with the like precision in what way the dis-

tinctions between race and race, between nation and nation,
began.   But all analogy leads us to believe that tribes, nations,
races, were all formed according to the original model of the family,
the family which starts from the idea of the community of blood,
but which allows artifical adoption to be its legal equivalent.   The
point is that, in all cases of adoption, naturalization, assimilation,
whether of individuals or of large classes of men, the adopted person
or class is strictly adopted into an existing community.   Their
adoption undoubtedly influences the community into which they are
adopted.   It at once destroys any claim on the part of that
community to purity of blood, and it influences the adopting
community in many ways, physical and moral.   A family, a tribe,
or a nation which has largely recruited itself by adopted members
cannot be the same as one which has never practised adoption at
all, but all whose members come of the original stock.   But the
influence of the adopting community on its adopted members is far
greater than any influence which they exercise upon it.   It cannot
change their blood; it cannot give them new natural forefathers;
but it may do everything short of this; it may make them, in speech,
in feeling, in thought, and in habit, genuine members of the
community which has artifically made them its own.   While there
is not in any nation, in any race, any such thing as strict purity of
blood, yet there is in each nation, in each race, a dominant element,
or rather something more than an element, something which is the
true essence of the race or nation, something which sets its standard
and determines its character, something which draws to itself and
assimilates to itself all other elements.   It so works that all other
elements are not co-equal elements with itself, but mere infusions
poured into an already existing body.   Doubtless these infusions
do in some measure influence the body which assimilates them; but
the influence which they exercise is as nothing compared to the
influence which they undergo.   We may say that they modify the
character of the body into which they are assimilated; they do not
affect its personality.   Thus, assuming the great groups of mankind
as primary facts, the origin of which lies beyond our certain
knowledge, we may speak of families and races, of the great Aryan
family and of the |731| races into which it parted, as groups which
have a real, practical, existence, as groups founded on the ruling
primaeval idea of kindred, even though in many cases the kindred

may not be by natural descent, but only by law of adoption. The Celtic, Teutonic, Slavonic races of man are real living and abiding groups, the distinction between which we must accept among the primary facts of history. And they go on as living and abiding groups, even though we know that each of them has assimilated many adopted members, sometimes from other branches of the Aryan family, sometimes from races of men alien to the whole Aryan stock. These races which, in a strictly physiological point of view, have no existence at all, have a real existence from the more practical point of view of history and politics. The Bulgarian calls to the Russian for help, and the Russian answers to his call for help, on the ground of their being alike members of the one Slavonic race. It may be that, if we could trace out the actual pedigree of this or that Bulgarian, of this or that Russian, we might find either that there was no real kindred between them, or we might find out that there was a real kindred, but a kindred which must be traced up to another stock than that of the Slave. In point of actual blood, instead of both being Slaves, it may be that one of them comes, it may be that both of them come, of a stock which is not Slavonic or even Aryan. The Bulgarian may chance to be a Bulgarian in a truer sense than he thinks for; he may come of the blood of the original Finnish conquerors, who gave the Bulgarian name to the Slaves among whom they were merged, while they adopted their Slavonic language. And if this or that Bulgarian may chance to come of the stock of the Finnish conqueror assimilated by his Slavonic subjects, this or that Russian may chance to come of the stock of Finnish subjects assimilated by their Slavonic conquerors. It may then so happen that the cry for help goes up and is answered on a ground of kindred which in the eye of the physiologist has no existence. Or the kindred may be real in a way which neither the suppliant nor his helper thinks of; the real kindred may have utterly passed out of the mind of either, while the cry is sent up and answered on the ground of a kindred which in this sense is purely imaginary. But in either case, for the practical purposes of human life, the plea is a good plea; the kindred on which it is founded is a real kindred. It is good by the law of adoption. It is good by the law the force of which we all admit whenever we count a man as an Englishman whose forefathers, two generations or twenty generations back, came to our shores as strangers. For all practical purposes, for all the purposes which guide men's actions, public or private, the Russian and the Bulgarian, kinsmen so long parted, perhaps in very truth no natural |732| kinsmen at all, are members of the same race, bound together by the common sentiment of race.   They belong to the same race, exactly as an Englishman whose forefathers came into Britain fourteen hundred years back, and an Englishman whose forefathers came only one or two hundred years back, are alike members of the same nation, bound together by a tie of common nationality.

And now, having ruled that races and nations, though largely formed by the working of an artificial law, are still real and living things, groups in which the idea of kindred is the idea around which everything has grown, how are we to define our races and our nations?   How are we to mark them off one from the other? Bearing in mind the cautions and qualifications which have been already given, bearing in mind large classes of exceptions which will presently be spoken of, I say unhesitatingly that for practical purposes there is one test, and one only, and that that test is language.   We may at least apply the test negatively.   It might be unsafe to rule that all speakers of the same language have a common nationality; but we may safely say that, where there is not community of language, there is no common nationality in the highest sense.   As in the teeth of community of language there may be what for all political purposes are separate nations, so without community of language there may be an artificial nationality, a nationality which may be good for all political purposes, and which may engender a common national feeling.   Still this is not quite the same thing as that fuller national unity which is felt where there is community of language.   In fact mankind instinctively takes language as the badge of nationality.   We so far take it as the badge, that we instinctively assume community of language as a nation as the rule, and we set down anything that departs from that rule as an exception.   The first idea suggested by the word Frenchman or German or any other national name, is that he is a man who speaks French or German as his mother-tongue.   We take for granted, in the absence of anything to make us think otherwise, that a Frenchman is a speaker of French and that a speaker of French is a Frenchman.   Where in any case it is otherwise, we mark that case as an exception, and we ask the special cause.   The rule is none the less the rule nor the exceptions the exceptions, because the exceptions may easily outnumber the instances which conform to the rule.   The rule is still the rule, because we take the instances which conform to it as a matter of course, while in every case which does not conform to it we ask for the explanation.   All the larger countries of Europe provide us with exceptions; but we treat them all as exceptions.   We do not ask why a native of France speaks French.   But when a native of France speaks as his mother-tongue some other tongue than French, when French is |733| spoken as his mother-tongue by some one who is not a native of France, we at once ask the reason.   And the reason will be found in each case in some special historical cause which withdraws that case from the operation of the general law.   So again, within the bounds of Great Britain, if we find any tongue spoken other than English, we at once ask the reason and we learn the special historic cause. In a part of France and a part of Great Britain we find tongues spoken which differ alike from English and from French, but which are strongly akin to one another.   We find that these are the survivals of a group of tongues once common to Gaul and Britain, but which the settlement of other nations, the introduction and the growth of other tongues, have brought down to the level of survivals.   So again we find islands which both speech and geographical position seem to mark as French, but which are dependencies, and loyal dependencies, of the English crown.   We soon learn the cause of the phaenomenon which seems so strange.   Those islands are the remains of a state and a people which had adopted the French tongue, but which, while it remained one, did not become a part of the French state.   That people brought England by force of arms under the rule of their own sovereigns.   The greater part of that people were afterwards conquered by France; but a remnant of them still clave to their connexion with the land which their forefathers had conquered....

|734| In the cases which we have just spoken of, the growth of the nation as marked out by language, and the growth of the exceptions to the rule of language, have both come through the gradual, unconscious working of historical causes.   There was no moment when any one deliberately proposed to form a French nation by joining together all the separate duchies and counties which spoke the French tongue.   Since the French nation has been formed, men

have proposed to annex this or that land on the ground that its
people spoke the French tongue, or perhaps only some tongue akin
to the French tongue.   But the formation of the French nation
itself was the work of historical causes, the work doubtless of a
settled policy acting through many generations, but not the work
of any conscious theory about races and languages.   It is a special
mark of our time, a special mark of the influence which doctrines
about race and language have had on men's minds, that we have
seen great nations united by processes in which theories of race and
language have really had much to do with bringing about their
union.   If statesmen have not been themselves moved by such
theories, they have at least found that it suited their purpose to
make use of such theories as a means of working on the minds of
others.   In the reunion of the severed German and Italian nations,
the conscious feeling of nationality, and the acceptance of a common
language as the outward badge of nationality, had no small share.
Poets sang of language as the badge of national union; statesmen
made it the badge, so far as political considerations did not lead
them to do anything else.   The revived kingdom of Italy is very
far from taking in all the speakers of the Italian tongue.   Lugano,
Trent, Aquileia, Trieste, Zara, form no part of the Italian political
body, and Corsica is not under the same rule as the other two great
neighbouring islands.   But the fact that all these places do not
belong to that body at once suggests the twofold question, why they
do not belong to it, and whether they ought not to belong to it.
History easily answers the first question; it may perhaps also answer
the second question in a way which will say Yes as regards one
place and No as regards another.   Ticino must not lose her higher
freedom; Dalmatia must not be cut off from the Slavonic mainland;
Corsica would seem to have sacrificed national feeling to personal
hero-worship.   But it is certainly hard to see why Trent and
Aquileia should be kept apart from the Italian body.   On the other
hand, the revived Italian kingdom contains very little which is not
Italian in speech.   It is perhaps by a |735| somewhat elastic view
of language that the dialect of Piedmont and the dialect of Sicily
are classed under one head; still, as a matter of fact, they have a
single classical standard, and they are universally accepted as
varieties of the same tongue.   But it is only in a few Alpine valleys
that languages are spoken which, whether Romance or Teutonic,

are in any case not Italian.   The reunion of Italy in short took in all that was Italian, save when some political cause hindered the rule of language from being followed.   Of anything not Italian so little has been taken in that the non-Italian parts of Italy, Aosta and the Seven German Communes, fall under the rule that there are some things too small for laws to pay heed to.

In the case of Germany the exceptions both ways are more numerous and more striking.   Still they are exceptions.   Wherever German-speaking people dwell outside the bounds of the revived German state, wherever that revived German state contains other than German-speaking people, we ask, and we can find the reason either way.   Political reasons forbade the immediate annexation of Austria, Tyrol, and Salzburg.   Combined political and geographical reasons, and, if we look a little deeper, ethnological reasons too, forbade the annexation of Courland, Livonia, and Esthonia.   Some reason or other will, it may be hoped always be found to hinder the annexation of lands which, like Zürich and Bern, have reached a higher political level.   Outlying brethren in Transsilvania or at Saratof come again under the rule "De minimis non curat lex." On the other hand, where French or Danish or Slave or Lithuanian is spoken within the bounds of the new Empire, it is almost wholly in corners, corners won by conquest and that mainly by recent conquest.   And on the principle that language is the badge of nationality, that without community of language nationality is imperfect, one main object of modern policy is to bring these exceptional districts under the general rule by spreading the German language in them.   Everywhere in short, wherever a power is supposed to be founded on nationality, the common feeling of mankind instinctively takes language as the test of nationality. We assume language as the test of a nation, without going into any minute question as to the physical purity of blood in that nation. A continuous territory, living under the same government and speaking the same tongue, forms a nation for all practical purposes. If some of its inhabitants do not belong to the original stock by blood, they at least belong to it by adoption.

The question may now fairly be asked, what is the case of those parts of the world where people who are confessedly of different races and languages inhabit a continuous territory and live under the same government?   How do we define nationality in such cases

|736| as these?   The answer will be very different in different cases, according to the means by which the different national elements in such a territory have been brought together.   They may form what I have already called an artificial nation, united by an act of its own free-will.   Or it may be simply a case where distinct nations, distinct in everything which can be looked on as forming a nation, except the possession of an independent government, are brought together, by whatever causes, under a common ruler.   The former case is very distinctly an exception which proves the rule and the latter is, though in quite another way, an exception which proves the rule also.   Both cases may need somewhat more in the way of definition.   We will begin with the first, the case of a nation which has been formed out of elements which differ in language, but which still have been brought together into an artificial nation.   In the other cases of which we have spoken thus far, the object which was consciously or unconsciously followed has been the formation of a nation marked out by language, and within whose bounds the use of any tongue other than the dominant tongue of the nation should be at least exceptional.   But there is one nation in Europe, one which has a full right to be called a nation in a political sense, which has been formed on the directly opposite principle.   The Swiss Confederation has been formed by the union of certain detached fragments of the German, Italian, and Burgundian nations.   It may indeed be said that the process has been in some sort a process of adoption, that the Italian and Burgundian elements have been incorporated into an already existing German body, that, as those elements were once subjects or dependencies or protected allies, the case is one of clients or freedmen being admitted to the full privileges of the *gens*.   This is undoubtedly true, and it is equally true of a large part of the German element itself.   Throughout the Confederation, allies and subjects have been raised to the rank of confederates.   But the former position of the component elements does not matter for our purpose.   As a matter of fact, the foreign dependencies have all been admitted into the Confederation on equal terms.   German is undoubtedly the language of a great majority of the Confederation; but the two recognized Romance languages are each the speech, not of a mere fragment or survival, but of a large minority forming a visible element in the general body.   The three languages are all of them alike recognized as national lan-

guages, though, as if to keep up the universal rule that there should be some exceptions to all rules, a fourth language still lives on within the bounds of the Confederation, which is not admitted to the rights of the other three, but is left in the state of a fragment or a survival. Is such an artificial body as this to be |737| called a nation? It is plainly not a nation by blood or by speech. It can hardly be called a nation by adoption. For if we chose to say that the three elements of all agreed to adopt one another as brethren, yet it has been adoption without assimilation. Yet surely the Swiss Confederation is a nation. It is not a mere power, in which various nations are brought together, whether willingly or unwillingly, under a common ruler, but without any further tie of union. For all political purposes, the Swiss Confederation is a nation, one capable of as strong and true national feeling as any other nation. Yet it is a nation purely artificial, one in no way defined by blood or speech. It thus proves the rule in two ways. We at once recognize this artifically formed nation, which has no common language, but each of whose elements speaks a language common to itself with some other nation, as something different from those nations which are defined by an universal or at least a predominant language. We mark it as an exception, as something different from other cases. And when we see how nearly this artificial nation comes, in every point but that of language, to the likeness of those nations which are defined by language, we see that it is the nation defined by language which sets the standard, and after the model of which the artificial nation forms itself. The case of the Swiss Confederation and its claim to rank as a nation would be like the case of those *gentes*, if any such there were, which did not spring even from the expansion of an original family, but which were artificially formed in imitation of those which did, and which, instead of a real or traditional forefather, chose for themselves an adopted one.

In the Swiss Confederation then we have a case of a nation formed by an artificial process, but which still is undoubtedly a nation in the face of other nations. We now come to the other class, in which nationality and language keep the connexion which they have elsewhere, but in which nations do not even in the roughest way answer to governments. We have only to go into the Eastern lands of Europe to find a state of things in which the notion of nationality, as marked out by language and national feeling, has altogether parted company from the notion of political government. It must be remembered that this state of things is not confined to the nations which are under the yoke of the Turk. It extends also to the nations or fragments of nations which make up the Austro-Hungarian monarchy. On the state of things under the Turk there is no need to enlarge |738| here. The essence of his rule is the trampling under foot of all national right. No one would be so unjust as to place the other great composite dominion on a level with his mere barbarian oppression. Yet that composite dominion is just as much opposed to those ideas of nationality towards which Western Europe has been long feeling its way. We have seen by the example of Switzerland that it is possible to make an artificial nation out of fragments which have split off from three several nations. But the Austro-Hungarian monarchy is not a nation, not even an artificial nation of this kind. Its elements are not bound together in the same way as the three elements of the Swiss Confederation. It does indeed contain one whole nation, in the form of the Magyars; we might say that it contains two, if we reckon the Czechs for a distinct nation. Besides these, there are Germans, Italians, Roumans, Slaves of almost every branch of the Slavonic race. Here, as on the other side of the Ottoman border, there is plenty of living and active national feeling; but, while in the West political arrangements for the most part follow the great lines of national feeling, in the East the only way in which national feeling can show itself is by protesting, whether in arms or otherwise, against existing political arrangements. Save the Magyars alone, the ruling race in the Hungarian kingdom, there is no case in those lands in which the whole continuous territory inhabited by speakers of the same tongue is placed under a separate national government of its own. And, even in this case, the identity between nation and government is imperfect in two ways. It is imperfect, because, after all, though Hungary has a separate national government in internal matters, yet it is not the Hungarian kingdom, but the Austro-Hungarian monarchy of which it forms a part, which counts as a power among the other powers of Europe. And the national character of the Hungarian government is equally imperfect from the other side. It is national as regards the Magyar; it is not national as regards the Slave, and the Rouman. There is indeed

one other nation, the Saxon, which is united under the rule of a
single power; but that power is one which has no right to the name
of government.   The whole Bulgarian nation is under the rule of
the Turk; but that simply means that the whole nation is given up
to the brigandage of the Turk.   The other nations of those parts
are cut up among various powers.   No one nation forms a single
national government.   One fragment of a nation is free under a
national government, another fragment is ruled by civilized
strangers, a third is trampled down by barbarians.   The existing
states of Greece, Roumania, and Servia are far from taking in the
whole of the Greek, Rouman, and Servian nations.   The mainland
of Illyria is unnaturally cut off from its Dalmatian mouths.   In all
these lands |739| there is no difficulty in marking off the several
nations; only in no case do the nations answer to any existing
political power.

In these lands too another element comes in towards the formation
of nationality of which, in that light, we know nothing in the
West.   In many cases religion takes the place of nationality; or
rather the ideas of religion and nationality can hardly be distinguished.   In the West a man's nationality is in no way affected by
the religion which he professes, or even by his change from one
religion to another.   In the East it is otherwise.   The Christian
renegade who embraces Islam becomes for most practical purposes
a Turk.   Even if he keep his Greek or Slavonic language, he remains
Greek or Slave only in a secondary sense.   Even the Greek or
Armenian who embraces the Latin creed goes far towards parting
with his nationality as well as with his religion.   In the Armenian
indeed we have come very near to the phaenomenon of the further
East, where names like Parsee and Hindoo, names in themselves as
strictly ethnical as Englishman or Frenchman, have come to express
distinctions which are religious rather than national, or rather
distinctions in which religion and nationality are absolutely the
same thing.   But this whole class of phaenomena presents far too
many subjects of enquiry to be dealt with cursorily at the end of an
article.   I merely point them out, as bringing in an element in the
definition of nationality to which we are unused in the West.   But
it quite comes within our present subject to give one definition from
the South-Eastern lands.   What is the Greek?   Clearly he who is
at once Greek in speech and Orthodox in faith.   The Hellenic

Mussulmans in Crete, the Hellenic Latins in some of the other islands, are at the most imperfect members of the Hellenic body. The utmost that can be said is that they keep the power of again entering that body, either by their own return to the national faith, or by such a change in the state of things as shall make difference in religion no longer inconsistent with true national fellowship.

Thus, wherever we go, we find language to be the rough practical test of nationality. The exceptions are many; they may perhaps outnumber the instances which conform to the rule. Still they are exceptions. Community of language does not imply community of blood; it might be added that diversity of language does not imply diversity of blood. But community of language is surely, in the absence of any evidence to the contrary, a presumption of the community of blood, and it is proof of something which for practical purposes is the same as community of blood. To talk of "the Latin race," is in strictness absurd. We know that the so-called race is simply made up of those nations which adopted the Latin language. The Celtic, Teutonic, and Slavonic races may conceivably have been formed by a like artificial process. |740| But the presumption is the other way; and if such a process ever took place, it took place long before history began. The Celtic, Teutonic, Slavonic races come before us as groups of mankind marked out by the test of language. Within those races we find nations marked out again by a stricter application of the test of language. Within the race we may have languages which are clearly akin to each other, but which need not be mutually intelligible. Within the nation we have only dialects which are mutually intelligible, or which at all events gather round some one central dialect which is intelligible to all. We take this standard of races and nations, fully aware that it will not stand a physiological test, but holding that for all practical purposes adoption must pass as equivalent to natural descent. And, among the practical purposes which are affected by the facts of race and nationality, we must, as long as man is what he is, as long as he has not been created afresh according to some new scientific pattern, not shrink from reckoning those generous emotions which, in the present state of European feeling, are beginning to bind together the greater as well as the lesser groups of mankind. The sympathies of men are beginning to reach wider than could have been dreamed of a century ago. The feeling which was once confined to the mere household extended itself to the tribe or the city.   From the tribe or city it extended itself to the nation; from the nation it is beginning to extend itself to the whole race. In some cases it can extend itself to the whole race far more easily than in others.   In some cases historical causes have made nations of the same race bitter enemies, while they have made nations of different races friendly allies.   The same thing happened in earlier days between tribes and cities of the same nation.   But, when hindrances of this kind do not exist, the feeling of race, as something beyond the narrower feeling of nationality, is beginning to be a powerful agent in the feelings and actions of men and of nations. A long series of mutual wrongs, conquest and oppression on one side avenged by conquest and oppression on the other side, have made the Slave of Poland and the Slave of Russia the bitterest of enemies.   No such hindrance exists to stop the flow of natural and generous feeling between the Slave of Russia and the Slave of the South-Eastern lands.   Those whose statemanship consists in some hand-to-mouth shift for the moment, whose wisdom consists in refusing to look either back to the past or onwards to the future, cannot understand this great fact of our times; and what they cannot understand they mock at.   But the fact exists and does its work in spite of them.   And it does its work none the less because in some cases the feeling of sympathy is awakened by a claim of kindred, where, in the sense of the physiologist or the genealogist, there is no kindred at all.   The |741| practical view, historical or political, will accept as members of this or that race or nation many members whom the physiologist would shut out, whom the English lawyer would shut out, but whom the Roman lawyer would gladly welcome to every privilege of the stock on which they were grafted.   The line of the Scipios, of the Caesars, and of the Antonines, was continued by adoption: and for all practical purposes the nations of the earth have agreed to follow the examples set them by their masters.

ELEVEN

GRANT ALLEN (1848–99)

Are We Englishmen?

Fortnightly Review
Volume 28, 1880, pp. 472–87

Allen was a prolific writer of fiction and non-fiction alike. The best remembered of some thirty novels is The Woman Who Did *(1895), a notorious vindication of female social nonconformity. The periodical press made many calls upon his talent as a popularizer of natural history, and in 1886 he published the volume on Darwin within the Longman's series of 'English Worthies' edited by Andrew Lang. In his writings Allen, the son of an Irish father and of a Scottish mother with French connections, took many opportunities of promoting Celticism after the manner of Ernest Renan and Matthew Arnold. In 1881 he issued a small monograph on* Anglo-Saxon Britain, *whose conclusions about the modern nation's racial heritage challenged the conventional wisdom of Freeman and his school. The following essay shows Allen trying to consolidate this reversal of the notion that the prosperity and success of Victorian Britain are attributable to some predominance of Anglo-Saxon over Celtic blood. This exercise in historical and economic ethnography attempts to show that, while the more Teutonic areas of the British Isles have been 'sinking to a position of a simple agricultural country', the Celtic territories have been expanding through internal migration and have risen into 'a great manufacturing region'. On this view, it is the Celt rather than the Anglo-Saxon who has been the more powerful driving force behind the triumphs of industrialization at home and of colonization in the wider world.*

Opinion always moves by see-saw.   First of all, it receives an
impulse in one direction, and then it suffers a reactionary rebound
toward the opposite side.   Next comes a second impulse, and after
it a second rebound.   Thus, slowly adjusting itself at each rhyth-
mical swing, it finally reaches an equilibrium.   The interesting
question of British ethnography has passed through the two primary
phases in such a rhythm; the object of the present paper is (if
possible) to give a slight fresh upward start to the side that is just
at this moment touching the ground.

Fifty years ago everybody spoke of "the Ancient Britons" as our
ancestors.   Histories of England began with the invasion of Caius
Caesar the dictator, and chronicled the advent of "the Saxons" as
a mere episode in our national life.   A wild philology derived
obviously Teutonic words from Keltic roots as glibly as it affiliated
Greek verbs upon a fanciful Hebrew origin.   The corporations of
English boroughs pretended to a sort of Apostolic succession from
Roman municipia; and the Tower of London traced its foundation
to a personage known in those innocent days as "Julius Caesar."
The fashion of ignoring the distinction between British and English,
a fashion derived from the influence of Tudor kings and strengthened
by the Union, led the whole world to talk of England as if it were
in reality Wales.   But during the present generation a great reaction
has set in.   Mr. Freeman has never ceased to beat into our heads
the simple fact that the English people and the English language
are English, and not Welsh, or any other like thing.   He has utterly
demolished that foolish word "Anglo-Saxon," which long hid from
our eyes the true continuity of English life.   He has shown us a
thousand times, and almost taught us to remember, that Alfred the
Great was an Englishman; and that the chronicle which probably
first took shape under his care, if not from his own pen, is written
simply in good old English, and not in any unknown Saxon tongue.
What Mr. Freeman sowed, Mr. Green watered; and every reader of
the weekly journals is now in a position to laugh Anglo-Saxons to
scorn, and to discourse of the reign of Aethelred as familiarly
as he discourses of Karl the Great or of the Holy Roman Empire.

In this reaction, however, as in every other, there is a great
danger of the pendulum swinging back too far on the other side,
and so overshooting the middle line of truth.   While fully allowing
|473| with Mr. Freeman that the so-called Angles, Saxons, and Jutes

who settled down in south-eastern Britain during or after the
decadence of the Roman power were all alike Englishmen, and all
spoke in its pristine purity the English mother tongue which we
ourselves use to the present day, it may yet be worth while to
inquire how far the existing nation known as English is really
composed of their direct descendants, and how far it has been
adulterated in later times by a foreign and, as Mr. Freeman doubtless
believes, an inferior admixture.   A simple instance will make the
question clear.   Champions of the modern school are fond of
laughing at those old-fashioned people who spoke of the dark-
skinned Silures and the blue-stained Brigantes as "our ancestors;"
but is it quite certain that they are not themselves equally wrong
in applying the same phrase to the men who came over with Aella
to Sussex, or with Ida to Northumbria?   If the first were not the
forefathers of the men who now live in Kent and Norfolk, neither
were the latter the forefathers of those who now live in Cornwall,
Inverness, or Connaught.   And since the British nation is at the
present day practically amalgamated into one, it is, to say the least,
rather provincial in Mr. Freeman and his followers entirely to ignore
every part of it save that which dwells between the Frith of Forth
and the English Channel.

I propose, therefore, to inquire here into the numerical proportion
of the Keltic to the Teutonic element in the British people as it now
exists at home and in the colonies.   And I hope to show that while
in language, laws, customs, and government we are preponderantly
or entirely English, yet in blood we are preponderantly if not
overwhelmingly Kymric and Gaelic.

The analogy of one among our tropical possessions will serve to
show how important is this distinction.   Jamaica has a population
of some five hundred thousand souls.   Of these, roughly speaking,
four hundred thousand are pure-blooded negroes, ninety thousand
are half-castes, and only ten thousand are Europeans, amongst
whom are included many Jews.   Yet the language, the laws, the
religion, and the government of Jamaica are purely English.   Three
years' search failed to disclose even a single word of African origin
in use in the island.   Were it not that the negro colour and features
show the true state of the case, a philologist and antiquarian would
naturally conclude that all the people in Jamaica were of unmixed
English origin.   But what an immense difference is implied in the

fact of their African blood! This example will suffice to suggest how dangerous it is to argue from language alone.

It will be well to begin with the most certain instances, and we may therefore first consider the case of the persons in the United Kingdom who still speak the Keltic languages; for though we must not conclude that a man who speaks English is necessarily an English-|474|man, we may fairly infer that a man who speaks Welsh, Erse, or Gaelic is at least not a Teuton. Now, most readers will probably be surprised to learn that one out of every fifteen inhabitants of the British Isles even in our own time employs some form of the old British tongue; yet such is actually the case. The population of England, Scotland, and Ireland at the last census amounted to thirty-two millions. But, at a meeting of the Statistical Society in 1879, Mr. E. G. Ravenstein showed most conclusively that two and a quarter millions among these still use some variety of the Keltic language. Astonishing as this fact will appear to many people, it is still undoubtedly correct.

Passing on from those persons who are still Keltic in tongue, let us next consider those who are undeniably Keltic in blood. Wales contains one and a quarter millions of inhabitants, and if we admit that two hundred and fifty thousand of these are of Teutonic extraction, we shall have allowed more than enough for the scattered Scandinavian and English or Anglo-Norman colonies of Pembrokeshire, South Wales, and Anglesey. This leaves us at least a million of pure Kelts in the Principality alone. The Highlands of Scotland contain a million and a half of people, all of whom are Keltic, with the exception of one hundred and fifty thousand Scandinavians in Caithness, Sutherland, and the Isles. Ireland contains five and a half millions, of whom we may allow a million as a large estimate for the Scandinavians of the coast, as well as for the English and Lowland Scotch element in Ulster and the Pale. So that here are seven millions of acknowledged Kelts still dwelling in virgin Keltic countries, and absolutely untouched by Teutonic colonisation.

Thus far, however, we have accounted for barely a quarter of our existing home population. To get a little deeper into the question we must go back to the historical origin of our present race-elements.

It is now pretty generally allowed that the people who inhabited these islands at the period of the Roman invasion consisted of two races, more or less distinct in various parts of the country. One of these, typified by the Silures, was that primitive dark-skinned and black-haired nation known as Euskarian, who probably migrated into Britain shortly after the close of the last glacial epoch. The other, typified by the Caledonii, was a light-haired, blue-eyed, and fair-complexioned race, the Kelts, an offshoot of the great Aryan family of Central Asia. Apparently the Keltic horde had crossed Europe through what is now Germany, made their wav over the North Sea, and settled in the eastern portion of South Britain, as the English did at a far later period. But just as the English language has spread over Keltic Cornwall, Wales, and Ireland, so, it |475| would seem, did the Keltic languages spread among the presumably less civilised Euskarian aborigines. Accordingly, at the time of C. Caesar, the whole of southern Britain spoke a single tongue, the Welsh; while in Ireland a cognate dialect, the Gaelic, was in use. From the more or less complete mixture of these two elements sprang the Kelt-Euskarian people, whom we may henceforth describe simply as Kelts. But it is worth while to remember that amongst their modern representatives the dark Euskarian type is far more common than the fair Aryan hair and skin.

When the Roman power broke down in Britain, and for some time before that event, a horde of Teutonic pirates began to swarm across the German Ocean, and colonise by force of arms the exposed eastern shore from Kent to Edinburgh, besides the whole south coast as far west as Southampton Water. These were the English, consisting of three tribes, the Jutes, the English proper, and the Saxons. Starting from a number of separate and exposed points, in Thanet, Wight, East Anglia, the Fen Country, and the Humber, they gradually spread, by the middle of the seventh century, over the whole eastern half of Britain south of the Forth. That, and that only, is ethnographically the true England, and its inhabitants the true Englishmen, much intermixed in the central portion with Scandinavian blood, but still, doubtless, partially Teutonic in some form or other to the backbone. Indeed, it would be hardly too much to say that there are no thoroughgoing pure Englishmen now left in Britain save among the so-called Scotch of the Lothians. The rest, even when free from Keltic blood, are either half Danish, like the men of the Midlands, or Jutes and Saxons, like the men of Kent and Sussex. It is important to remember that only about one-third of the British Isles has ever been fully colonised by people bearing the English name, and that even these have afterwards undergone much adulteration. Nevertheless, for brevity's sake, we shall here call all Teutons in Britain Englishmen, just as we call all non-Teutons Kelts.

I allow, then, that if you draw a straight line from Edinburgh to Southampton, all the people to the east of it were, roughly speaking, English in the early Middle Ages, though I will attempt to show hereafter that they have been flooded at a later date by a peaceful but overwhelming Keltic invasion. Even at this early period, however, they may have been English by courtesy only, in part; for we cannot be sure that in Kent and East Anglia themselves, where the Anglicizing tendency has gone the furthest, the Keltic aborigines were utterly exterminated. Many facts, indeed, look quite the other way. It is true Mr. Freeman, like every other writer from Gibbon downwards, makes a great point of the single definite statement in the English Chronicle with regard to the capture of Pevensey: |476| "Aella and Cissa beset Anderida, and offslew all that therein dwelt, nor was there thenceforth one Briton left." But then we have to consider three things: first, that this entry was made, presumably from tradition, hundreds of years after the event; secondly, that it refers to the treatment of a single town; and thirdly, that the very fact of such special mention would go to prove that in the writer's opinion the course pursued was an unusual one. Again, it is quite possible that while the fighting men were killed, the women and children were spared as slaves. In this way they might easily have become the ancestors at least of half-castes between the Keltic and English races. To be sure, Canon Stubbs has been at great pains to show that Englishmen would not marry Welshwomen; but such an argument would have little weight with any person who knows anything practically of slaveholding communities. To revert to the analogy of Jamaica: no white man there ever marries a negress, and yet there are no less than nine mulattoes to every white person, man, woman, or child, in the whole island—a truly astounding proportion. It would thus be quite possible to have a community only one-tenth of whom were pure English in blood, and which was yet wholly English in name, in language, and in feeling.

Indications of such a mixture even in the most Teutonic parts of England are undoubtedly strong. All our rivers, and most of the other natural features of the country, bear Keltic names, such as Stour, Ouse, Thames, or Don.   Now these names could only have been gained by intercourse with the conquered race, which is inconsistent with the notion of extermination.   Many even of the towns and territorial divisions retain their primitive titles, as in the case of London, Lincoln, Kent, and Wight.   Evidence like this, strong in itself, becomes even stronger when we remember the similar case of Ireland, where only the Keltic names of places will soon remain, or contrast it with that of Jamaica, where not a single African word survives.   Moreover, there are several traces of scattered Welsh communities up and down in Teutonic England to a late date—"Little Britains," as they have been appropriately called.   Mr. Guest has shown that the valleys of the Avon and Frome, near Bath, formed such an intrusive wedge of purely Welsh nationality.   Even Mr. Freeman himself is a little troubled at the appearance of "British robbers" in the Fen Country at a period when, according to his theory, they ought all long since to have been eaten up bodily by the English invaders, though he is inclined to smother up the difficulty by arguments that are verbal and not real.   The physical appearance of the English in the true England bears out the like conclusion; but as this is a point where individual observers are apt to be misled by their own predispositions, I am happy to be able to quote so unprejudiced a scientific observer as the late Professor Phillips. |477| He thus describes one of the three physical types of man in Yorkshire, after sketching two others of obviously Teutonic origin: "Persons of lower stature and smaller proportions; visage short, rounded; complexion embrowned; eyes very dark, elongated; hair very dark.   (Such eyes and hair are commonly called black.)   Individuals having these characters occur in the lower grounds of Yorkshire, as in the valley of the Aire below Leeds, in the vale of the Derwent, and the level regions south of York.   They are still more frequent in Nottinghamshire and Leicestershire, and may be said to abound amidst the true Anglians of Norfolk and Suffolk. . . . .   Unless we suppose such varieties of appearance to spring up among the blue-eyed races, we must regard them as a legacy from. . . . the older Britons, amongst whom, as already stated, the Iberian [Euskarian] element was conjecturally admitted."   It should be added that provincial words of Keltic origin abound in Yorkshire.

However this may be, I shall waive all such considerations, and allow that during the first few centuries after their settlement the people of south-eastern Britain had a fairly good claim to the title of pure-blooded Englishmen. But the case is widely different with regard to the northern and western half of Great Britain, as well as with regard to all Ireland. In the west, the English slowly conquered, it is true; but they certainly never exterminated the Kelt-Euskarian race. There are three convenient divisions of England proper, by means of which we may most easily deal with the question of westward extension. These three divisions are Wessex, Mercia, and Northumbria—the south, the midlands, and the north.

Beyond Wessex lay the Keltic kingdom of West Wales. It included Cornwall, Devonshire, and Somerset; and still earlier Dorset, Wilts, and Hants. Now everybody admits that the Cornish men are Kelts, as they still spoke a Keltic dialect till comparatively recent times. But it is not so well known that the population in the other West Welsh counties is even now essentially Keltic, though Mr. Freeman himself allows nearly as much in a grudging way. The fact is, the West Saxons merely imposed their authority over the Kelts of West Wales, just as the English have done over the Kelts of Ireland. The people remain the same as ever, though their language, laws, and customs have been Anglicized. The inhabitants of Devonshire retained their Keltic name of Defenas under the early English kings. Many of them still spoke Cornish in Queen Elizabeth's reign. Alfred the Great in his will leaves to his younger son "the land at Adrington, and at Dean, and at Theon, and at Amesbury, and at Downe, and at Stourminster, and at Gidley, and at Crewkern, and at Whitchurch, and at Axmouth, and at Branscombe, and at Collumpton, and at Twyford, and at Milbourne, and at Axminster, and at Southsworth, and at Litton, and all the lands |478| that thereto belong, that is, all which I have amongst Welsh-kin, except Cornwall." Now, these places are scattered about in Wilts, Hants, Somerset, Dorset, and Devon, all of which were still simply Welsh-kin to Alfred. All the Keltic personal peculiarities are strong to the present day throughout this district, and even the Keltic names lingered on amongst the lower orders in some parts till the date of the Norman Conquest, as we see in the manumissions of serfs and other legal documents.

The population of Cornwall at the last census was three hundred and sixty-two thousand, all of whom we may count as Kelts; for though there is undoubtedly a small body of English and Norman immigrants, yet they may be fairly balanced against the Cornish men in neighbouring counties, as Cornwall is actually decreasing in number of inhabitants through emigration elsewhere. The other three pure West Welsh shires—Somerset, Dorset, and Devon—have a joint population of a million and a quarter souls; and if we allow that the unreckoned Kelts of Wilts and Hants (which I give in to the Teutonists) balance such of these as are of English descent, we have a gross Keltic total for the south-western counties, including Cornwall, of nearly a million and three-quarters of persons.

Mercia, the great midland kingdom, consisted, as its name imports, of the March or boundary against Wales proper. But here, again, we have on the extreme west an almost undoubted Welsh strip of country between the Severn and the modern boundary-line. Monmouthshire is as Keltic in blood as any part of the principality. Herefordshire and Shropshire are full of Keltic faces and Keltic names. Even Cheshire is far from thoroughly Teutonic. Gloucester, Worcester, and Stafford show signs of imperfect Anglicization. The English clan names, as elements in local nomenclature, form one of the surest marks of Teutonic colonisation, and they are almost entirely wanting in Western Mercia; they abound in Kent, Sussex, and East Anglia; grow rare in Cheshire, Worcestershire, and Herefordshire; and all but utterly disappear in Monmouth. The English, in fact, only conquered and settled in these districts by slow degrees, and their supremacy was clearly one of overlordship, not of active colonisation. The laws of Offa, King of Mercia, show us the two races dwelling side by side, and mentioned by name—the one as a superior conquering caste, the other as an inferior but still legally recognised body. And here, as elsewhere, we may be pretty sure that the serfs far outnumbered their lords.

The population of Cheshire, Shropshire, Herefordshire, Monmouthshire, Gloucestershire, and Worcestershire amounted in 1871 to very nearly two million souls. I shall liberally allow that one-half of |479| these were English, though I do not for a moment believe that they were, and we have here another million of Kelts to add to our capital account. An *ex parte* pleader would be quite justified in claiming the whole body at once, but I prefer to be generous.

Lastly, then, we arrive at Northumbria.   Opposite and to the west of this early English kingdom lay the Welsh principality of Strathclyde, stretching from Glasgow far into the heart of what is now the midland counties.   The Northumbrian kings overran the whole of this district, except the southern portion, which fell to the share of Mercia.   But they never destroyed its Keltic nationality, and the country still bore the general name of Cumberland, that is to say the land of the Cymri, which is now restricted to one of its shires.   At a later period the southern half, which at present forms part of England, was overrun by Norwegian pirates, who, however, probably came unaccompanied by their wives or children, and must therefore have intermarried with the native population, as we know they did in Teutonic England.   The northern half, now a part of Scotland, was granted to the Scottish kings—themselves of Irish descent—by the West-Saxon overlords.   All the linguistic evidence goes to prove that the whole of this northern Cumbria, from the Mersey to the Clyde, and from the central dividing-ridge to the sea, is still essentially Keltic in blood.   Welsh words survive abundantly, not only in the names of places, but also in the popular dialect. The physique of the Lancashire men and the folk of Ayr belongs distinctly to the Keltic type, only slightly interfused with a Norse element.

Now the modern population of this teeming tract, including as it does the great cities of Glasgow, Liverpool, and Manchester, besides many lesser but still important towns, is of course very large.   Moreover, in addition to the original Keltic blood which it derives from the early Welsh inhabitants, it has received in modern times an enormous accession of Irish settlers, about whom I shall have more to say a little further on.   Lancashire, Cumberland, and Westmoreland contained in 1871 no less than three millions and odd inhabitants.   Of these I shall only claim two-thirds, which again is far less than I might do if avariciously inclined.   For the south-western division of Scotland, including Glasgow and the thickly-inhabited Clyde district, I shall be satisfied with only half a million Kelts.   We thus get a total Cumbrian figure of two and a half millions.

Putting together these three totals—a million and three-quarters for the Cornish and other West Welsh; a million for the Border counties; and two and a half millions for Strathclyde—we reach a grand total of five and a quarter millions.   This, then, is our present position.   We have seven millions of acknowledged Kelts, living in |480| Keltic countries, and still calling themselves Scotch, Welsh, or Irish; and we have five and a quarter millions of unquestionable Kelts living in England or the Lowlands, and passing as Englishmen or Lowlanders.   Again, to put it geographically, we have, as at present advised, a comparatively pure Teutonic belt on the east and south, an intervening mixed belt just beyond the central ridge, and a comparatively pure Keltic belt in the west and north, as well as in the greater part of Ireland.

During the Middle Ages, and up to the growth of the modern industrial system, such was really the approximate distribution of the two races.   Indeed, there can be little doubt that if a trustworthy census of Britain had been taken in the days of Henry VI., it would have disclosed a large preponderance of the Teutonic element.   In those days the south-eastern and strictly English part of the island was by far the most important.   Trade was centred on Kent, London, East Anglia, and the Yorkshire coast.   The people were mainly agricultural, and they throve chiefly on the level secondary and tertiary plains of the eastern half; whereas the Kelt was forced to content himself with the rugged primary hills of the north and west.   But the great social revolution by which Britain became a manufacturing country exercised an immense reaction in favour of the older race.   In our island mineral wealth is almost entirely confined to the primary rocks; hence we have seen a complete reversal of the original distribution taking place during the last two centuries.   Lancashire has become the thickest seat of population in Great Britain.   The West Riding of York has outstripped the fertile valley of the Ouse and the flat plains of Holderness.   Lincolnshire and East Anglia have fallen back to the position of mere agricultural countries, while South Wales has developed into a wealthy mining tract.   Birmingham and the Black Country stand almost alone among the great manufacturing districts as lying within the Teutonic belt; yet even Birmingham is scarcely outside the dubious Mercian border, while Staffordshire stands well within the debatable land.   The westward direction given to our commerce by the intercourse with America and the Cape route to India has aided in the same change.   Glasgow and the Clyde have superseded Edinburgh and the Forth.   The cotton trade with the Southern

States has made Liverpool and Manchester; while the sugar traffic with the West Indies has given new youth to the more ancient port of Bristol.   To put it briefly, in the Middle Ages agricultural England turned eastward to the continent, in our own day industrial England turns westward to the ocean.

Accordingly, it is not surprising that students of early English history should almost always over-estimate the importance of the Teutonic element, especially under the influence of reactive feeling |481| against the puerilities of older writers.   The English Chronicle shows them an English people, Teutonic in language, laws, and feelings, and mainly Teutonic in blood.   It represents this people as occupying the whole England of that day, and bounded to the west by a small remnant of Welsh nationality in Wales or Cornwall, interfused on the border with a dominant English aristocracy, whose names alone, to the exclusion of the servile race, find record for the most part in the national annals.   Led away by these facts, they forget the immense revolution which has since completely reversed the relative importance of the two races.   They forget that England has merged into Britain, and Britain into the Empire; that Glasgow, Dundee, and Aberdeen, Belfast, Cork, and Dublin, Montreal, Toronto, Melbourne, Sydney, and Auckland, are now great mercantile and university cities, busy centres of British life and thought, while Winchester, Lichfield, and Canterbury have fallen back to the level of mere cathedral towns.   They forget that, while Teutonic Britain has been sinking to the position of a simple agricultural country, Keltic Britain has been rising to that of a great manufacturing region.   They forget that, while the Teuton has been staying at home in Kent or Suffolk, the Kelt has been pouring into London, Glasgow, Manchester, Leeds, or Birmingham, invading the mines, the factories, or the docks, and colonising Australia, Canada, or California.   It is this great peaceful return-tide of the Kelt to the lands occupied by the Teuton, and this great overflow of the Kelt into lands where the Teuton is all but unknown, which really make our nation to-day British in a far truer sense than it is English. But all this naturally escapes the eyes of closet ethnologists, who never take into consideration any facts of life later than the reigns of the Tudors.

In the first place let us look at the Kelts in England and the Scotch Lowlands.   It is a notorious fact that the most purely

Teutonic shires, such as Sussex and Norfolk, are those where there is least movement of the indigenous population. The people increase but slowly, and mostly live and die on their own soil. On the other hand, in the most Keltic counties, as, for example, in Cornwall, there is little increase or even a positive decrease in the stated population, because, in spite of the large families usually reared by Kelts, most of the children go elsewhere to seek their livelihood. While the lazy, stupid, and slow-headed Teuton, as we seem him in the eastern counties or the south coast, stops at home on whatever wages he can earn, the active, enterprising, and intelligent Kelt seeks in a new quarter for better employment and higher pay than he can obtain among his own people. I am aware that these are not the conventional epithets of either race, but it is well now and again to hear the other side of a foregone conclusion. Now London is |482| very largely recruited with servants, small shopkeepers, artisans, drivers, and other persons following the most useful occupations, from the south-western counties, the West Wales of early history. The overflowing population of Devon, Dorset, Somerset, and Cornwall pours into that district which Mr. Freeman will not allow us to call the metropolis, in immense numbers. I have been at the trouble for many years to make inquiries into this subject, both in London itself and in the south-western counties, and though the question is one on which it is difficult to obtain definite statistics, I have no ground for doubting, from the information I have obtained, that fully thirty per cent. of the three millions of Londoners are either of West Welsh or other Keltic descent. I find, too, that large numbers of these people are settled in Brighton, Portsmouth, Southampton, and the other southern watering-places and seaport towns. Not a few are to be found in Bristol and in the South Welsh district. Altogether, West Wales is one of the most prolific sources of our southern urban population; while, on the other hand, I can find very few traces of any modern Teutonic incursion from other parts of England into Devonshire or Cornwall. Except a few invalids at Torquay or Weymouth, and a few well-to-do residents at Plymouth and Devonport, nobody has any reason for immigrating into this mainly agricultural tract, whose own people are more than sufficient to fill its not very numerous towns. The labouring class in the west is almost entirely native.

Similarly, from Wales and the border counties, a great stream of emigration has long set in, both towards London and towards the manufacturing districts, of which Birmingham and Manchester form the centres.   In Liverpool Welshmen swarm; but what is still more noticeable is the general diffusion of the Welsh nationality in thousands of unsuspected cases amongst all the large towns of England, east, west, north, and south.   In many instances these persons have no idea of their Keltic origin, as they have often been Anglicized for generations, or come originally from the Border; but their true derivation is clearly proved by their surnames.   Indeed, nomenclature, like language, is in this case the very best of evidence; for though all men with Teutonic names are not necessarily Teutons, yet all men with Keltic names are undoubtedly Kelts.*   Now all such common names as Evans, Bevan, Parry, Owen, Bowen, Griffith, Griffiths, Rice, Reece, Price, Preece, Lloyd, Pritchard, Hughes, Pugh, Howell, and Powell, besides such rarer ones as Bethell, Meredith, Vaughan, Pennant, Llewelyn, Gwyn, Wynne, |483| Morgan, Prothero, and Maddock, are sure signs of Keltic origin.   I have long been in the habit of observing and noting down surnames, both on shops and signboards and in the ordinary intercourse of life, and also of consulting and comparing directories or other lists of names.   From all these I have become convinced that the Welsh Keltic element in our principal towns is far larger than is usually suspected; and I have found such names in abundance, even in the most Teutonic parts of the island.   It should be added that many other common patronymics, such as Richards, Williams, Watkins, Jones, Davies, and Thomas, though not so uniformly Welsh as those already cited, afford good presumptive evidence of Keltic origin. Similarly, in the case of originally Cornish families, they may often be detected by the names of Vivian, Trevelyan, Trelawney, Thackeray, or Pengelley, as well as by most of those beginning with the traditional "Tre, Pol, and Pen."   Any philologist who takes the trouble to watch all the names with which he comes in contact will be astonished at the results which he will obtain.   Indeed, only the student of nomenclature can rightly appreciate the extreme com-

* It may be objected that in many instances such persons will be English on the mother's side; but as married daughters lose the father's name while sons preserve it, this argument cuts both ways. Here, where our object is merely to estimate the comparative amount of Keltic blood, two half Kelts may be fairly held as the equivalent of one Kelt.

plexity of our existing population.   The London Directory shows
a perfectly surprising number of Keltic names, either Welsh, Scotch,
or Irish; and even provincial directories contain far larger proportions than would be ordinarily supposed.   It is hardly necessary to
observe that none but tourists have yet notably invaded North
Wales, and South Wales supplies the greater part of her industries
for herself, while the margin of deficiency is made up by Keltic
importations from Ireland.

Cumbria has mainly kept the mills of Lancashire at work, and
has helped in its northern portion to form the population of
Glasgow.   But in the West Riding of York, once a rugged and
desolate mountain tract, a vast mass of people have collected over
the rich coal measures.   These are in part native half-caste Kelts,
in part immigrants from elsewhere.   On the whole, there can be
little doubt that Keltic blood either predominates or at least holds
half the ground throughout the great manufacturing tract which
stretches from Liverpool to Leeds.   I have found on inquiry many
Welsh, Dorsetshire, and Devonshire hands among the operatives in
a few mills which I have happened to visit; but I know little of this
region personally.   The dialect at least has numerous Keltic traces.

So much for the Cymric Kelts.   And next we come to their
brethren, the Gaels of Scotland and Ireland.   Now, it is notorious
that Glasgow is crowded with Highlanders, and that they form a
large element in Edinburgh, as well as in several of the southern
cities.   For many generations the Gael has been moving southward,
and he now shares the Lowlands with the true Englishman of the
Lothians, and the half-caste Cymri of Strathclyde.   In all parts of
England |484| where occupation is to be had there is a fair sprinkling
of Macdonalds, Mackenzies, and Macdougalls, as well as of Camp-
bells, Gordons, Camerons, and Skenes.   Here, again, it is necessary,
for a fair comprehension of the question, to keep a look-out upon
the names in streets or directories; and in the case of so-called
Scotchmen it is essential to distinguish between the Teutonic patro-
nymics of the Lothians and the true Gaelic clans of the north.   But
a careful comparison of directories, coupled with inquiries among
gangs of workmen, will show an unsuspected Gaelic invasion, not
only of London, but also of Manchester, Liverpool, Birmingham,
and many other great towns.

As to the Irish, we all know that they have long overflowed all our larger cities, and have even spread into some rural districts. There is a great Irish colony in Marylebone and the Tower Hamlets, and others of less extent in the east and south of London. In Liverpool, in Manchester, in Glasgow, they form a very considerable proportion of the population. The Scotch census for 1871 estimates their number in the principal towns of Scotland at from ten to thirty per cent. of the whole body of inhabitants, and since that date they have become powerful enough to set up Home Rule candidates in more than one Scotch or English borough. Wherever they find a footing they increase with extraordinary rapidity, and in many cases the memory of their origin dies out in the second generation.

The conclusion forced upon me by all these facts, and others like them observed for many years, is this: Even in the most Teutonic portion of England the town population consists in very large part of Kelts, either Welsh, semi-English, Gaelic-Scotch, or Irish. The census of 1871 returned the urban population in the 198 large towns of England at thirteen millions, as against only ten millions in the small towns and rural parishes. How large a proportion of these may be Keltic it would be rash to guess exactly without better data than those which we now possess; but I do not hesitate to say, on the evidence of nomenclature, that it must be quite large enough to turn the scale heavily in favour of the Keltic race, even in the British Isles themselves.

Let us now turn for a moment to the Colonies. It is common to speak of the "Anglo-Saxons" as the great colonising race, but when we look at the facts such pretensions will not for a moment hold water. It is the Kelt who colonises. Personal experience and observation of names enable me to say that by far the largest number of Canadians are of Irish, Highland Scotch, Welsh, or Breton extraction. Examination of directories and other lists of names convinces me that the same is the case with Australian and New Zealand colonists. The imperial census of 1870 gives Canada nearly four millions of inhabitants, and Australasia two millions. |485| About two millions more may be allowed for the white inhabitants of our tropical dependencies and minor colonies. An overwhelming proportion of all these eight millions are certainly Keltic; so that "the great Anglo-Saxon race," whose energy spreads it over every part of the world, may be regarded as an ingenious myth. Even in England itself colonists go rather from the Keltic western half than from the Teutonic east. Devonshire and Somerset are great feeders of Canada and New Zealand.

What, then, is the final result at which we have arrived? A small body of Teutonic immigrants descended some time about the fifth century and onward on the eastern shore of South Britain. They occupied the whole coast from the Forth to the Isle of Wight, and spread over the country westward as far as the central dividing ridge. Though not quite free from admixture with the aborigines, even in this limited tract, they still remained relatively pure in this their stronghold, and they afterwards received a fresh Teutonic reinforcement by the Danish invasion. Westward of the central line they conquered and assimilated the aborigines, upon whom they imposed their language and laws, but whom they did not extermi-nate. In the extreme west and in Ireland the Kelts long retained their language and nationality undisturbed. During the Middle Ages the English people formed by far the most powerful body in the island; and even now they have imposed upon all of it their name and language. But since the rise of the industrial system the Kelts have peacefully recovered the numerical superiority. They have crowded into the towns and seaports, so that at the present day only the rural districts of Eastern England can claim to be thoroughly Teutonic. The urban population consists for the most part of a mixed race. Moreover, since intermarriage is now so very frequent, it seems probably that almost all English families, except those of the stationary agricultural class in the east, have at least some small proportion of Keltic blood. In the upper classes, where numerous intermarriages are universal, this proportion is, doubtless, everywhere very great. Out of Britain the Kelts have it all their own way.

It may be objected, however, by Teutonic enthusiasts, that these facts only show a numerical balance in favour of the conquered race. All the energy, intellect, and power, all the literature, science, and art, they will say, are on the side of the "Anglo-Saxon." Now it cannot be denied that, up to a comparatively late period, Teutonic and Anglicized Britain bore away the palm in most of these respects. It could hardly be otherwise, seeing that the Keltic language has always been a mere provincial dialect, or rather three or four provincial dialects, spoken for the most part by the lower orders in remote regions of the country. But it is practically impossible to |486| say how much of English literature or English science is due to Anglicized Kelts.   It is impossible to guess whether a Shakespeare born in Warwickshire, a Watt born in Strathclyde, or a Scott from the border clans, had or had not a mixture of English and Keltic blood.   In most cases, away from the east coast, we may be pretty sure that at least some such mixture has at some time taken place.   It is seldom, however, that a familiar name, like William Makepeace Thackeray, Humphry Davy, Owen Jones, Colin Campbell, or Daniel O'Connell, bears its Keltic origin unmistakably upon its face.   On the other hand, it cannot be denied that if we look at the undoubtedly Keltic names we shall find they have each supplied of late centuries as large a proportion of distinguished men in all departments of life as most of the Teutonic patronymics, which may or may not indicate Teutonic blood.*   Taking a few such names at random, and looking them up in a Biographical Dictionary, I find under Owen, Edward Owen the painter, John Owen the epigrammatist, John Owen the Independent, Richard Owen the palaeontologist, Robert Owen the socialist, Robert Dale Owen the essayist, and William Owen the artist.   Half-a-dozen Welsh, Scotch, and Irish names yield like results.   Byron, Carlyle, Darwin, all bear Keltic patronymics.   Long since, in examining official historical documents relating to India for a Government purpose, it struck me that our Indian empire (*valeat quantum*) had been mainly acquired and governed by men bearing Highland-Scotch names.   A glance through our peerages will show how large a number of those persons who raise themselves to the House of Lords or to the dignity of knighthood by professional distinction are of Keltic extraction.   And it must be remembered that the Anglicized and therefore undiscoverable Kelts always bear a heavy proportion to the obvious cases.   Similarly, if we take the Keltic counties, we shall find that Devonshire alone has given us so many distinguished men as Marlborough and Albermarle amongst statesmen; Drake, Davis, Raleigh, Hawkins, and Grenville amonst navigators or dis-coverers; Sir Joshua Reynolds, Prout, Haydon, and Eastlake amongst artists; Hooker and Jewel amongst theologians; Herrick, Gay, and

* At the period when surnames first became general, in the thirteenth and fourteenth centuries, the Anglicization of West Wales and the border counties had proceeded so far that many or most of the Keltic families in these districts bear English or Anglo-Norman names.

Coleridge amongst poets; and Newcomen, Buckland, and Clifford amongst men of science. Wherever the Kelt has a fair field and no disfavour, he is able on the average to compete on a tolerable equality with his Teutonic compeer. In the colonies he has certainly gained the upper hand in every case. In Canada the reins of government pass always from a Macdonald to a Mackenzie: in Australia they are held by a Duffy or an O'Shaughnessy.

|487| The fact is, Keltic blood has so long been regarded as in some way obviously inferior to Teutonic, that most of us are ashamed to acknowledge it, even if we suspect its presence. The idle, ignorant, superstitious Kelt has been so often contrasted with the clear-headed, energetic, pushing Anglo-Saxon, that everybody has hastened to enroll himself under the victorious Anglo-Saxon banner. A great many people are scandalized when they learn that most British subjects are not Christians, but Mahommedans or Hindus; they will doubtless be equally scandalized when told that most true British people are not "Anglo-Saxons," but Kelts. Yet in reality the Kelts in many parts of Britain have proved themselves just as orderly, industrious, and enterprising as their Teutonic fellow-countrymen. Coal, not blood, is the true differentiating agent. If we contrast Essex or Norfolk with Cornwall, Lancashire, and South Wales, I do not see that the comparison tells very forcibly in favour of the English race. "Silly Suffolk" is the conventional phrase for the most purely Teutonic county in Britain. And there is no reason why that Keltic race, which just across the Channel has produced the great, free, and noble French nation, should be incapable in the British Isles of producing anything better than the caricature of Ireland in which Tory prints are fond of indulging. Are we quite sure that geographical position and English misrule have not done more than Keltic blood to produce the unfortunate condition of the Irish peasantry at the present day? An Advocatus Diaboli and apologist of Flogging Fitzgerald may be ready to use every argument, down to the argumentum baculinum against the wretched Kelt, but good Liberals like Mr. Freeman should not, even by implication, countenance such national injustice.

A fair recognition of the strength of the Keltic element in England itself—an element which, as I believe, has done much to differentiate our national character from that of the slow and ponderous continental Teutons—may help to break down this unhappy prejudice of race. I trust, therefore, that I may succeed in giving the pendulum some small impulse, which, even if it a little overshoots the mark, may yet help in bringing the see-saw of opinion one degree nearer to the equilibrium of truth. And we may sum up the result here indicated in a single sentence: though the British nation of the present day is wholly Teutonic in *form*, it is largely and even preponderantly Keltic in *matter*.

INDEX

This selective index makes no claim to completeness. It aims simply to assist readers in making prompt reference to the most significant persons and themes covered by the volume.